Critical Theories of the State

Clyde W. Barrow

Critical Theories of the State

Marxist, Neo-Marxist, Post-Marxist

The University of Wisconsin Press

The University of Wisconsin Press
2537 Daniels Street
Madison, Wisconsin 53718

3 Henrietta Street
London WC2E 8LU, England

7   6   5   4   3

Printed in the United States of America

Library of Congress Cataloging-in-Publication Data
Barrow, Clyde W.
    Critical theories of the state : Marxist, Neo-Marxist,
Post-Marxist / Clyde W. Barrow.
    220 p.   cm.
    Includes bibliographical references and index.
    ISBN 0-299-13710-4   ISBN 0-299-13714-7
    1. State, The.   2. Socialism.   3. Communist state.   4. Radicalism.
5. Welfare state.   6. Political development.   I. Title.
JC251.B32   1993
320.1—dc20   92-34761

To my wife, Trini

Thanks!

Contents

Figures

Tables

Acknowledgments

Critical Theories of the State started as a set of preliminary notes for an undergraduate seminar which I first taught at the University of Massachusetts–Dartmouth in 1988. Two years later, at the request of seminar students, the notes were expanded into a series of short papers and placed in the library for reserve reading. It was not long thereafter that I decided to rework the papers into their current form and publish them as a short book designed for courses in state theory and political development. Thus, the many students who inspired this work deserve my sincere thanks. Moreover, in each of the last three years, a special student has emerged in the seminar, and each warrants special mention for his or her exceptional contribution to the development of this text. Joe LaValley, who sparked my interest in several strains of post-Marxist theory, has gone on to graduate studies in sociology at the University of California, Los Angeles. Darin Conforti, who initiated countless conversations on the works of Claus Offe and the new social movement theory, is now a graduate student in political theory at the State University of New York–Albany. Lynn Miller, who also served as my research assistant for almost two years, is now off to the University of Washington to begin graduate work in geography. I wish them the best of luck in the future.

The manuscript has also benefited from the thoughtful and insightful comments of three reviewers. Richard Bensel, Samih Farsoun, and Erik Olin Wright all contributed their considerable expertise to the preparation of the final text. Barbara Hanrahan, senior editor at the University of Wisconsin Press, has supported and encouraged the project patiently, since it was delayed for a year by my frequent forays into the turbulent and chaotic morass of Massachusetts state politics. My colleagues at the University of Massachusetts–Dartmouth have been notable for maintaining a combination of free inquiry, political expression, and social activism that is still rare on American campuses. I must also express my gratitude to the librarians and library staff who cheerfully lent their assistance throughout this project: Shaleen Barnes, Jane Booth, Jo-Ann Cooley, Paige Gibbs, Catherine Fortier-Barnes, Kate Jones-Randall,

Ross LaBaugh, Charles McNeil, Julie Miller, and Linda Zieper. Peggy Silva, Fera Karakaya, and Bill Kerry all provided invaluable technical assistance while I opened up new frontiers of computer illiteracy. My thanks to Robin Whitaker for lending her notable skills as a copy editor. Finally, I owe an immeasurable debt to my wife, Trini.

List of Abbreviations

AAA   Agricultural Adjustment Act

AALL   American Association for Labor Legislation

BAC   Business Advisory Council

BC   Business Council

CC   U.S. Chamber of Commerce

CED   Committee on Economic Development

CFR   Council on Foreign Relations

NAM   National Association of Manufacturers

NIRA   National Industrial Recovery Act

NRA   National Recovery Administration

RT   regulation theory

SSAT   social structure of accumulation theory

Critical Theories of the State

Introduction

This book is an introduction to the major theoretical approaches currently utilized by Marxist scholars as frameworks for the conduct of empirical or historical research on public policy and political development. The book is not intended as a comprehensive survey of the entire field of state theory, but is focused on plain Marxist, neo-Marxist, and post-Marxist theories of the state.[1] Three types of individuals are most likely to find the book useful. First, university students should find the book helpful in defining and formulating research problems on the state. Second, scholars who are not specialists in state theory but who are seeking to stay abreast of an important literature will find a concise summary and history of the Marxian contribution to that field. Finally, the new emphasis in social science on theoretically informed policy studies will commend the present survey to scholars working in various specialized fields of public policy and comparative political development.

Design and Scope of the Text

There are certainly some people who will question the value of yet another rendering of the state of state theory. Consequently, it is worth noting that the scope and design of this text differs from similar books in several ways.[2] First, there are certainly several quasi texts of varying quality already on the market, but the existing books serve more as platforms for advanced theorizing, and, thus, they tend to presume a fair degree of familiarity with previous literature on the state. It is perhaps hard for senior scholars to remember just how difficult it is to read authors such as Ralph Miliband, Nicos Poulantzas, or Claus Offe for the first time as a graduate or undergraduate student. Indeed, for those scholars who have labored on state theory throughout their careers, it may come as a surprise to note that most undergraduates and even some graduate students were not even born in the heyday of the Miliband-Poulantzas debate, the watershed event which captured the attention of so many graduate students in the late 1960s and early 1970s. Given

3

this long history, a brief reprise of the literature now seems in order. However, more important, I have chosen to write a survey that is uncompromisingly designed as an introductory orientation for the novice. Thus, one important difference between this book and similar ones is the level on which it is written.[3] Similarly, I have attempted to render an often obscure and jargon-laden literature as accessible as possible without sacrificing its conceptual or technical integrity.[4]

Second, both for brevity and for theoretical reasons, I have dispensed with the orthodox ritual of retracing the genealogy of Karl Marx's and Friedrich Engels's thinking on the state. Several of the existing works have already done an excellent job of this task.[5] The result of such analyses has made it painfully evident, as Bob Jessop concludes, that Marx "did not offer a theoretical analysis of the capitalist state to match the scope and rigour of *Das Kapital*. His work on the state comprises a fragmented and unsystematic series of philosophical reflections, contemporary history, journalism and incidental remarks."[6] Thus, although reading *Capital* and other works by Marx will always have its place in Marxian political theory, we are well beyond the point of thinking that such readings will yield a well-defined Marxist theory of the state.[7] Quite the contrary, as I will demonstrate in subsequent chapters, there are real tensions in Marx's thought that allow for the articulation of several competing approaches to the state.

Third, therefore, this text is further distinguished from similar books by its emphasis on the historical and logical development of the competing approaches.[8] Rather than focusing on specific concepts (e.g., hegemony or autonomy) and analyzing the use of those concepts across competing schools of thought, I have opted for modular presentations of entire theories. This strategy has made it possible to clarify more effectively the kinds of hypothetical assumptions that are made by the proponents of each theory and to draw out the contrasting logics of explanation that underlie each approach. This process has been facilitated by reconstructing particular schools of thought around a highly selective examination of specific theorists who are taken to represent the competing theoretical approaches. The advantage to this technique is that it enables the text to maintain a sharpness of focus and a logical continuity in presentation that would not otherwise be possible.

Finally, the text has been constructed with a specific historical and analytic focus in mind, namely, the origins of the modern welfare state and its contemporary crisis. A wide-ranging debate still rages among Marxists over how to periodize the stages of capitalist development and how to classify the forms of capitalist state that presumably correspond to these different stages. Nevertheless, there is agreement that since the Great Depression political development in the advanced capitalist societies is distinguished from previous periods by the rise of the welfare state. The concept of the welfare state has been defined theoretically in different ways and has been applied to many different types of democratic polities. Yet, for purposes of orienting the reader, one can identify the welfare state with two sets of activities that were absent from the liberal state of nineteenth-century laissez-faire capitalism.[9]

Redistributive policies are the first set of welfare-state activities. On this point, Saundra K. Schneider notes, there is consensus that an important element of the welfare state is its new responsibility for "providing certain services, benefits, and assistance to its citizens who are unable to help themselves—the sick, the old, the young, the injured, and the unemployed. Furthermore, within the societies identified as welfare states, similar types of programs have been adopted in roughly the same sequence and have been expanded in the same general direction."[10] The core of the welfare state is structured by five policy initiatives that have typically been adopted in the following historical sequence: workmen's compensation, sickness and disability benefits, old-age pensions, unemployment insurance, and family allowances.[11] Moreover, when redistributive policies are adopted by states, one of the most visible features of welfare capitalism is the absolute and relative increase in the size of the public-sector economy.

However, it is worth noting that welfare states have not generally redistributed income *among* classes as much as they have evened out income throughout the lifetime of individuals *within* classes. The programmatic nucleus of the welfare state redistributes income among age groups, between those with children and those without children, between the healthy and the sick, and between the employed and the unemployed.[12] Thus, income is largely redistributed across the life cycle of individuals to provide a "social safety net" during periods of greatest need, such as unemployment, child rearing, sickness, and retirement. What is important, however, is that the majority of welfare state benefits, such as unemployment insurance and social security, are tied to the length of previous work force participation, to prior wage and salary levels, and not specifically to need. The longer one has worked continuously on a full-time basis and the higher one's average income, the larger the benefits that will be received from these programs. In this respect, Arthur Stinchcombe observes that capitalist welfare states are "redistributive only in the sense that insurance generally is redistributive. It mostly takes from the lucky and the young to give to the unlucky and the old, and except for administrative expenses and interest earnings does not change expected lifetime incomes . . . In general, social insurance does very little to redistribute from the rich to the poor." [13]

Although welfare states have provided an increasing number of goods and services outside the market on the basis of need entitlements (e.g., family allowances and health care), generally speaking, the redistribution of wealth and income *among* classes has been left to private organizations that still compete for their relative shares in the marketplace. The most prominent examples are the trade unions and employers' associations that explicitly negotiate the division of production between wages and profits. The welfare state has confined itself mainly to codifying the rules of collective bargaining, supervising the process of collective bargaining, and enforcing the terms of otherwise privately negotiated contracts between employers and workers. Nevertheless, the institutionalization of collective bargaining has resulted in very little redistribution of income among classes in most of the welfare states and even less redistribution of wealth over the course of the last century. [14]

Consequently, in assessing the social origins and political meaning of the welfare state, it must be observed that its redistributive activities have not been at the direct expense of the private sector. The private sector has continued to grow in absolute terms so that private capital accumulation continues to take place even within welfare economies. The public sector has merely expanded more quickly in welfare economies to the degree that a larger and larger share of growth has been channeled into the public sector. [15] Furthermore, this growth has usually been part of a Keynesian macroeconomic strategy for managing effective demand in order to sustain or increase consumer and government demand for privately produced goods and services (e.g., military hardware, health care, housing). Indeed, welfare policies are typically linked to economic development and labor market strategies that simultaneously provide a minimum level of economic security for individuals and promote national economic growth, increased labor productivity, and higher profits for private businesses. Frequently, the growth of the public sector has even resulted in the state's direct absorption of the costs of private production. For instance, insofar as new production techniques require a more highly educated work force, public education may be viewed as a public subsidy to private business, because education defrays labor costs. Likewise, the state has largely absorbed the costs of retraining workers displaced by automation and technological innovation and has thus reduced the potential costs of technical innovation to private business. From this perspective, one may view private business as a major beneficiary of the welfare state.

A second set of welfare state activities is regulatory policies. The welfare state's regulatory activities are primarily directed at mitigating neighborhood effects produced by private individuals and organizations, that is, at arbitrating disputes over private actions that directly alter the immediate conditions of life of other individuals and groups within a society. State regulations may thus involve anything from protecting the rights of women and children in the household to imposing environmental standards on factory emissions. Most critical theorists would agree that as the regulatory activities of the welfare state have expanded in scope the distinction between public and private spheres of life has been steadily eroded across an ever-widening range of social activities. The welfare state has expanded its involvement not only in the regulation of economic relations, such as those between labor and management or those between the corporation and the environment. The state has become similarly involved in also regulating institutions of civil society that are primarily concerned with the development of personal identity and normative values, such as the family, education, and the Church. In this social sphere, the welfare state has been more and more directly involved in the regulation and promotion of specific normative values (e.g., abortion and racial integration) and in the maintenance of specific family structures (e.g., through day care, maternity leave, and family allowances).

Furthermore, the necessity of administering the welfare state's wide range of redistributive and regulatory policies has resulted in a concomitant expansion of the state's institutional apparatus throughout most of the twentieth century. In a process that Max Weber describes as a "quantitative" expansion of the state apparatus, the state has become physically bigger in terms of both the number, size, and complexity of its institutions and the numbers of civilian and military personnel employed by the state.[16] The welfare state is a leviathan state, whether measured by public expenditures, the increase of state personnel, or the expansion of its regulatory, taxing, military, and educational institutions. Moreover, as state activities have grown wider in scope, the state's institutional capacities have simultaneously penetrated more deeply into the economic and social orders. As Weber describes it, there has also been a qualitative development of relations between the state apparatus and civil society, a relation in which the state, metaphorically, has pushed its institutional rhizomes ever more deeply into the soil of civil society.[17]

This introductory description of the welfare state leaves open the question of its social origins and class-theoretic nature. Whether the welfare state is a socially neutral mechanism for balancing the claims of society and private capital, a first step on the road to socialism, or a control mechanism for diffusing opposition to capitalism (and that "saves capitalism from itself") remains a point of continuing debate among theorists and policy analysts. The political interpretation and theoretical explanation of the welfare state are still unresolved issues that will be discussed from various perspectives in the subsequent chapters.[18]

In chapter 1, a school of thought that I refer to as plain Marxism interprets the state as an instrument of class domination. In this view, the state serves the interests of whatever class controls its central institutions, such as the chief executive, the civil bureaucracy, the police, armed forces, and schools. Thus, these "instrumentalists" explain the welfare state as a form of "corporate liberalism" designed by the capitalist class to undercut the historically more radical demands of the working classes. In chapter 2, on the other hand, scholars associated with the structuralist neo-Marxist approach conceptualize the state as an arena of class struggle. The state's relative autonomy from particular social groups enables it to mediate social conflict and, therefore, to function as a "factor of cohesion" which regulates the equilibrium between competing classes within the social system. Thus, neo-Marxist structuralists explain the welfare state as a form of capitalist regulation that partly responds to the demands of workers while also functioning to constrain state policies within limits that are compatible with a capitalist mode of production. Chapter 3 reconstructs the derivationist or capital logic school, which conceptualizes the state as an "ideal collective capitalist." According to this approach, the state's main function is to provide the general legal framework for a capitalist economy (e.g., private property and contract law) and to supply market deficiencies (e.g., infrastructure) which capitalists cannot provide for themselves. From this perspective, the welfare state is explained by the ever-increasing failure of capitalist economies to generate self-sustaining private-sector economic growth.

Chapter 4 examines a group of post-Marxist scholars who employ a systems-analytic approach to the state. This particular type of post-Marxism argues that welfare states must simultaneously promote capital accumulation and maintain democratic legitimacy. Therefore, to the extent that these dual systemic imperatives are often mutually contradictory, the state emerges as an increasingly incoherent institutional matrix that necessarily generates a steady stream of policy failures. In failing to perform its functions adequately, the state is seen as tending toward a multiplicity of potential crises. Finally, chapter 5 analyzes a post-Marxist approach called organizational realism. Organizational realism views the state as a political organization that seeks intrinsically to control territory and people. This approach maintains that all states seek to maximize their autonomous institutional powers and to advance the interests of state officials in controlling more resources, people, and territory. Consequently, organizational realists view economic and international crises as potential opportunities for state officials to initiate policies that increase their autonomy from the economically dominant capitalist class. Thus, by taking control of additional economic resources during crises and using them to enhance the state's strength, state officials may actually find it advantageous to establish new client relationships with subaltern classes, which, they claim, is evidenced in the construction of the welfare state.

Methodology and the State

It must be emphasized that no particular interpretation or explanation of the state is definitively "proven" by the historical and empirical evidence used to illustrate the competing claims of different approaches. Indeed, one of the more significant repercussions of the many postpositivist critiques of social science is the increased recognition by political theorists that "facts" never speak for themselves.[19] Instead, the ideological power of theories is their ability to reduce the complexity of historical developments and empirical data to a few orderly relationships that explain these developments and data.[20] In reducing the complexity of a particular object—for example, capitalism or the state—we are designating certain questions, problems of historical interpretation, and empirical phenomena as being worthy of further investigation. Robert R. Alford and Roger Friedland point out that because "a theory focuses upon a particular factor as historically important, . . . the empirical manifestations of that factor become important, and they are singled out for investigation."[21] Thus, in line with Mark Warren's recent suggestion, this work adopts the premise that "political scientists need to develop a greater awareness of how their theories constitute their problems and even their findings."[22] The best way to achieve this methodological objective is to make the theories into objects of study.[23]

Political theories have an analytic and a methodological dimension. The analytic dimension of a political theory consists of key concepts that select, name, and logically interrelate a specified range of phenomena—in this instance, a range of phenomena identified as the state. However, in selecting and interrelating phenomena, political theories simultaneously put forward specific claims about *how* various events and phenomena are related to one another. Either these claims can be accepted as unproblematic philosophical presuppositions, or they can be viewed as provisional hypotheses that further research may confirm, revise, or falsify. Hence, political theories must also advance a methodological position that enables scholars to specify what kinds of research and evidence are necessary to test those hypothetical claims and to provide rules about what counts as an adequate explanation of the state.

The focus of this text has been rigorously confined to an examination of the various ways in which these two dimensions—analytic and methodological—have been conceptualized and linked together to construct competing theoretical approaches to the state. The central problem at the analytic level of state theory is to define what range of phenomena are encompassed by a concept of the state. This may at first seem like an easy task to accomplish, as it once did to me, until midway through a course on "Class, Power, and the State" a sophomore timidly asked me: "What is the state anyway?" When posed in so direct a manner, one is forced to acknowledge that the existing literature provides no single answer to that question. In fact, as noted above, there are many different, sometimes overlapping, and often incompatible concepts of the state prevalent in the theoretical literature.

Therefore, this text regards "the state" as an essentially contested concept.[24] What is important, as Russell Hanson notes, is that the main thing which sets essential contests apart from other theoretical disputes in the social sciences is the fact that each contestant's usage of a concept has merit.[25] No single usage of the concept is self-evidently correct, nor does any one usage necessarily exclude other usages in different contexts. Because there is currently no discernable principle for evaluating even the comparative superiority of any one concept of the state as opposed to others, the text rejects the idea that there is any metatheoretical position from which to arbitrate the current dispute.[26] Moreover, the inconclusive (and often vacuous) results of previous forays into the metatheory of the state make it highly dubious whether there is any grand synthesis that can transcend the existing array of competing theories.[27] Indeed, it is my contention that there is no single, overarching synthetic standpoint from which the state is fully comprehensible.

Quite the contrary, the text lends support to John Gray's hypothesis that "essentially contested concepts occur characteristically in social contexts which are recognizably those of an ideological dispute."[28] In this case, what is most often at stake in the essential contest is not simply a concept of the state, but also the validation of particular political strategies; that is, each Marxian concept of the state tends to be associated with a specific type of socialist politics. Thus, as Robert Grafstein has argued: ". . . essential contestability does not characterize political concepts by accident . . . concepts are essentially contestable because they are political."[29] Put simply, political theorists are contesting the concept of the welfare state, because the welfare state is contested in politics.

This observation defines a second major thesis that constrains the theoretical focus of the text. The text is designed from a standpoint, advanced most explicitly by George Lukács, that being a Marxist "does not imply the uncritical acceptance of the results of Marx's investigations."[30] However, contrary to Lukács's more famous dictum, the following chapters reject the claim that Marxist theory refers exclusively to a method. Rather, Marxist theories, like other theories, are constituted by the irreducible fusion of a specifiable analytic *and* methodological dimension. Moreover, throughout the text I maintain that what is peculiarly "Marxist" about Marxist theories is the conceptual constellation constituting its analytic dimension. What is Marxist about Marxism is concepts such as the relations of production (i.e., the foundation of Marxist definitions of class), surplus value and exploitation, and the tendency for the rate of profit to fall, among others.

On the other hand, as Eduard Bernstein pointed out nearly a century ago, the text firmly adheres to the thesis that there is no such thing as a Marxist methodology.[31] Methodological approaches such as power structure analysis, structural functionalism, systems analysis, and organizational realism are in no way peculiar attributes of Marxism. Consequently, I argue that the methodological debates which continue to divide Marxists into competing theoretical camps are not substantially different from the methodological debates in mainstream social science.[32]

Hence, a chief objective of the text is to demonstrate the way in which specific concepts of the state are linked to particular methodological assumptions. The way in which the analytic and methodological dimensions intersect each other constitutes different approaches, while each approach points toward a different empirical and historical research agenda. The text aims to identify the key methodological presuppositions of each approach and so specify what kinds of evidence count in its explanation of the state. From this perspective, it becomes evident that essential contests over the meaning of the state are, simultaneously and irretrievably, debates about social science methodology. I do not resolve these issues, since, as indicated above, pending some unforeseen paradigmatic revolution there is no metatheoretical principle on which to arbitrate these methodological contests.[33] However, what one can do is clarify methodological assumptions and thus internally specify the kinds of hypotheses that require testing in order to sustain the plausibility of a theoretical position. Implicit in this approach is a distinction between the truth and meaning of theories that is best summarized by Brian Fay:

> Even though what it means for a proposition to be true is a result of human conventions, and even though these conventions could have been otherwise than they are, and even though they contain ideological components, it does not follow that this proposition cannot be objectively true in an important sense. Thus, men decide what it means to say that "it is raining outside," but men do not decide, *given this meaning,* whether this proposition is true, i.e., they do not decide whether it is raining—for *that* they have to look and see.[34]

However, Claus Offe finds that a radical dissention within the field of state theory has made it impossible for any one theoretical approach to "monopolize definitions of Marxism and its limits" effectively.[35] Similarly, in their comprehensive survey of the state theory literature, Alford and Friedland conclude that "if there was ever a hegemonic perspective called Marxism, there is one no longer."[36] In the absence of either an intellectual consensus or a compelling political orthodoxy, it is not possible to agree even on what counts as an adequate theory of the state. The following chapters accept that dissention and seek to explain its irreducibility within Marxian political theory.

CHAPTER ONE

Plain Marxism: The Instrumentalist Approach[1]

The executive of the modern State is but a committee for managing the common affairs of the whole bourgeoisie.
—*Marx and Engels*, Communist Manifesto, *1848*

The most succinct statement of instrumentalist theory is Paul Sweezy's assertion that the state is "an instrument in the hands of the ruling class for enforcing and guaranteeing the stability of the class structure itself."[2] The basic thesis of the instrumentalist approach is that modern capitalists are able to formulate public policies which represent their long-term class interests and to secure the adoption, implementation, and enforcement of those policies through state institutions. Thus, instrumentalist theory offers a straightforward and simple claim that the modern state serves the interests of the capitalist class because it is dominated by that class.

The Methodology of Power Structure Research

Most instrumentalists employ the method of power structure research.[3] Power structure research is a methodological approach which views the organized control, possession, and ownership of key resources as the basis for exercising power in any society. Key resources typically consist of wealth, status, force, and knowledge.[4] Moreover, in every society, control over these key resources is institutionalized through specific (and often competing) organizations of the economy, society, government, and culture.

What is important is that institutions organize power in a society by vesting the individuals occupying certain positions with the authority to make decisions about how to deploy the key resources mobilized by that institution. For instance, as an economic institution, the modern corporation vests its board of directors and executive officers with the authority to allocate any economic resources which the corporation

13

owns or controls. Likewise, government vests specific public officials with the authority to employ administrative coercion or police force against anyone who fails to comply with the law. Similarly, educational institutions certify specific individuals as possessing expertise in particular fields of knowledge. In this sense, the individuals who occupy positions of institutional authority in a society control different types of power: economic power, political power, ideological power. Thus, power can be imputed to particular groups of individuals to the degree that they control resources such as wealth, force, status, or knowledge. A power structure consists of a patterned distribution of resources that is regularized by the institutions within a particular society.

Power structures can be conceptualized along with two methodological axioms:

Axiom$_1$:   The more widely dispersed the institutional control of key resources, the more reasonable it becomes to describe a power structure as egalitarian.

Axiom$_2$:   The more concentrated the institutional control of key resources, the more reasonable it becomes to describe a power structure as one dominated by a ruling class.

A key methodological assumption of power structure analysis is that patterned distributions of key resources institutionalize the levels of power that specific individuals can potentially deploy against other individuals or that they can deploy in realizing their objectives at any given time and place.[5] The research agenda generated by this analytic framework is driven by the further assumption that one can develop empirical maps of a power structure by measuring the relative degrees of power controlled by different groups of individuals. Relative amounts of power are indicated by the degree to which those who control a particular resource (e.g., wealth) are able to monopolize (1) the control of that key resource which defines them as a social group, and (2) the control of other key resources that potentially supply other groups with competing sources of power.

Thus, for example, a simple indicator of economic power would be the distribution of wealth and income among different groups or classes in society. One way to ascertain social status would be to measure the social reputation accorded certain occupational groups, such as corporate executives, lawyers, and professors.[6] The most effective way to chart linkages between sources of power is to measure the degree to which specific groups of individuals hold overlapping positions of authority. For example, do those groups who control knowledge and information, such as professors, also command greater social prestige, or do they simultaneously control positions of state power? If so, a power structure analysis would infer that such groups control more power than if they did not hold overlapping positions of authority in society.[7]

It should be emphasized that there is nothing necessarily "Marxist" about the methodology of power structure research.[8] First, the question of whether or not key resources are actually dispersed or concentrated in a particular society is not necessarily presupposed as part of the methodological approach. As a result, the method of power structure research has often been employed to test hypotheses put forward by pluralist, polyarchist, and Marxist theorists alike.[9] Second, the method of power structure research does not assign a relative analytic weight to any of the key resources. Thus, a power structure methodology provides no indication a priori whether wealth, knowledge, coercion, or status should be conceptualized as equivalent and coequal sources of power (as in pluralist theory) or whether any one power source should be assigned a stronger analytic weight in conceptualizing an empirical power structure. However, a specifically Marxian deployment of power structure analysis is typically informed by two additional theoretical principles.

These principles, taken from Marx's *Capital* (volume 1), are the Principle of Commodification and the General Law of Capitalist Accumulation.[10] The Principle of Commodification refers to the idea that in capitalist societies all use values are potentially convertible to exchange values. As a historical phenomenon, commodification is the tendency of the capitalist mode of production to extend market relations to a wider and wider range of social phenomena, thus making it possible to convert capital (i.e., money) to other types of use values.[11] The importance of this principle to a theory of the state is its implication that wealth and income (i.e., capital) are always a potentially generalizable source of power in capitalist society. Capital is convertible to other forms of power to a degree that is not true of social status, political influence, or knowledge.[12] For example, an individual or social group that controls capital can utilize its market power to obtain legal talent, social prestige, technical consultation, and political office. On the other hand, as any student will know, knowledge is not so readily convertible to money or political power. Consequently, in Marxian theory, capital is presumed to be the single most important, though not the only, source of power in a capitalist society. For that reason, the ownership of capital is accorded prior analytic weight in the explanation and analysis of power structures.

The General Law of Capitalist Accumulation simply refers to the historical tendency for capital and other productive assets to become concentrated and centralized in the hands of fewer and fewer individuals in the regular course of capitalist economic development.[13] Thus, if one combines the Principle of Commodification with the General Law of Capitalist Accumulation, one would expect that, as a consequence of its control of capital, the capitalist class will have a greater relative capacity to deploy an array of power resources on its own behalf *under normal circumstances*. As a result, there is a theoretical expectation that other sources of power will be pulled into the orbit of the capitalist class in one of two ways. Capital can be converted to direct *control* of other resources (e.g., state offices and higher education), or it can be used to *influence* those who control other resources (e.g., campaign contributions, consultant positions, and research grants). This means that under normal circumstances the capitalist class will be able to mobilize and deploy a variety of key resources in greater and more efficient concentrations than other classes in society. This expectation is the theoretical basis for Ralph Miliband's postulate that ". . . in the Marxist scheme, the 'ruling class' of capitalist society is that class which owns and controls the means of production and which is able, by virtue of the economic power thus conferred upon it, to use the state as its instrument for the domination of society."[14]

David Gold, Clarence Lo, and Erik Olin Wright point out that this theoretical approach to defining the state requires that one be able to answer three questions: (1) What is the nature of the class which rules? (2) What are the mechanisms which tie this class to the state? (3) What is the concrete relationship between state policies and ruling class interests?[15] Hence, the instrumentalist research agenda can be formalized in three hypotheses:

(H₁)   There is a capitalist class defined by its ownership and control of the means of production.

(H₂)   The capitalist class uses the state to dominate the rest of society.

(H₃)   State policies further the general interests of the capitalist class in maintaining their domination of society.

Power Structure: The Economic Base

For the most part, plain Marxists have directed their research activities toward generating evidence that lends support to each of these hypotheses and thus builds a cumulative case for the instrumentalist thesis. The initial step, as suggested in the first hypothesis, is to demonstrate that an economically dominant class does exist in capitalist society.[16] As Domhoff notes, if the capitalist class is to be viewed as a real historical actor, then one must be able to identify empirically "an observable, differentiated, interacting social group with more or less definite boundaries."[17]

In contemporary analyses, the corporation supplies an initial reference point for identifying the capitalist class. Corporations emerged as the dominant economic institutions in capitalist societies by the end of the nineteenth century. By the late 1920s, the bulk of U.S. economic activity, whether measured in terms of assets, profits, employment, investment, market shares, or research and development, was concentrated in the fifty largest financial institutions and the five hundred largest nonfinancial corporations.[18] Baran and Sweezy refer to this key sector of the U.S. economy as *monopoly* capital in order to distinguish it from the millions of lesser corporations and individual small businesses constituting *competitive* capital.[19]

Typically, members of the capitalist class are identified as those persons who manage corporations and/or those who own corporations. Thus, the capitalist class is an overlapping economic network based on institutional position (i.e., management) and property relations (i.e., ownership).[20] The wealthy families who own large blocks of corporate stock and the high-ranking managers of those same corporations are usually estimated to compose no more than 0.5–1 percent of the total U.S. population.[21] This small corporate elite stands in contrast with those classes who neither own nor manage productive capital in the United States, namely, industrial workers, the poor, many white-collar professionals, and service-sector employees. This highly diversified working class makes up about 85 percent of the U.S. population.[22]

In these terms, few scholars would any longer dispute that the United States has a corporate elite. Furthermore, most scholars would agree that corporate elites wield immense economic power through their authority to allocate corporate resources within individual firms and by deploying those same resources toward political, educational, and cultural goals. However, for power structure analysts, the key objective is to determine whether corporate owners and managers constitute a coherent ruling class, or whether they are simply a loose agglomeration of privileged special interests. For the most part, neo-Marxists and post-Marxists who employ other approaches to the state have adopted the view that corporate elites are inherently incapable of organizing themselves as a class. Instead, they argue, market rivalries between individual companies and conflicts of interest between different industries are seen as mechanisms that direct corporate elites toward pursuing the specific interests of their particular company or industry.[23]

Thus, a key issue in contemporary power structure research is whether or not corporate elites have a capacity to formulate their general class interests and to act then as a coherent organizational entity in pursuit of those interests. As Beth Mintz observes, this challenge has required more recent studies of the internal structure of the U.S. capitalist class to "concentrate on one organizing question: are there mechanisms for cohesion capable of transforming a series of important actors into a unified social class?"[24] The primary thrust of this research has been to evaluate the potential for coordinated action among corporate elites on the basis of, first, shared economic interests and, second, a set of common social experiences and cultural values. The first type of research is called positional analysis, and the latter is called social analysis.

Positional Analysis

The most common model of U.S. capitalist class formation is based in a concept of financial groups. Paul A. Baran and Paul Sweezy define a financial group as a "number of corporations under common control, the locus of power being normally an investment or commercial bank or a great family fortune."[25] There are a variety of indicators for identifying linkages between individual corporations and corporate elites, but, as Mintz notes, "the most popular in this regard are investigations of interlocking directorates."[26] Private corporations, such as banks, industrial firms, and commercial enterprises, are governed by boards of directors elected by shareholders. The board of directors exercises the proprietary, or ownership, function of the corporation. Directors have the legal authority to make decisions concerning wages, working conditions, and terms of employment in the corporation, to establish capital investment policies, to set goals for profitability, product prices, and decide virtually any other matter related to the disposition of a corporation's assets. Interlocking directors are individuals who simultaneously sit on two or more corporate boards of directors. An interlocking directorate is said to exist whenever a stable network of interlocking directors is identified among a specific group of corporations.[27]

The theoretical importance of interlocking directorates is twofold. First, it is hypothesized that interlocking directorates provide a linking mechanism for intercorporate coordination and planning in the monopoly capital sector. Second, it is theoretically plausible to infer that interlocking directors are more likely than their noninterlocking counterparts to "think in terms not only of the narrow interests of the individual corporation but also of the good of the class as a whole."[28] This is because their position within the corporate network is tied simultaneously to several different companies that often represent several different industries. Thus, interlocking directors are much more likely than other elements of the corporate elite to be the agents of classwide interests.

The intercorporate agent established by interlocking directorates is often referred to as finance capital.[29] The reason for this designation is that the officers, directors, and owners of financial corporations (e.g., banks, securities firms, and insurance companies) are usually at the center of interlocking directorates in the monopoly sector as indicated by their number of interlocks and the geographic scope and industrial distribution of their interlocks.[30] However, it should be emphasized that the concept of finance capital does not refer exclusively to persons or institutions in the financial sector; it simply designates the asymmetrical balance of power that exists between the financial and nonfinancial sectors of the monopoly capitalist class.

At present, the financial-groups model has generated a sizable amount of evidence to support claims that U.S. corporate elites are currently organized into several classwide financial groups. As the general model would suggest, the internal structure of each group is dominated by one or more financial institutions which occupy the center of each group.[31] An example is provided in figure 1.1. Previous research indicates that by 1935 eight major financial groups (three national and five regional) had been constructed in the United States.[32] Furthermore, additional research has recently suggested that despite the potential for rivalries between financial groups there is an emerging pattern of coordination between them.[33]

A systemic division of labor between U.S. financial groups is apparently based in three classes of financial institutions: New York money-center banks, regional commercial banks, and major insurance companies. Research findings indicate that elites attached to regional commercial banks are at the center of dense pockets of corporate inter-

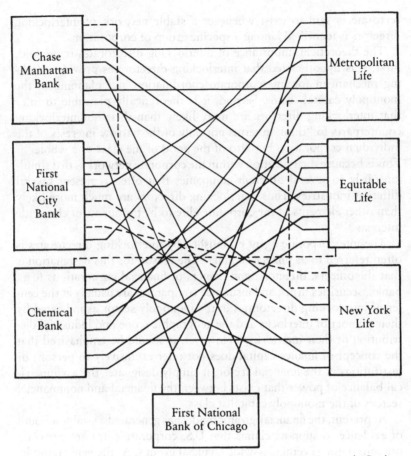

Figure 1.1. Interlocking directorates among the core financial institutions in the Rocke-feller Group

Source: Knowles, "The Rockefeller Financial Group," pp. 343–46.

Note: Each line designates an individual who sits on the boards of directors of the con-nected institutions (i.e., an interlocking director). Knowles ("The Rockefeller Financial Group") also establishes that the financial institutions shown in Figure 1.1 had effective control of at least forty-four nonfinancial corporations among the Standard & Poor's 500.

locking at the local level. Furthermore, these densely interlocked re-gional groups are increasingly connected to the larger money-center banks by a series of bridging links created by the country's largest insur-ance companies. The regional orientation of monopoly capital is thus "organized by the major regional banks whose interests are rooted in the local economic environment and whose position in the interlock

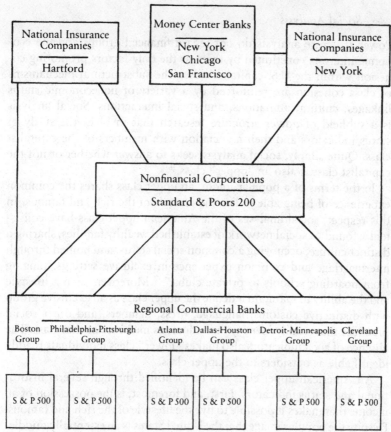

Figure 1.2. A financial groups model of the capitalist class

Sources: Constructed as a summary of the literature as presented by Mintz, "United States of America," pp. 207–36; and Knowles, *Superconcentration/Supercorporation*, pp. 2–13.

network reflects its role in local capital allocation." However, regional and "local orientations are transcended by the bridging function of the major insurance companies which link the regions into a coherent whole."[34] The result is a functionally integrated intercorporate system that supplies the internal mechanisms for unifying finance capital (see figure 1.2). Moreover, as Michael Schwartz observes, the importance of this corporate power structure to a theory of the state is that the "centralization of the economic sector provides the foundation upon which corporate domination of American life is constructed."[35]

Social Analysis

Power structure analysts do not regard financial groups and the economic interests constituted by them as the only factors promoting cohesion within the U.S. capitalist class. The substructural mechanisms of class cohesion are reinforced by a variety of noneconomic status linkages, cultural affiliations, and social interactions. Social analysis is a subfield of power structure research that involves the study of status indicators and their association with members of the capitalist class. Quite simply, social analysis seeks to answer whether or not the capitalist class is also an "upper" class.[36]

In the terms of a popular idiom, an upper class shares the common experience of being able to live the lifestyle of the rich and famous. In this respect, social analyses of the American upper class have consistently found "a social network of established wealthy families, sharing a distinct culture, occupying a common social status, and unified through intermarriage and common experience in exclusive settings, ranging from boarding schools to private clubs."[37] Moreover, such a lifestyle and the ability to maintain it define the upper class as an exclusive group with distinctive customs, language, dress, manners, and other social practices that readily identify individuals as members of that class. The absence of such indicators also makes "lower" class individuals readily identifiable as outsiders to the upper class.

An American upper class can be identified through several institutional and status indicators. First, and foremost, is the possession of an income that makes it possible to live the lifestyle of the rich and famous. Despite the popular image that the United States is an essentially middle-class society, the fact is that the top 1.0 percent of American families own 61 percent of all outstanding corporate stock in the United States, and 41 percent of total personal income goes to the top one-fifth of families in the United States.[38] It should be pointed out that this distribution of wealth and income has not changed substantially since the 1920s (see tables 2.1 and 2.2 in the next chapter) and that inequalities of wealth and income actually grew larger during the 1980s.[39]

Likewise, empirical and historical studies have revealed that the U.S. social upper class betrays many of the characteristics that one would associate with a hereditary aristocracy. Indeed, E. Digby Baltzell has concluded that the American upper class may be appropriately called a business aristocracy.[40] For example, wealth tends to be accumulated and transmitted from one generation to the next through inherited estates. Similarly, contrary to the popular American myth of poor girls marrying rich boys and vice versa, the reality is that the social upper class tends to intermarry within its own ranks to the exclusion of other classes. Members of the social upper class also distinguish themselves from the rest of society through various forms of conspicuous consumption: wearing expensive clothes, dining at exclusive restaurants, sponsoring debutante balls for their daughters, throwing lavish gala parties, making large charitable contributions, driving luxury automobiles, and vacationing at restricted spas and resorts.[41] The subhypothesis underlying such research is that, the more these status indicators overlap with the capitalist class (as defined by economic relations to production), the more the capitalist class is likely to perceive a broader range of common interests distinct from those of the rest of society; in other words, members of the capitalist class are more likely to be class conscious.

However, Mintz cites the fact that 70 percent of U.S. corporate executives are not upper class by family origin to effectively emphasize the analytic difference between the corporate elite and the social upper class.[42] The implication of such findings is that the analytic linkage between corporate elite membership and upper-class membership must be viewed as contingent on the degree to which "members of the upper class also occupy positions in or around large companies."[43] The general findings have been that most members of the upper class are also members of the corporate elite (though not all members of the corporate elite are necessarily members of the upper class). Members of the upper class nearly always derive their large incomes and, hence, the ability to live a lavish lifestyle from their positions as owners or managers of corporations; that is, the rich are rich because they are members of the capitalist class.

However, this should not be taken to imply that all members of the corporate elite are necessarily welcomed into the exclusive social and cultural circles of the capitalist upper class. In fact, not all members of the corporate elite are immediately welcomed into the social institutions that define the upper class. One can find frequent examples of individuals who are members of the corporate elite but who are not socially integrated into the noneconomic institutions of the upper class. This distinction is often conceptualized as a division between "new money" and "old money" within the U.S. capitalist class. New money capitalists, often referred to as barbarians or cowboy capitalists, are thus sometimes in conflict with the old money capitalists, who are frequently called the patricians or Brahmins of the class.

However, social analysis indicates that here, too, there are a variety of intraclass mechanisms constantly at work to assimilate new money barbarians into the social networks of the upper class. Their selective admission into upper-class social institutions is designed to socialize new corporate elites gradually into the higher circles of the capitalist class.[44] For instance, individuals with the proper educational credentials will be more readily accepted into the social circles of the class. Proper credentials are usually identified with Ivy League university degrees, especially those from Harvard, Yale, Princeton, Penn, and Columbia.[45] In time, as new money barbarians adopt the lifestyle, attitudes, and manners of the upper class, they receive invitations to participate in the elite world of private social clubs, gala parties, and debutante balls.[46] Their social integration into the class is solidified when they buy homes in exclusive neighborhoods, send their children to the right preparatory schools and academies, make sizable contributions to charity, and either they or their children marry into established upper-class families. Thus, the social integration of the capitalist class is an ongoing process that is continuously taking place from generation to generation.

The State or Capital: Who Governs?

A second hypothesis of instrumentalist theory is the claim that the capitalist class is able to use the state to dominate the rest of society and in so doing to constitute itself as a ruling class. However, to test such a hypothesis, two further concepts (in addition to the capitalist class) must be assigned clearly demarcated referents. It is necessary to define what power structure analysts mean by "the state" and "ruling class."

For instrumentalists, the state is a multidimensional concept with three levels of meaning. Each dimension of the concept refers to one component of an interconnected network of territorial, institutional, and ideological phenomena that are collectively called the state system. At its most basic level, the state is a *sovereign political territory*, namely, a nation-state like the United States or France. However, as a sovereign political territory, the state is maintained, governed, and administered by a *state apparatus*.[47] The modern state apparatus consists of a number of specific institutions that may be grouped into four state subsystems:

1. the governmental subsystem, consisting of elected legislative and executive authorities;
2. the administrative subsystem, consisting of the civil service bureaucracy, public corporations, central banks, regulatory commissions, and "private" professional associations that

exercise government-delegated regulatory authority;
3. the coercive subsystem, consisting of the military, police, judiciary, and intelligence agencies; and
4. the ideological subsystem, consisting of schools, universities, and government-financed cultural and scientific organizations.[48]

Finally, and equally important, the state is a state of mind that scholars call *legitimacy*. The legitimacy of a state is ultimately expressed in people's willingness to comply with decisions made by the state apparatus, and, if necessary, to risk their lives defending the common territory of the state.[49] Thus, a ruling class may be defined as a clearly demarcated social class (H_1) which has power over the state apparatus and over the underlying population within a given territory.

Power structure analysis has identified five political processes which cumulatively enable the capitalist class to exercise political domination through the state apparatus and to wield power over the underlying population. These five processes are called the colonization process, the special-interest process, the policy-planning process, the candidate-selection process, and the ideological process. The processes constitute a network of mechanisms that establish and maintain a state-capital conjuncture in instrumentalist theory.

One of the most direct indicators of ruling-class domination is the degree to which members of the capitalist class control the state apparatus through interlocking positions in the governmental, administrative, coercive, and ideological apparatuses. *Positional control of the state apparatus is particularly important in instrumentalist theory, because the theory locates state power within the state system's institutional apparatus.* As Miliband emphasizes: "It is these institutions in which 'state power' lies, and it is through them that this power is wielded in its different manifestations by the people who occupy the leading positions in each of these institutions."[50] For this reason, according to Miliband, instrumentalists attach considerable importance to the social composition of the state elite. The class composition of a state elite creates "a strong presumption . . . as to its general outlook, ideological dispositions and political bias" in the way it will wield state power.[51]

From this perspective, one way to measure the degree of potential class domination is to quantify the extent to which members of a particular class have colonized the state apparatus. One measures the colonization process simply by counting heads, namely, by quantifying the degree to which the means of political decision-making are controlled by members of a particular class. Thus, an analysis of the colonization process seeks to find out whether or not members of the capitalist class also hold most of the decision-making positions in the state apparatus; that is, does the class which wields economic power also control state power?

Instrumentalists have often relied heavily on colonization studies for their explanation of state-capital conjunctures. Indeed, in the eyes of critics, instrumentalism is synonymous with the concept of colonization. As a consequence, two of the most frequent criticisms of the approach have concerned the importance of colonization to instrumentalist theory. First, instrumentalists have been roundly criticized for suggesting that the state is totally dominated by finance capital, thereby implying that the state lacks the autonomy ever to act against the capitalist class on behalf of other classes. If this accusation were correct, then instrumentalism would be incapable of explaining instances in which other classes (e.g., competitive capital or workers) have made real inroads against finance capital through institutional or policy reform.[52] A second major criticism is made on empirical grounds. Finance capitalists do not directly control most positions in the state apparatus. However, the first criticism has confused the theory of instrumentalism with its empirical findings.[53] The second criticism has wildly exaggerated the empirical claims made by proponents of the theory.

Contrary to often-made assertions, adherents of instrumentalist theory have considered the process of colonization an important one, precisely because they begin with the explicit presumption of an analytic separation of class and state. As Domhoff has recently pointed out, the basic assumption of power structure research is that the state "might well be independent of the upper class and the big-business community; otherwise, all the empirical digging, network tracing, and content analysis that constitutes the field of power structure research makes no sense whatsoever theoretically."[54] Likewise, Miliband agrees that "the first step in the analysis is to note the obvious but fundamental fact that this [capitalist] class is involved in a *relationship* with the state, which cannot be *assumed* in the political conditions which are typical of advanced capitalism," namely, political democracy.[55]

The analytic autonomy of the state means that, from the instrumentalist perspective, any relationship between class and state is a historically contingent one. As Domhoff further observes: "What this means empirically is that there can be no general theory of the relationship between state and ruling class"; that is, the state in capitalist society is not necessarily either capitalist or democratic.[56] Consequently, it becomes theoretically important to know who actually controls state power at any given time. Moreover, it is the autonomy of the state as a separate power source that opens up the theoretical possibility that noncapitalist classes might actually "seize" state power under certain circumstances, whether through elections or revolution, and then be able to deploy that power against the capitalist class.

Likewise, despite the importance of colonization to the theory, instrumentalists have always made circumscribed empirical claims about the degree to which capitalists colonize the state apparatus. For instance, Ralph Miliband finds that businessmen have not "assumed the major share of government" in most advanced capitalist democracies.[57] For that reason, he argues, capitalists "are not, properly speaking, a 'governing' class, comparable to pre-industrial, aristocratic and land-owning classes."[58] Consequently, if capitalists are a ruling class, it is not primarily (or at least exclusively) because they colonize the state apparatus. Instead, the colonization of certain key positions is merely one weapon, albeit an important one, in the arsenal of ruling-class domination. Moreover, given the empirical results of instrumentalist analyses, colonization alone is clearly insufficient to account for capitalist domination of the state. Rather, what instrumentalists have persistently argued is that capitalists are "well represented in the political executive and in other parts of the state system" and that their occupation of these key positions in the apparatus enables them to exercise *decisive influence* over public policy.[59]

The fact that finance capitalists usually control the executive branch of government and the administrative-regulatory apparatuses is considered particularly important for both historical and theoretical reasons. In historical terms, political development of the state apparatus has been marked mainly by the growth of its regulatory, administrative, and coercive institutions over the course of the last century. While these institutions have grown in size, numbers, and technical complexity, the state's various subsystems have achieved greater autonomy from government in their operations. The growth of independent administrative and regulatory subsystems within the state has occurred because governments, especially legislatures, have found it increasingly difficult to maintain any central direction over the many components of the state system. The historical result is that the center of state power has shifted from the legislative to the executive branch of government and to independent administrative or regulatory agencies.

This development is theoretically important in instrumentalist theory, partly because the very basis of state power is concentrated in those

institutions (i.e., administration, coercion, knowledge) and partly because it is those institutions that the capitalist class has colonized most
successfully. Thus, the actual extent of power that capitalists achieve by
colonizing executive and administrative posts has been magnified by the
internal power structure of the contemporary state system, that is, by
the imperial presidency and the emergence of "independent" regulatory
agencies. This magnification of their state power provides monopoly
capitalists with a platform from which to initiate, modify, or veto a
broad range of national policy proposals.

Miliband certainly recognizes that a potential weakness of even this
limited claim is the fact that capitalists usually colonize only the top
command posts of government and administration. Consequently, additional processes must be at work if instrumentalism is to provide an
adequate account of state-capital conjunctures. The colonization process is clearly unable to explain the operational unity of the entire state
system. In other words, one must be able to identify the mechanism that
leads a number of relatively autonomous and divergent state subsystems
to operate as if they were a single entity called *the* state.

First, a mechanism must be identified to explain how the state elite
(i.e., those capitalists occupying top command posts) maintain the intra-
institutional unity of the state apparatuses. Indeed, the loose connection
of lower-level career administrators to the state elite is indicated by
Miliband's description of them as servants of the state. In fact, these
"servants" are frequently conceptualized as a separate professional-
managerial class composed of lower- and middle-level career state managers.[60] Miliband observes: "The general pattern must be taken to be
one in which these men [i.e., state managers] do play an important part
in the process of governmental decision-making, and therefore constitute a considerable force in the configuration of political power in their
societies."[61] Likewise, a problem of systemic unity derives from the disparate organization of the contemporary state apparatus. To the extent
that the state system is viewed as a web of decentered institutions, one
must account for how the state elite and state managers are able to maintain some overarching interinstitutional cohesion that is "capitalist" in
its content.[62]

Miliband has attempted to explain the coherence of the state system
by suggesting that its operational unity is primarily ideological, that is,
a state of mind. He argues that most state elites, including those who
are not members of the capitalist class, "accept as beyond question the
capitalist context in which they operate." Consequently, their views
on public policy "are conditioned by, and pass through the prism of,

their acceptance of and commitment to the existing economic system." In Miliband's account, the ideological commitments of state elites and state managers are of "absolutely fundamental importance in shaping their attitudes, policies and actions in regard to specific issues and problems with which they are confronted." The result of their underlying ideological unity is that "the politics of advanced capitalism have been about different conceptions of how to run the *same* economic and social system." [63]

Yet, by relying on the subhypothesis that the state's systemic unity is primarily ideological, two additional problems surface for instrumentalist theory. First, theoretical treatments of the state have too often assumed that those capitalists who serve as state elites have a coherent political vision. [64] However, if this claim is to be anything more than mere assertion, specific mechanisms must again be identified that facilitate political class consciousness by capitalists. Moreover, if capitalists are class conscious, then one should also be able to identify and reconstruct their specific political ideology.

Second, instrumentalist theory must likewise account for the pro-capitalist nature of the state managers' ideological commitments. Miliband nominally resolves the second problem by reference to the workings of an ideological system. The ideological system is an institutional matrix that includes the state's ideological apparatus (i.e., schools and universities) and private institutions such as churches, the mass media, and other opinion-shaping networks. As with the economic and state systems, the ideological system's command positions are colonized by the capitalist class. [65] Miliband considers the ideological system, particularly the state's ideological apparatus, an important mechanism for socializing state managers, especially because higher educational credentials are a stringent requirement for holding advisory, policy-analysis, or decision-making positions in the administrative and coercive apparatuses. Likewise, many of the most important positions in state management require applicants to pass confidential security checks. Evidence of "anticapitalist" commitments will usually be interpreted as a disqualification for holding many state managerial offices. The result of both checking educational credentials and screening ideologies is that state managers "are not likely to be free of certain definite ideological inclinations, however little they may themselves be conscious of them." Therefore, at best, state managers are never likely to occupy more than a narrow spectrum of ideological commitments ranging from strong conservatism to weak reformism. It is these ideological commitments that make the state managers, "within their allotted sphere, the conscious or unconscious allies of existing economic and social elites."[66]

Instrumentalist theory has been much maligned for leaning so heavily on the role of ideology in its explanation of intrastate cohesion. Likewise, the explanatory power of the colonization process depends upon the class consciousness of state elites. The criticisms are not without merit, but they are polemical oversimplifications that again misrepresent the instrumentalist position. More often than not critics have based their arguments on the assumption that ideology is the *only* source of intrastate cohesion proposed by instrumentalist theory. Yet, ideology has never been advanced by instrumentalists as the only factor involved in explaining the state's operational unity.[67] Rather, the ideological process is nearly always viewed as one factor that operates in conjunction with the other political processes mentioned earlier.

State and Capital: The Policy-Formation Process

According to both Domhoff and Miliband, the state always operates within a broader political system that is largely defined by the special-interest process, the policy-planning process, and the candidate-selection process. Considerable importance has always been attached to the workings of the political system, precisely to the extent that the capitalist class does not control most positions within the state apparatus. Domhoff, for instance, has long emphasized that, although members of the upper class directly control major corporations, foundations, universities, and the executive branch of the federal government, "they merely have influence in Congress, most state governments, and most local governments."[68] Consequently, their ability to wield a decisive influence on public policy is heavily dependent on the ability of capitalists to organize their interests within the political system and to deploy key resources toward influencing state elites and state managers through the political system.

The special-interest process refers to the actions of formal organizations that are created to represent the interests of individual companies, wealthy families, specific industries, and trades in the political system. Domhoff suggests a series of subhypotheses about business organizations that participate in the special-interest process. He argues that business organizations will pursue one or a combination of four objectives in this process. Their first and overriding goal is to secure special tax breaks and tax loopholes that reduce the tax burden of an individual firm or industry. Their second objective is to thwart the actions of regulatory agencies that are viewed as too costly or as a threat to private control over investment decisions. A third objective is to funnel self-serving advice and information selectively to state officials to influence which facts are available to government decision-makers. Finally, a fourth objective of the process is to secure favorable legislation for a particular company or industry (e.g., antitrust exemptions, tariffs) through legislative bodies. All these objectives, in Domhoff's analysis, constitute the short-term interests of capitalists in maintaining or increasing the immediate profitability of their particular company or business sector.[69]

The theoretical goal in studying the special-interest process is to measure the extent to which organizations representing finance capital, competitive capital, labor, and other groups actually influence public policy decisions. Domhoff notes that one can observe and study the special-interest process through two kinds of case-study research. One research approach is to start with a specific family, corporation, or industrial association and follow its favor-seeking operations through whatever combination of congressional committees, regulatory agencies, and executive bureaucracies is necessary to secure the desired governmental action. The other approach focuses on a specific regulatory agency, congressional committee, executive department, or advisory committee in order to determine how various special interests impinge upon its decision-making process.[70]

Influence is usually measured by the number and significance of special-interest "wins." A win occurs whenever state officials reject proposals that are opposed by a particular special interest, substantially modify a proposal in ways recommended by a special interest (in order to accommodate its objections), or adopt a proposal supported by a special interest. Although such an approach seems simple enough, Domhoff readily admits that, even when scholars agree on the facts of a case, its theoretical meaning is not necessarily self-evident, because legislative and regulatory decisions are, as often as not, the outcome of conflict, compromise, and accommodation. Therefore, most empirical and historical case studies rarely constitute "pure" wins or losses for any special interest. The result, as Domhoff concedes, is that studies of the special-interest process often supply "excellent evidence for the thesis that a ruling class dominates government in corporate America" but only to the degree that "a theorist is predisposed to a ruling-class view."[71]

Consequently, Domhoff suggests that one must develop a sliding scale on which to measure case studies. Insofar as no case study ever fully supports either the pluralist or the ruling-class thesis, one should regard both theses as ideal types. The pluralist model is one in which corporate special interests *rarely* win or at least win no more often than other groups under ideal conditions. The ruling-class model is one in which corporate special interests *always* win under ideal conditions. One must then judge the evidence on the basis of which model more closely approximates the factual situation.

If one adopts this approach, there are two reasons to argue that a ruling-class model of business dominance is best supported in the United States by case studies of the special-interest process. First, the *frequency* of wins indicates that corporate special interests have seldom lost in direct confrontations with other groups. This is not to say that there are no instances in which government acts against special interests, but such examples, in Domhoff's view, are few and far between.[72] Moreover, in cases where monopoly capital does suffer a partial defeat, the victories belong even less frequently to the majority—workers and consumers; rather, they typically represent "some minor victories for small business forces," that is, competitive capital.[73]

Second, one must also offer a theoretical assessment of the *magnitude* of wins and losses by corporate special interests. On this point, Domhoff concludes that, even where strong populist leaders gain a foothold in the state apparatus, they have not been able to defeat corporate special interests on the most important issues.[74] This view is echoed by Murray Edelman's finding that "few regulatory policies have been pursued [in the United States] unless they proved acceptable to the regulated groups or served the interests of these groups."[75]

However, even if one accepts these findings, case studies of the special-interest process do not necessarily indicate the existence of a capitalist ruling class.[76] The major point of contention has been whether or not there is any coordinating mechanism in the political system that can be identified as a classwide political process. For instance, Grant McConnell has argued that case studies of the special-interest process actually prove that the state apparatus is an uncoordinated agglomeration of special-interest policy networks. If so, this would imply that the capitalist class never does act as a class in politics but only in special-interest factions pursuing short-term interests that often undermine the long-term stability of the capitalist system.[77] Thus, to the degree that corporate special interests are often in competition with one another, Fred Block maintains that "to act in the general interest of capital, the state must be able to take actions against the particular interests of capitalists."[78] A state apparatus of the sort described by McConnell would be so tightly welded to competing special interests that it would be unable to direct public policy toward the general interests of the entire capitalist class.

Instrumentalists have responded to this theoretical challenge with the concept of a corporate policy-planning network. The corporate policy-planning network is increasingly seen as an important mechanism for mediating sectoral conflicts within finance-monopoly capital. The planning process takes place within an overlapping institutional matrix of public agencies and private associations. Policy-planning groups are described as intermediate organizations, because they mediate between various special interests within the capitalist class and between the capitalist class and the state. As distinct from the special-interest process, policy planning is a mechanism wherein "the various sectors of the business community transcend their interest-group consciousness and develop an overall class consciousness."[79] The members of these organizations are viewed as the political inner circle of the capitalist class and as the nucleus of a power elite that actively represents the class in politics. The concept of a power elite, as employed by Domhoff, thus refers to "the leadership group or operating arm of the ruling class and high-level employees in institutions controlled by members of the ruling class."[80]

The most important U.S. power elite planning organizations are the Council on Foreign Relations (CFR), the Committee for Economic Development (CED), the Conference Board, the Business Council, and the Business Roundtable. These groups are usually financed through corporate contributions and draw the bulk of their membership directly from the financial groups and the upper class. In addition, the most important members and officials of these groups frequently overlap to create an ongoing planning network. The objective of these organizations is to bring together leading members of the capitalist class from the entire country to discuss general problems of concern to all members (see table 1.1). Thus, planning organizations identify the long-term interests of the capitalist class in regard to issues of general import. Hence, for example, planning organizations seek to define common national goals on issues such as Third World development, international trade policy, public education, national defense, health care, and labor relations (see figure 1.3).

The capitalist inner circle is assisted in the technical aspects of policy planning by academic advisors and technical experts who are occasionally invited to join the planning organizations and to become members

Table 1.1. Members of the Business Roundtable

Abbot Laboratories	Eli Lilly	Pacific Telesis
Aetna Life & Casualty	Emerson Electric	J. C. Penney
Air Products and Chemicals	The Equitable	Pennzoil
Alcoa	Exxon	Pepsico
Allied-Signal	Federal Express	Perkin-Elmer
American Brands	Fluor	Pfizer
American Cyanamid	FMC	Phelps Dodge
American Electric Power	Ford	Philip Morris
American Express	Florida Power & Light	Phillips Petroleum
American Home Products	Gannett	Potomac Electric Power
American International Group	Gencorp	PPG Industries
AT&T	General Electric	Primerica
Ameritech	General Mills	Proctor & Gamble
Amoco	General Motors	Promus Companies
American Airlines	Georgia-Pacific	The Prudential
Anheuser-Busch	BF Goodrich	PSI Energy
ARA Services	Goodyear	Public Service of New Mexico
Armstrong World Industries	GTE	Quaker Oats
Asarco	Halliburton	Raytheon
Asea Brown Boveri	Hallmark	Reader's Digest
Ashland Oil	M. A. Hanna	Reynolds Metals
Atlantic Richfield	Harris	RJR Nabisco
BankAmerica	Hercules	Roadway Services
Bankers Trust	Hershey Foods	Rockwell International
Baxter International	Hewlett-Packard	Rohm and Haas
Bechtel	Honeywell	Ryder System
Bell Atlantic	Household International	Santa Fe Pacific
Bellsouth	Humana	Sara Lee
Bethlehem Steel	Illinois Tool Works	Scott Paper
Black & Decker	Ingersoll-Rand	Sears
Boeing	Inland Steel	Shell Oil
Boise Cascade	IBM	Sifco Industries
BP America	International Paper	A. O. Smith
Bristol-Myers Squibb	ITT	Southern California Edison
Browning-Ferris	Jack Eckerd	The Southern Company
Burlington Northern	Johnson & Johnson	Southwestern Bell
Capital Cities/ABC	K Mart	Springs Industries
Carolina Power & Light	Kellogg	Super Valu Stores
Carter Hawley Hale Stores	Kerr-McGee	Tenneco
Caterpillar	Kroger	Texaco
Certainteed	Litton Industries	Texas Industries
Champion International	LTV	Texas Utilities
Chase Manhattan	Manufacturers Hanover	Textron
Chemical Banking	Marriott	Time Warner
Chevron	Marsch & McLennan	Times Mirror
CIGNA	Martin Marietta	The Travelers

Table 1.1. Members of the Business Roundtable (*continued*)

Citicorp	McGraw-Hill	TLC Beatrice
Cleveland-Cliffs	MCI	TRW
Coca-Cola	McKesson	United Air Lines
Colgate-Palmolive	Mead	Union Camp
Columbia Gas	Merck	Union Carbide
Conagra	Merrill Lynch	Union Pacific
Control Data	Metropolitan Life	Unisys
Cooper Industries	Milliken	United Parcel Service
Corning	3M	United Technologies
CPC International	Mobil	United Telecom
CSX	Monsanto	Unocal
Dana	J. P. Morgan	Upjohn
Dayton Hudson	Morgan Stanley	USX
Deere	Motorola	Warnaco
Delta Air Lines	Nalco	Warner-Lambert
Dial Corporation	National Intergroup	Waste Management
Digital Equipment	NCNB	Wells Fargo
Dow Chemical Company	NCR	Westinghouse
Duquesne Power & Light	Norfolk Southern	Weyerhauser
Dresser Industries	Norton	Whirlpool
Du Pont	NYNEX	Williams Companies
Duke Power	Olin	Xerox
Dun & Bradstreet	Owens-Corning	Zenith Electronics
Eastman Kodak	Pacific Enterprises	
Eaton	Pacific Gas & Electric	

Source: *The Business Roundtable* (New York: Business Roundtable, June 1991), pp. 3–5.
Note: All member companies are represented by their chief executive officer. Member companies are chosen with "the goal of having representation varied by category of business and by geographic location. Thus, the members, some 200 chief executive officers in all fields, can present a cross section of thinking on national issues." *The Business Roundtable*, p. 1.

of the power elite. These advisors are usually drawn from well-known "ideological satellites" such as major universities, foundations, and privately financed research institutes or think tanks. These "intellectuals" are offered other inducements to assist the capitalist class, such as lucrative speaking honoraria, endowed university professorships, mission-specific research grants, positions as corporate consultants, positions on boards of directors, and lobbying fees. Likewise, high-ranking state managers and emerging legislators are often invited into the planning

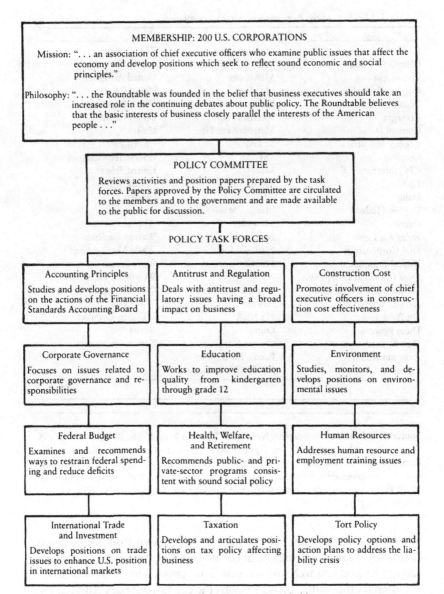

MEMBERSHIP: 200 U.S. CORPORATIONS

Mission: ". . . an association of chief executive officers who examine public issues that affect the economy and develop positions which seek to reflect sound economic and social principles."

Philosophy: ". . . the Roundtable was founded in the belief that business executives should take an increased role in the continuing debates about public policy. The Roundtable believes that the basic interests of business closely parallel the interests of the American people . . ."

POLICY COMMITTEE

Reviews activities and position papers prepared by the task forces. Papers approved by the Policy Committee are circulated to the members and to the government and are made available to the public for discussion.

POLICY TASK FORCES

Accounting Principles	Antitrust and Regulation	Construction Cost
Studies and develops positions on the actions of the Financial Standards Accounting Board	Deals with antitrust and regulatory issues having a broad impact on business	Promotes involvement of chief executive officers in construction cost effectiveness

Corporate Governance	Education	Environment
Focuses on issues related to corporate governance and responsibilities	Works to improve education quality from kindergarten through grade 12	Studies, monitors, and develops positions on environmental issues

Federal Budget	Health, Welfare, and Retirement	Human Resources
Examines and recommends ways to restrain federal spending and reduce deficits	Recommends public- and private-sector programs consistent with sound social policy	Addresses human resource and employment training issues

International Trade and Investment	Taxation	Tort Policy
Develops positions on trade issues to enhance U.S. position in international markets	Develops and articulates positions on tax policy affecting business	Develops policy options and action plans to address the liability crisis

Figure 1.3. Policy-planning structure of the Business Roundtable.

Source: Data from *The Business Roundtable* (New York: Business Roundtable, June 1991), pp. 1–2.

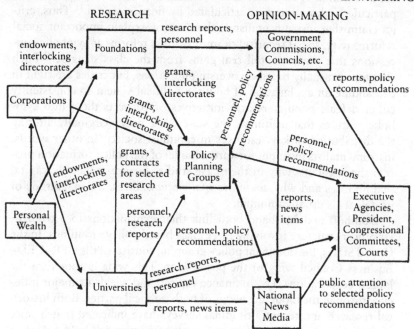

RESOURCES   DECISION-MAKING   LAWMAKING
          RESEARCH   OPINION-MAKING

Figure 1.4. The policy planning network
Source: From *The Powers That Be* by G. William Domhoff. Copyright © 1978 by G. William Domhoff. Reprinted by permission of Random House, Inc.

network, where they are trained and socialized to become the spokespersons, allies, and future executive leaders of the power elite.

Domhoff argues that the most important institutional and policy reforms of the last century have usually emerged from this or similar policy-planning networks. Domhoff contends that the very foundations of the U.S. welfare state are linked directly to the proposals, members, and political support of the planning network. For instance, Domhoff argues that the Social Security Act of 1935, usually considered the cornerstone of the U.S. welfare state, was primarily the work of the Business Advisory Council and its allies. The architects of postwar foreign policy came from the Council on Foreign Relations.[81] The central position of intercorporate planning groups in mediating the policy-formation process is illustrated by figure 1.4.

However, it should not be assumed that there is no conflict, negotiation, or compromise involved in the process of securing classwide policies. Critics have charged that instrumentalists see state policies solely "as a reflection of the interests of certain groups in the capitalist class," particularly those interests articulated by finance capital.[82] Thus, critics claim that instrumentalism either cannot explain important social reforms (e.g., social security) or must dismiss reforms as symbolic concessions that do not entail real gains from the class struggle.[83] Such charges are usually based on oversimplifications, but critics are right in demanding an explanation of how the political system so consistently either defeats popular reform initiatives or converts them into symbolic gestures that legitimate the state while only marginally altering the distribution of key resources in capitalist society. In other words, instrumentalists must put forward a model of the policy-formation process that explains why in their case studies finance-monopoly capital seldom loses and why, *under normal circumstances*, the magnitude of its defeats is usually minimal.

Domhoff and Miliband both link their explanations to a triangular power structure involving three class-based policy groupings. In the United States, the dominant policy grouping consists of the CFR–CED–Business Council wing of the power elite. This wing is rooted in the largest corporations (i.e., in finance capital) and wields its major influence through the moderate wings of both political parties. Both historical research and recent attitudinal surveys have indicated that finance capitalists and members of its policy-planning network hold a distinct political outlook called corporate liberalism. Useem notes that corporate liberalism as a political ideology is not rooted "in a commitment to reform, nor in an enlightened acceptance of labor and government opponents, but rather in the recognition that the entire business community and the future of the private economy will best prosper if it assumes a posture of compromise" with other policy groupings.[84]

A competing policy grouping is anchored by the National Association of Manufacturers (NAM) and the U.S. Chamber of Commerce (CC). This policy grouping represents an ultraconservative wing of the power elite and is supported by smaller corporations (i.e., medium-sized competitive capital) and small businesses. It wields its influence through ultraconservative Republicans and southern Democrats. Finally, a loose-knit progressive coalition is rooted in middle-class liberal organizations, trade unions, and university intellectuals. The social democratic grouping wields its marginal influence through a progressive wing of the Democratic party.

Each of the three policy groupings can be understood as creating stable political whirlpools that draw other groups into the current of their leadership on major issues. Furthermore, each policy grouping has established a base of power within the state apparatus. As already noted, the corporate liberal bloc is usually strongest in the executive branch of government and in the administrative and regulatory apparatus. The major strength of the ultraconservatives has typically been in Congress, although during the last decade they have increasingly captured the executive branch. The progressive coalition does not have any significant stronghold in the state, but must rely on a few Democratic, union, and university mavericks for its feeble voice in the United States.

The power structure that is institutionalized by the political system and by the patterns of representation within the state apparatus yields a corporate liberal model of policy formation. Within this model, the preferences of the corporate liberal bloc generally decide the outcome of any conflicts over public policy because of the relatively stable balance of power among the three policy groupings. For example, Domhoff contends that whenever popular demands for policy or institutional change reach crisis proportions, the corporate liberal wing of the power elite will respond with a reform initiative or propose substantive modifications to any plan already initiated by progressives. Corporate liberals will then seek to enlist the support of progressives for the liberals' own plan or withhold support from the progressive plan until it is modified to meet liberals' objections. Because progressive policy blocs lack any substantial base of power within the American state, progressives always have to choose eventually between the options of no reform at all or the corporate liberal plan. Thus, the progressives' dependence on support, leadership, and initiative from the corporate liberals ultimately forces them to accede to a corporate liberal variant of any reform proposal.[85]

On the other hand, if the corporate liberal bloc decides reform is politically unnecessary or objectionable, it will retain its natural conservative alliance with the NAM-CC bloc and present a united power elite in opposition to any progressive coalition. Because the ultraconservative policy bloc always maintains a hard line in defense of a minimalist state and free markets, when the power elite is united progressives are frozen out of the policy-making process completely, or ultraconservatives are able to destroy progressive initiatives within Congress while corporate liberals sit by silently.[86] In both scenarios, finance capital (i.e., the corporate liberal wing of the power elite) exercises the "decisive influence" over policy outcomes either by actively supporting moderate reform and compromise or by passively refusing to support any reform.

However, to complete this policy-formation model, one must be able to specify the circumstances in which corporate liberals will either initiate or accept a reform agenda instead of remaining aligned with the ultraconservatives. One must also be able to specify the limits of reform that will be acceptable to capitalists. Generally, instrumentalist theory has operated on the assumption that corporate liberals are most likely to pursue a reform agenda under two conditions:

(H_{3a}) The larger the scale of mass popular revolt the more likely corporate liberals are to initiate or accept reform policies.

(H_{3b}) Corporate liberals will initiate reform proposals that promote their long-term interests and will tolerate reform proposals that do not contravene their long-term interests.

In addition, Frances Fox Piven and Richard A. Cloward have found that significant reforms are most likely to occur when the required mass mobilizations take place outside the existing power structure and, thus, circumvent the patterns of class representation institutionalized by the state apparatus.[87] In this context, social-reform policies are necessary to restore political order and to preserve the long-term stability of the existing political system.

Sweezy's statement that capitalists seek to use the state to enforce and guarantee the class structure itself offers a way to conceptualize the long-term interests of the capitalist class. The major dividing line in the class structure of a capitalist society is the distinction between that class which owns the means of production (i.e., capital) and those classes who must work for capitalists. It is this separation of the working class from the means of production which allows the capitalist to pay workers less than the value of what they produce. Consequently, the long-term interests of the capitalist class fundamentally include:

1. the protection of private control over the means of production, that is, maintaining the existing relations of production; and
2. the retention of private control over investment decisions and capital allocations.[88]

In this respect, corporate liberals may answer popular discontent with economic, social, or political reforms, so long as these policies restore popular quiescence and at the very least do not contravene the long-term interests of capitalists. For the most part, the long-term interests of capitalists can be accommodated or even promoted so long as economic and social policies operate through the private market and offer market incentives for business participation in government programs. Thus, for example, corporate liberals will nearly always demand that current or prior labor-market participation, as opposed to need, be a condition of eligibility for access to social spending programs (e.g., Social Security, unemployment insurance). Social spending programs that link public benefits to long-term employment create market inducements that discipline workers to remain in the labor force and provide a self-financing funding mechanism that is regressive and nonredistributive.[89]

Likewise, the implementation of state policies through private service providers (e.g., Medicare, public housing) creates new opportunities for the private sector to maximize profits by supplying public services. In addition, linking the implementation of economic and social policies to private markets means that any effective state policy must rely on the cooperation or partnership of private capitalists.[90] Otherwise, the implementation of public policies through the marketplace can be sabotaged by refusals to participate in government programs or to supply public services. In this manner, a welfare system has been created which responds to popular demands for economic and social reform, but which in its implementation must continually distribute benefits to the corporate sector (e.g., urban renewal for private developers, health care for private hospitals) while distributing program costs to service recipients (e.g., user fees, Social Security taxation).

The Welfare State: Corporate Liberalism or Social Democracy?

The conflict between corporate liberal and progressive policy blocs may be understood in terms of two competing social policy models. Walter Korpi has drawn on the work of Richard Titmuss[91] to clarify the differences between the corporate liberal model of social policy and a progressive or social democratic model of social policy. As a social philosophy, corporate liberalism "is based on the assumption that private markets and the family constitute the natural channels through which the needs of citizens are to be met. Social policy is to enter only when these natural mechanisms do not function and then only as a temporary substitute."[92] Yet, as opposed to corporate liberalism, proponents of a social democratic welfare state are explicitly committed to social policy that offers citizens public services outside the market on criteria of need.

Thus, an important objective of the social democratic welfare state is to redistribute key resources in society in a way that does not rely ex-

clusively on market allocations.[93] Most important, a social democratic
welfare state will not only seek to ameliorate the economic uncertainty,
individual hardships, or social and environmental effects of unregulated
markets but will also aim to reduce the class inequalities arising out of
a capitalist economy. The implication, according to Korpi, is that the
social democratic nature of a welfare state must be measured by "the
extent to which equality in basic conditions of living has been achieved
among the citizens."[94]

Yet, most comparative research on the welfare state has focused only
on the levels, timing, and growth of welfare services. This focus has
occurred partly because these variables are easily quantifiable and comparable, but also because most scholars have assumed that the welfare
state is a generic phenomenon. However, the key variables may well
be qualitative historical differences in the kind of welfare states that
emerge in particular countries as opposed to their mere size and time
of origin. Historical and theoretical assessments of the kind of welfare state that prevails in a particular country are certainly much more
elusive than mere quantitative comparisons. Nevertheless, the current
qualitative research suggests that the dominance of one or the other
of the two competing strategies of social policy is strongly, though not
exclusively, the result of whether labor or capital is the governing class.
In this respect, the axis of conflict between big business and big labor,
between corporate liberal and progressive policy blocs, does not necessarily involve the issue of whether to pursue regulatory and welfare
policies. Instead, the major political conflict between labor and finance
capital is over the kind of welfare state which favors the respective
interests of each.

In the United States, for example, James Weinstein argues that the
ideal of a liberal social order was first formulated by "the more sophisticated leaders of America's largest corporations and financial institutions."[95] Weinstein's historical study emphasizes that the strategy of
corporate liberalism was a conscious and successful political movement
by finance capital to control and influence the state's economic and
social policies. Most important, corporate liberalism was explicitly put
forward by finance capitalists as a coordinated set of counterproposals
to undercut the appeal of populism, socialism, and working-class rebellion. Thus, Weinstein regards the liberal welfare state as a means
of securing the existing order against more radical and revolutionary
transformations.

Weinstein and other adherents of the corporate liberal model thus
acknowledge that the original impetus for liberal reforms came from

the working class, but they emphasize that few policy or institutional reforms have ever been (or ever will be) enacted without the tacit approval or active guidance of finance capitalists represented by the policy-planning network. Consequently, in the corporate liberal historiography of American political development, finance capital is considered the chief historical agent of political reform.[96] Even when finance capital does not initiate welfare-state reforms, the class is still able to set the terms on which working-class demands will be met through its decisive influence in the policy-formation process.[97]

A variety of policy histories now exemplify Weinstein's original corporate liberal thesis. For example, one of the most controversial aspects of the modern welfare state has been the expansion of public relief expenditures for the poor. While conservative scholars, journalists, and politicians have persistently berated U.S. social welfare programs as "socialistic," Frances Fox Piven and Richard A. Cloward offer a radically different historical interpretation. Piven and Cloward argue that relief from poverty is a secondary objective in most social welfare programs and that the primary objective is to stabilize (and thus protect) the existing economic and political order. According to Piven and Cloward, "historical evidence suggests that relief arrangements are initiated or expanded during the occasional outbreaks of civil disorder produced by mass unemployment [e.g., 1930s and 1960s], and are then abolished or contracted when political stability is restored [e.g., 1980s]." They conclude that "expansive relief policies are designed to mute civil disorder, and restrictive ones to reinforce work norms" once civil order is restored.[98]

Similarly, liberal scholars have persistently emphasized the role of public schools as training grounds for democratic citizenship and as channels of equal opportunity for the children of working-class and poor families. Joel H. Spring offers historical evidence, on the contrary, to suggest that finance capital (through its policy-planning organizations) has played a dominant role in aligning American public education with its own interests. Spring maintains that big business views education "as one institution working with others to assure the [continued] progress and efficient operation of the social system."[99] The objectives of big business have been achieved by constructing a stratified system of unequal educational opportunity that sorts out students by class background and then channels them to private industry with the appropriate vocational skills and normative values. Thus, the rise of public education and education policy are seen as a "human resource" development strategy in which state allocations of human resources reproduce the existing social order while creating the symbolism of equal opportunity.[100]

However, proponents of a social democratic model argue that democratic political arrangements make it at least possible for a highly organized working class to capture the state and to use it as a non-market instrument for redistributing income and services away from the economically and socially privileged. Hence, proponents of the social democratic model have suggested that differences in the size and type of welfare states can be accounted for under instrumentalist theory by the strength of social democratic labor movements and their ability to occupy positions within the state apparatus.[101] In Korpi's social democratic model, the two most important indicators of working-class mobilization are "the proportion of the labor force that is unionized and the proportion of the electorate which supports the parties of the left (defined as the traditional social democratic parties and those to their left)."[102]

Yet, as instrumentalist theory would anticipate, Korpi emphasizes that a heavily unionized work force and even a strong working-class party, although necessary, are not sufficient either to indicate or to effect a real shift in the state power structure. Instead, the indicators of a genuine capture of state power by social democrats are:

1. the relative *length of time* during which labor governments are in power (i.e., the degree of stability and continuity in the presence of working-class parties in government), and
2. working-class *control of the political executive* and other administrative or regulatory centers of state power.

Hence, consonant with instrumentalist theory, the social democratic model "asserts that partisan control of the executive branch of government, rather than sheer electoral support . . . is the primary means by which class forces are politically translated into policy outcomes." In order to effect a shift in the power structure, a highly mobilized working class must physically displace capital from its key sector in the state apparatus and thereby neutralize finance capital's executive veto power. Needless to say, a significant political implication of this model is that "it is deemed possible for the subordinate class to peacefully conquer the state and to exploit such conquests to intervene in class conflict on the side of labor."[103] Korpi thus claims that in those countries "where the working class has been strongly mobilized and has achieved a relatively stable control over government, a crucial decrease in the difference between the power resources of the main classes has occurred." [104]

There has been a tendency to see corporate liberal and social democratic analyses of the welfare state as mutually exclusive *theories* of the welfare state; however, they should instead be viewed as complementary instrumentalist *models* of the welfare state. This view is possible to the extent that the two models indicate relative differences between the development of state-capital relations in the United States and those in Europe, the most notable example evidenced in the low levels of unionization and the absence of a true working-class party in the United States.[105]

Criticisms and Rejoinders

There is probably no other theory of the state that has been more criticized than instrumentalism. Unfortunately, the simplicity of the instrumentalist thesis has enabled many critics to oversimplify instrumentalist theory. G. William Domhoff has recently shown that scholars so often misrepresent and confuse plain Marxism that what passes for instrumentalism today is little more than a caricature of the theory.[106] Indeed, over the last three decades, Marxist critics have all but dismissed the approach for being "too pedestrian and unmistakably American." [107] However, this chapter suggests that instrumentalism remains a fruitful avenue of empirical and institutional research, particularly in conceptualizing the "exceptional" underdevelopment of the U.S. welfare state.

The list of potshots, strawman distortions, and polemical misrepresentations is a long one. However, for purposes of analytic summary, one can identify three types of criticisms that have been persistently directed at instrumentalist theory. These are: (1) criticisms based on methodological fiat, (2) claims that instrumentalism has failed to take into account certain theoretical issues or is unable to explain specific political phenomena, and (3) claims that various case studies contravene or fail to support the theory.

First, criticisms by methodological fiat are derived from a priori claims that the assumptions of a different approach to the state are in some way superior to those of power structure methodology and its reliance on conscious historical agency to explain state policies. On this point, some of the bitterest polemics have centered on the explanatory significance that should be accorded to empirical studies of capitalist and state elites and to historical investigations of policy formation and institutional reform. For instance, Nicos Poulantzas claims that the studies of interlocking directorates, planning groups, policy formation, and institutional reform are methodologically suspect, because they "give the impression" that "social classes or 'groups' are in some way reducible to *inter-personal relations*" between individuals rather than being constituted as objective relations of production. Along these lines, Poulantzas berates instrumentalist theory for offering explanations of the state and public policy that are "founded on the *motivations of conduct* of the individual actors." [108] Bob Jessop explains that the major theoretical implication of Poulantzas's criticism is that in instrumentalism "the class nature of the capitalist state depends entirely on [contingent] factors external to the state itself" and thus implies that there is nothing *necessarily* capitalist about the state. [109]

However, this objection illustrates the way in which arguments about the class nature of the state have been intermixed with disputes about social science methodology. The point to be made here is the extent to which Poulantzas's objections make sense only if one is uncompromisingly committed to the underlying methodological assumptions of structural functionalism and to the absolute exclusion of other methodological approaches. Steven Lukes has pointed out that Poulantzas's methodological criticisms of instrumentalist theory can be accepted at face value only if one postulates a strict dichotomy between structural determinism and historical agency that requires scholars to choose either explanations derived from structure or explanations grounded in agency.

Yet, on what basis does one make such an uncompromising choice? Poulantzas supports his methodological position by pointing out that even where socialist parties have held power for substantial periods of time such societies have remained capitalist in their property relations while their social policies have done very little in regard to actual reduction of class inequalities. For Poulantzas, this implies that far more must be at work in the operations of the state and social policy than mere occupation of the state apparatus by the personnel of a particular class.

Yet, making a case that more is at work in the operations of the state than conscious and organized class agency is a far weaker claim than the methodological assertion that agency is irrelevant. Poulantzas's critique may point to an explanatory limitation in instrumentalist theory, but it does not establish a basis for a wholesale rejection of the theory. On the contrary, Lukes suggests that the more fruitful line of inquiry is to explore "the complex interrelations between the two, and allow for the obvious fact that individuals act together and upon one another within groups and organisations and that the explanation of their behaviour and interaction is unlikely to be reducible merely to their individual motivations."[110]

Nevertheless, even in the context of Lukes's proposed rapprochement between agency and structure most Marxists continue to insist that instrumentalism is flawed in its theoretical claim that capitalist rationality is "located in the consciousness of some sector of the ruling class."[111] Theda Skocpol, a leading proponent of organizational realism, asserts that U.S. capitalists "lack the political capacity to pursue class-wide interests in national politics."[112] Claus Offe, a systems theorist, has elevated this historical claim to an a priori principle by postulating that "the 'anarchy' of competition-geared capitalist production" makes it "extremely unlikely" that a capitalist class interest could emerge from among the competing special interests of various business groupings.[113] Yet, after all is said and done, methodological decrees do not answer historical evidence supporting the claim that power elite planning groups do manage to articulate a classwide interest in the policy-formation process.

Unfortunately, when adherents of the corporate liberal model generate historical and empirical evidence to support their hypotheses, the evidence is often contemptuously dismissed as conspiracy theory.[114] Yet, the power elite identified by instrumentalist theory routinely discusses public policy in the minutes and conventions of business associations and trade groups, through the policy statements of planning groups, in newspaper editorials and magazine interviews, the publications of various lobbying organizations, the hearings of congressional committees, and in many other public forums. The conspiracy objection is generally flawed insofar as it equates any organized and conscious political action by businessmen with conspiracy. The fact is that businessmen are not lacking in political consciousness and are not totally ignorant of their common interests to the extent that most Marxists stipulate in competing theories.[115]

Moreover, the conspiracy objection also relies on the unstated assumption that conspiracy is always an unacceptable explanation. On this point, it is worth saying a word in defense of "conspiracy theories," since few scholars are willing to soil their academic reputations with such controversial notions. It is easy to point to any number of harebrained conspiracy theories. One can always invoke Lyndon LaRouche's claim that Queen Elizabeth and Henry Kissinger are the linchpins of an international drug trade or Frank Zappa's theory that the CIA developed AIDS to wage biological warfare on Castro's Cuba. Indeed, it is easy to make the abusive, *ad hominem* argument that all conspiracy theories should be thrown into the same scrap heap with such nonsense.

However, it is equally nonsensical in this day and age to pretend that conspiracy does not take place at high levels of finance, industry, and government. It should not be necessary to remind scholars constantly of the Church committee hearings on the CIA, of Watergate, Irangate, Love Canal, the Ford Pinto, defense industry scams, Charles Keating of Lincoln Savings and Loan, and many other conspiratorial scandals that surface in newspaper headlines every year. In fact, conspiracies take place in government and industry so frequently and at such high levels of decision-making that the corporate liberal model probably understates the real influence of business in American society. At a minimum, the assertion that conspiracy can never provide an explanation for important policy decisions is on weak ground historically. Quite the contrary, the substantial evidence that does exist, and this comes mainly from bungled conspiracies, suggests that secrecy and conspiracy have been increasingly institutionalized in a subterranean world of state and business policy.

A second set of objections to instrumentalist theory are those which rest on claims that it is inherently unable to explain various phenomena that a theory of the state must explain. These criticisms generally rest on the underlying view that the instrumentalist approach has been constructed on either a defective concept of the state or an incomplete picture of class struggle. However, as this chapter has sought to demonstrate, most of these criticisms are aimed at a theoretical strawman that has been made plausible only by constant reference to Sweezy's somewhat misleading metaphor of the state as a tool in the hands of the capitalist class.

However, the emphasis on class-conscious elites as the decisive influence in policy formation has also led to charges that instrumentalist theory results in a static analysis which lacks an internal dynamic for explaining social or political change.[116] Yet, such critiques tacitly ignore Domhoff's and Miliband's reliance on a tripartite model of class segmentation and class struggle. Furthermore, even though the corporate liberal model emphasizes the decisive influence of finance capital in the current power structure, this thesis is always balanced against the potential for shifts in power structure as a result of exceptional mobilizations or demobilizations of power resources among the three policy groupings. In this context, the oft-repeated assertion that instrumentalist theory has no place for the working class in explanations of public policy is sheer nonsense. Thus, for example, the myriad accusations that instrumentalist theory is inherently unable to explain important policy reforms are ridiculous.[117] The corporate liberal model has been used successfully to explain reforms as diverse as Social Security, foreign policy, and public education.[118]

As a result, the focus of future debates should not be whether instrumentalism is analytically sufficient to account for public policy formation or institutional development. Theoretical debate will be more fruitful to the extent that it continues down the current path of more limited engagements centering on whether or not actual case studies and other empirical evidence support or deviate from the expectations of the two instrumentalist models. However, to make this claim leads back to the treacherous question: what counts as proof? To this point, no one has proposed a metatheoretical principle that could establish in advance a point at which the cumulative evidence of case studies can be said to support instrumentalist theory.

Nevertheless, we can dispel an increasingly common misconception about the ability of counterfactual case studies to "falsify" the corporate liberal model of the state. The polemical ground of current falsification strategies is the assumption that in the corporate liberal model "all outcomes consciously serve the interests of identifiable business elites." [119] This reconstruction of the model implies that if one can find a single counterfactual instance in which the state fails to act in the general interests of capital then the model is falsified and instrumentalist theory is rendered suspect. Skocpol has suggested that as counterfactual case studies accumulate it will be revealed that the corporate liberal model has rested on the specious methodological practice of "selecting" examples and evidence that are compatible with the model.[120]

The methodological problem with Skocpol's accusation is that the current falsification strategy also relies on selective case studies. The fact is that antagonists of the corporate liberal model can be accused of the same selective gamesmanship inasmuch as their own approach rests on the accumulation of counterfactuals. Moreover, the problem of falsification is far more ambiguous than the mere accumulation of counterfactual case studies, for as ongoing debates about the Social Security Act and the Wagner Act demonstrate, it is not clear even which specific cases count as counterfactuals. Both proponents and opponents of the corporate liberal model are holding up the same case studies as evidence to support their theoretical positions (See Chapter 5.)

Yet even if counterfactuals could be sorted out from other case studies by scholarly consensus, the results would not necessarily offer a decisive falsification of the corporate liberal model. The corporate liberal model and instrumentalist theory have never claimed that *all* outcomes serve the interests of the capitalist class. That rendition of the corporate liberal model is mainly a polemical exaggeration designed to bolster the theoretical importance of what otherwise might be the utterly mundane conclusions of some counterfactual case studies. The actual claim of the corporate liberal model is that *most* policy outcomes, especially the most substantively important outcomes, will serve the interests of the capitalist class under normal circumstances.

Furthermore, these claims are not either/or propositions easily judged by the nomological criteria of "falsification" that still naively underpin behavioral and positivist social science. In the first place, it is not necessarily clear what policies count as substantively important decisions as opposed to unimportant decisions. However, even if this question can be resolved, the existence of counterfactuals alone is not sufficient to contravene any but the strawman rendition of instrumentalist theory. Instead, the real evidentiary questions concerning counterfactuals are more ambiguous: Within what range can counterfactual case studies be viewed as exceptional deviations from the model—anomalies, to use Thomas Kuhn's language? And at what point does the cumulative evidence of counterfactuals disprove the model? One can speculatively postulate ideal end points of analytic certainty where all cases either support the model or contravene the model. The empirical and historical reality of social science, however, is that it is always bogged down in the evidentiary marshlands between these two ideal points.

CHAPTER TWO

Neo-Marxism: The Structuralist Approach

Individuals are dealt with only in so far as they are the personifications of economic categories, embodiments of particular class-relations and class-interests.
—*Marx*, Capital, *1867*

The structuralist approach to the state starts from the assumption that capitalist societies are inherently prone to crises which originate in regular cycles of economic stagnation and/or in continual outbreaks of class war between capital and labor.[1] Because of this underlying tendency toward crisis, structuralists argue that the state must intervene politically to maintain economic stability and to mediate class struggles in capitalist societies. The structuralist thesis, as summarized by Ernest Mandel, is that the function of the state is to protect and reproduce the social structure of capitalist societies (i.e., the fundamental relations of production) insofar as this is not achieved by the automatic processes of the economy.[2] Consequently, structuralists argue that state policies and state institutions are best understood by their "function" in maintaining the capitalist system. The main goal of institutional and policy analyses informed by a structuralist approach is to analyze how the effects of state institutions and state policies operate to fulfill this general maintenance function.[3]

The Basic Concepts of Structuralism

Structuralists postulate that every mode of production can be analyzed in terms of the functional interrelations between its economic, political, and ideological structures.[4] A structure consists of one or more institutions that fulfill specific economic, political, or ideological functions necessary to sustain a particular mode of production. The economic structure of a capitalist society is constituted primarily by the relationships that organize the production and distribution of commodities, namely, private property and the market. Its political structure consists of the institutionalized power of the state.[5] The ideological instance refers both to the subjective consciousness of individual social actors and to the collective thought systems that exist in a given society.[6] A

51

stable capitalist society is one in which all the structures function as an integrated system to maintain "capitalist" relations of production and, hence, the ability of capitalists to appropriate surplus value from workers.

However, structuralists note that as a result of its internal development, various "contradictions" are constantly at work within the system to generate crises of capital accumulation and simultaneously to undermine ruling class domination. While there remains a great deal of debate among structuralists concerning the exact nature and source of these contradictions, most theorists identify one or all of three possible factors as the source of crises: (1) economic crisis, (2) class struggle, and (3) uneven development.[7]

There is now an extensive economics literature on the problem of capital realization crises, and it is far beyond the purpose of this work to offer a summary or analysis of that literature.[8] It is sufficient to note that the central theme running through most of this literature is an attempt to explain what Marx described as the "tendency for the rate of profit to fall."[9] Investment and job creation in capitalist economies are induced by the prospect of capitalists being able to realize profits. Economic crisis models have argued that, for various reasons, capitalist economies periodically exhaust their capacity to generate profits and, hence, their economic growth.[10] Thus, in order to restore private capital accumulation, structural adjustments become necessary for the state (e.g., Keynesian intervention) and ideological instances (e.g., consumerism).

To a certain degree, the economic crisis and class struggle perspectives often overlap insofar as economic stagnation can accelerate and intensify class struggle as during the Great Depression. On the other hand, adherents of "the class struggle perspective" have often emphasized that capitalist class relations are exploitative and antagonistic *precisely because surplus value appropriation by capitalists is successful* during periods of economic growth. Hence, in principle, class struggles may occur independently of economic crises. Indeed, class-struggle theorists have emphasized that it is the inherently exploitative character of capitalist *production* relations that creates a structural tendency toward class solidarity among workers and capitalists. Yet, at the same time, the process of capital *circulation* generates a structure of fragmentation among capitalists over the distribution of surplus value and among workers over the distribution of wages, salaries, and opportunities. Hence, the marketplace, as opposed to production sites, generates centrifugal tendencies within all classes that divide them into competing "fractions" (e.g., skilled vs. unskilled workers, finance capital vs.

industrial capital).[11] For this reason, the intensity and success of class struggle by workers or capitalists may be viewed more as an organizational (i.e., political and ideological) variable than as a dependent effect of economic crisis.

Finally, capitalist societies are usually structured by a historical process of uneven development. Although scholars frequently refer to particular societies as feudal or capitalist, historical social formations are rarely constituted as pure modes of production. Rather, the core of most social formations is defined by the relative dominance of one mode of production. Consequently, scholars often refer to the nineteenth-century United States as a capitalist society, but this does not exclude the fact that many noncapitalist economic relations (e.g., slavery) persisted at the "periphery" of the U.S. social formation, particularly in the South. Similarly, although late nineteenth-century U.S. capitalism was dominated by large-scale industry, small-scale agriculture (i.e., a petit-bourgeois class) continued to exist alongside the corporate sector as a structural "survival" from earlier stages of U.S. capitalist development.[12] Thus, historical social formations usually consist of a dominant mode of production that is hierarchically linked to a periphery of subordinate modes of production and to previous historical stages of the dominant mode of production.[13] This results in a historical class structure and in patterns of political conflict that are actually far more complex than the analytic two-class model that Marx considers typical of "pure" capitalism. Most important, it suggests that the state must intervene through a variety of political and ideological mechanisms to maintain the dominance of capitalist economic relations.

Furthermore, because structuralism postulates the relative separation of economic, political, and ideological structures, each level of a social formation may also develop unevenly according to its own internal structural rhythm or time sequence. Thus, for example, the banking laws of a particular country might hinder further economic development because they lag behind the current functional requirements of capital accumulation. This contradiction between the forces and relations of production constitutes a structural disjuncture between the political and economic levels. By the same token, the ideological activities of intellectuals might at times lead to the introduction of policy proposals (e.g., guaranteed annual income) which eliminate incentives to work for low wages and, hence, undermine an underlying functional requisite of private capital accumulation. In this case, a contradiction between the forces and relations of production would be constituted as a disjuncture between the political and ideological levels. A possible solution, in the first case, would be to update banking laws and, in the second case, to terminate radical intellectuals from their academic positions. In both cases, the objective would be to restore a functional equilibrium between the contradictory instances.

In this regard, the structural effects of crisis tendencies are visible in the social dislocations that disrupt the functional stability of all capitalist social formations. Whether one identifies the contradictions of capitalism with structural economic crises, class struggle, uneven development, or a combination of all three factors, it is the ever-present phenomena of crisis that, for structuralists, raises the question of how the reproduction of capitalism is even possible for any extended length of time. The structuralist answer to this puzzle is that in a capitalist social formation the state functions as *"the regulating factor of its global equilibrium as a system."* [14] Poulantzas suggests that

(H_1) the state fulfills a general maintenance function by *"constituting the factor of cohesion between the levels of a social formation."* [15]

The Poulantzian hypothesis has often been criticized as an analytic tautology which begs the question of how (and even if) state institutions and policies fulfill a general maintenance function. This criticism is partly warranted, particularly in regard to Poulantzas's most abstract formulations of the hypothesis. [16] However, there are at least three formulations of the Poulantzian hypothesis that can be tested by analyzing the operational objectives of state institutions and state policies. Each of these formulations is derived, respectively, from the three perspectives on crisis theory mentioned earlier.

First, Poulantzas argues that contrary to the mythology of neoclassical economic theory, the economic level of capitalist societies has never "formed a hermetically sealed level, capable of self-reproduction and possessing its own 'laws' of internal functioning." Rather, the economic level of capitalist societies is only relatively autonomous of the other levels. Consequently, he argues, *"the political field of the State* (as well as the sphere of ideology) *has always, in different forms, been present in the constitution and reproduction of the relations of production."* [17] Along these lines, Poulantzas claims that

(H_{1a}) the state's major contribution to reproducing the economic relations of a capitalist social formation is the effect of its policies on the reproduction of labor power and the means of labor. [18]

Second, Jill S. Quadagno has drawn on the class-struggle perspective to argue that, if Poulantzas's general hypothesis were operationalized, structuralist theory would further expect that

(H$_{1b}$)   the state acts as a mediating body to preserve and enhance capitalist interests.[19]

Quadagno claims that state policies contribute to the reproduction of labor power and the means of labor partly by mediating disputes between antagonistic classes and between competing fractions of capital. The state preserves the capitalist system as a whole by effecting compromise policies which yield unequal benefits to the politically dominant power bloc in a capitalist society, but it also confers on workers real tangible benefits that are necessary to the reproduction of labor power (e.g., education, family allowances). Hence, according to Quadagno, the structuralist concept of political power "can be [empirically] derived by analyzing how state managers respond to different power blocs, by examining the existing economic and political constraints unique to a particular period and to a particular state action, and by assessing how working-class demands get incorporated into social policy."[20]

Third, Poulantzas clearly accepts the principle of uneven development as an important structural element of state institutions and state policies. Poulantzas maintains that uneven development within capitalist societies results in an unstable equilibrium between the economic, political, and ideological instances. As a result, Poulantzas argues that

(H$_{1c}$)   "this [structural] equilibrium is never *given* by the economic as such, but is maintained by the state."[21]

The state must often intervene with policies or institutional reforms in order to reestablish equilibrium between the various levels. Thus, for example, the state might initiate curriculum reform in public schools, such as computer literacy or engineering scholarships, to bring the ideological level into a time sequence that corresponds to the functional requirements of capitalist accumulation. In this example, the "operational objective" of curriculum reform would be realized empirically in the creation of a labor force that previously did not exist but is necessary to capital accumulation in a postindustrial economy.[22]

The operational objectives of state policy are realized through three "modalities of the state function." The modalities of the state function identify the structural levels in which the effects of state policies are realized: (1) the technicoeconomic function at the economic level, (2) the political function at the level of class struggle, and (3) the ideological function at the cultural level.[23] In the example above, the effects of curriculum reform are an ideological mode of the state that makes it possible for capitalists to continue purchasing the necessary labor power and, thus, to realize surplus value through its ongoing exploitation. In a similar manner, Poulantzas offers the general hypothesis that,

(H₂)   at whatever level the state's modalities are exercised, the state function is oriented "with particular reference to the productivity of labor."[24]

The modalities of the state function are always implemented through three functional subsystems of the state: the judicial subsystem, the ideological subsystem, and the political subsystem. Poulantzas argues that in capitalist societies the judicial subsystem is constituted as a set of rules which facilitate market exchanges by providing a "framework of cohesion in which commercial encounters can take place" (e.g., property and contract law, fair business practices, etc.).[25] The state's ideological subsystem functions primarily through public educational institutions, and the strictly political subsystem consists of institutions engaged in "the maintenance of political order in political class conflict" (e.g., electoral laws, the party system, law enforcement).[26] The state's modalities each constitute political functions insofar as their operational objective is the maintenance and stabilization of a society in which the capitalist class is the dominant and exploitative class. As Poulantzas notes, "it is to the extent that the prime object of these functions is the maintenance of this unity that they [i.e., the functions and their modalities] correspond to the political interests of the dominant class."[27]

It should be emphasized as a point of considerable methodological significance that structures (i.e., the levels of capitalist society) are not reducible to the economic, political, or ideological *institutions* that compose them.[28] On this point, David Gold, Clarence Lo, and Erik Olin Wright observe that the concept of "structure does *not* refer to the concrete social institutions that make up a society, but rather to the *systematic functional interrelationships among these institutions.*" Hence, a structural analysis consists of more than a narrative history of a particular institution or an analysis of the policy-formation process. It requires one to identify "the functional relationship of various institutions to the process of surplus-value production and appropriation."[29] Gordon L. Clark and Michael Dear correctly note that explanatory references to function must be taken as theoretical statements about the operational objective(s) of a particular policy or institution, whereas operational objectives designate the means by which a particular policy or institution contributes to the process of private capital accumulation.[30]

The Structuralist Concept of the State

The functional necessity of policy conjunctures between state power and capitalist interests is a postulate derived from an *analytic distinction* between the concepts of state power and the state apparatus.[31] Poulantzas defines state power as the capacity of a social class to realize its objective interests through the state apparatus.[32] Thus, Jessop observes that "state power is capitalist to the extent that it creates, maintains, or restores the conditions required for capital accumulation in a given situation and it is non-capitalist to the extent that these conditions are not realised."[33] In this respect, the objective effects of state policies on capital accumulation and the class structure are the main indicators of state power.[34]

On the other hand, the state apparatus is identified with two relations that are analytically (though not functionally) distinct from state power. Poulantzas defines the state apparatus as: "(a) the place of the state in the ensemble of the structures of a social formation," that is, the state's functions, and "(b) the *personnel of the state*, the ranks of the administration, bureaucracy, army, etc."[35] The state apparatus is thus a unity of the effects of state power (i.e., policies) and the network of institutions and personnel through which the state function is executed.[36]

The *functional unity* between state power and the state apparatus is emphasized by Poulantzas with the observation "that structure *is not the simple principle of organization which is exterior to* the institution: the structure is present in an allusive and inverted form in the institution itself."[37] This indicates that for Poulantzas the concept of the state apparatus intrinsically includes the functions executed through state institutions and by state personnel. Hence, unlike instrumentalist or organizational theorists, structuralists have generally insisted that the concept of state power is not reducible merely to governmental institutions and state personnel. Quite the contrary, Poulantzas argues that "the institutions of the state, do not, strictly speaking, have any power."[38] Bob Jessop echoes this view with his observation that "the state is a set of institutions that cannot, *qua* institutional ensemble, exercise power."[39] Instead, state institutions are viewed only as arenas for the exercise of political power and exist as such only by virtue of their functional role in capitalist society.[40] Jessop notes that an important implication of this view is that neither the state nor state elites should be seen as historical agents capable of exercising political power toward noncapitalist objectives.[41]

It is from this methodological perspective that Poulantzas and other structuralists criticize the instrumentalist approach to the state. Poulantzas concludes that if state institutions are not seen as the repository of state power, but merely as structural channels for the realization of its effects, then the direct participation of members of the capitalist class in the state apparatus, even where it exists, is not the most important aspect of political analysis. Rather, as Poulantzas claimed in his famous debate with Ralph Miliband, "if the *function* of the state in a determinate social formation and the *interests* of the dominant class in this formation coincide, it is by reason of the system itself: the direct participation of members of the ruling class in the state apparatus is not the *cause* but the *effect,* and moreover a chance and contingent one, of this objective coincidence."[42] The implication, as Roger King concludes, is that "state bureaucrats are constrained to act on behalf of capital because of the logic of the capitalist system, irrespective of their personal beliefs or affiliations."[43]

The Mechanisms of Functional Constraint

The concept of automatic functioning was a formidable analytic hurdle in the development of structuralist theory, because it required a concept of functional constraint able to satisfy the stringent requirements of this methodological assertion. Consequently, if structuralism is to avoid the worst kind of functionalist metaphysics, it must be able to specify a structural mechanism that requires the state to function automatically as a capitalist state even though capitalists do not directly hold most, or sometimes any, governmental offices.[44]

In an early critique of Poulantzas, Amy Beth Bridges proposed two constraint mechanisms that have since become widely accepted in the structuralist literature, mainly through the works of Fred Block and Charles Lindblom. Bridges's first hypothesis is that

(H₃)   the state necessarily serves the interests of the capitalist class, because the state's own fiscal functioning is immediately dependent on the economy.[45]

Structural theorists have identified two sources of fiscal dependency. First, Block notes the state's tax capacity is dependent on the overall performance of the economy. When the economy slows down or declines, the state will have difficulty maintaining adequate revenues to finance its own operations.[46] When the economy is growing, the state can generate revenues with much less tax effort and, thus, with much less resistance from business or the public. Second, Ernest Mandel has consistently emphasized that all modern capitalist states rely on short-term borrowing and long-term deficit financing as regular components of public budgeting. Consequently, he argues, escalating public debt increasingly forges "a golden chain" between state and capital, because no government could last more than a month without knocking on the doors of the major banks.[47]

In addition, however, Bridges also suggests that

(H₄)   the state necessarily serves the interests of the capitalist class, because the state's legitimacy is dependent on the economy.[48]

Citizens generally view the state's personnel and policies as being responsible for their economic prosperity or lack thereof. Consequently, during economic downturns support for a regime declines. In democratic states, the party in power is likely to be ousted in the next election because of its poor economic performance, and in nondemocratic countries rising opposition may destabilize a regime if poor economic conditions persist for too long. Paradoxically, the ease with which party regimes can be ousted in most democratic countries may well make democratic states more responsive to the needs of capitalists and, hence, make democracy what Lenin called "the best possible shell" for a capitalist state.

The key to the functioning of both mechanisms is the fact that in a capitalist economy the ownership of productive assets is largely private as opposed to public. In other words, although the state depends on the private economy for its own revenues and is held accountable for the performance of the economy by its citizens, actual decisions about investment, job creation, and wages (i.e., economic growth) are made by private capitalists. However, capitalists do not invest unless there is a reasonable guarantee that their capital is physically (and legally) secure and that it will return a profit to them. Thus, state policies and the stability of the state are both central to creating a favorable "business climate" and, hence, to maintaining enough "business confidence" to sustain investment and economic growth (for example, hypotheses

1 and 2 above).[49] Where state policies undermine business confidence, private business people will either refuse to invest or, more likely, redeploy their capital toward economies in which they have political as well as economic confidence.

In this manner, the marketplace will automatically trigger punishment for unfavorable state policies in the form of reduced investment, unemployment, declining public revenues, and lower standards of living for everyone. In addition, because states are more likely to rely on deficit financing during economic downturns, business confidence may further constrain tax and expenditure policies because of investors' unwillingness or reluctance to finance the public debt. Most important, these punishments will be inflicted spontaneously and without any prior coordination among capitalists, simply because individual managers and owners will decide that it is no longer prudent or profitable to invest their assets in an unfavorable business climate. Meanwhile, political regimes that maintain favorable business climates will be automatically rewarded, because increased private investment will produce economic growth, rising public revenues, and high levels of regime support from the public.[50]

The concept of "capital flight" is a key element in structural theory that greatly clarifies the structuralist distinction between state power and the state apparatus. As used by Bridges, Block, and Lindblom, the explanatory power of the capital flight concept is that it reinforces Poulantzas's claim that political power is constituted outside the state apparatus in capitalist relations of production, namely, in the private control of productive assets.[51] Moreover, as Bridges concludes, such a concept makes it "impossible to conceive of a state functioning against the interests of the bourgeoisie . . . short of removing the basis of their power, that is, control of the means of production."[52]

Michael H. Best and William E. Connolly suggest that the functional constraints are particularly evident at the state level in the United States during cyclical economic downturns.[53] As an illustration, Best and Connolly call attention to the mid-1970s recession, when liberal governors like Michael Dukakis in Massachusetts, Ella Grasso in Connecticut, Hugh Carey in New York, and Jerry Brown in California were forced to go against their own ideological inclinations because of the functional constraints imposed on their policy options. Each governor was faced with declining revenues, growing expenditures for welfare, and inflated prices for state services; yet each governor gave high priority to welfare cuts while seeking to retain or expand other programs which offered inducements to corporate and financial investors. In each case, when tax increases finally became unavoidable, the taxes were generally regressive and fell most heavily on working- and middle-class taxpayers already hit by inflation, high tax rates, and the threat of unemployment. One may easily argue that the same pattern was repeated during the 1990–92 recession by liberal governors such as Lowell Weicker in Connecticut, James Florio in New Jersey, Mario Cuomo in New York, and Ann Richards in Texas. The implication, as Best and Connolly conclude, is that the policy options available to the state "are very limited whether its incumbent officers are liberal or conservative in ideology." [54]

In this respect, the structuralists' ability to locate class power outside of the state (i.e., in the relations of production) poses a serious challenge to the social democratic model discussed in chapter 1. As discussed in the previous chapter, the social democratic model hinges on three assumptions: (1) that workers can win control of the state apparatus through democratic elections, (2) that the state apparatus is the repository of state power, and (3) that the autonomous state power can be used to shift the control of productive assets from capital to labor peacefully and gradually. However, Adam Przeworski has utilized a rational choice model to demonstrate that capital flight also imprisons the collective action of the working class in terms of the state policies their parties can implement. [55]

Gradualist state policies designed to shift the control of productive assets away from capital quickly lower business confidence and thus trigger the automatic recoil of capital flight. Therefore, the short-term effect of socialist policies is often unemployment and economic suffering for the very workers these policies are designed to benefit. While this trend continues, workers and their state representatives will be forced to choose between two alternatives: They can move more rapidly and more forcefully to seize the means of production, although this means choosing the uncertain outcomes of revolution, potential violence, further suffering, and economic decline. Or they can end capital flight by negotiating compromise policies with the capitalist class.

The logic of collective action suggested in Przeworski's model reveals that it is "more rational" to negotiate tangible concessions from capital in exchange for leaving production relations intact. [56] In fact, Lindblom concludes that "in so far as policy has successfully pushed into areas of which business people disapprove, it has often had to be offset by new benefits or supports to business." [57] The outcome is a political and economic system that remains "capitalist" even where socialist governments have been in power for many decades.

The idea of policy-makers as prisoners of the market has proved to be a compelling concept that explains why, as a general rule, the state tends to promote private capital accumulation regardless of the particular governing elite. In their hardest variants, the structuralist analyses of Poulantzas and Przeworski have tended to rationalize collective action and decision-making to the point that only one rational choice or functional policy outcome is possible. The functioning of the market so imprisons decision-making that the composition of state elites, the policy-formation process, and indeed the entire superstructure of instrumentalist theory is considered irrelevant.

This "hard" structuralism depends on a concept of functional constraint "so absolutely compelling as to turn those who run the state into the merest of functionaries and executants of policies imposed upon them by 'the [capitalist] system' ".[58] However, the hard formulation of structuralism, often polemical in its intent, tends to exaggerate the automatic functioning of the market's trigger mechanism.[59] First, capitalists do form associations to plan policy, lobby, and engage in a variety of political activities. Hence, Roger King muses, "if business is inevitably privileged in the political systems of advanced capitalist societies, why does it require associations?"[60] A deterministic formulation of structural theory cannot explain this simple political reality. Second, Colin Crouch calls attention to the fact that capitalists often deeply mistrust the state even though it is supposedly a capitalist state.[61]

These challenges have been met with "softer" versions of structuralism, such as that of Fred Block and Stephen Elkin, who see the market's automatic trigger mechanism as merely promoting a natural alliance between state and capital. However, to forge and maintain this alliance in practice, capitalists must rely on a variety of "subsidiary structural mechanisms," which, as Block describes them, are not substantially different from Domhoff's "processes of domination."[62] Indeed, it is one thing to say that capital flight commands the undivided attention of state policy-makers, but it is another for state elites to know what business "needs" to restore its confidence. If state elites are to do anything more than throw stones in the dark, there must be institutionalized mechanisms for business to communicate those needs to policy-makers. To this extent, political processes such as lobbying, candidate contributions, propaganda campaigns, and consulting are necessary "transmission belts" between capital and the state. Furthermore, before business can communicate its interests to the state, it must at some level know what it needs from the state, that is, what policies will impact it negatively and what policies will satisfy its requirements.

In addition, soft structuralism therefore recognizes that the social composition of a state elite, as well as the ideology of state managers, will at least influence the strength or weakness of the state-capital partnership. The power structures emphasized by an instrumentalist approach can at least influence the timing of policy responses to fluctuations in business confidence and the types of policy adjustments that are forthcoming, and they can affect whether or not the state exerts its full capacities on behalf of capital. For example, having direct representation in the executive apparatus is certainly a more favorable political position than not having it, because this position allows capital to veto unfavorable policy initiatives and thus to preempt declines in business confidence. Without direct representation, it is always possible that unfavorable policies will be implemented or that policies required by business interests will not be forthcoming from the state when needed.[63] Hence, the subsidiary mechanisms emphasized by instrumentalists turn out to be required for the effective functioning of the major mechanisms pointed out by structuralists.

Block's distinction between major and subsidiary structural mechanisms opens the possibility of an analytic rapprochement between structuralist and instrumentalist theories. Nevertheless, the explanatory logic of structuralist theory continues to focus scholarly research on different aspects of the same historical and empirical phenomena. The two types of research emphasized by structuralist theory are called form analysis and policy analysis.

Form Analysis

Form analysis is linked to the structuralist assumption that each mode of production requires a particular type of state to fulfill the functional requirements of system maintenance specific to that mode of production. In principle, one should be able to identify feudal, capitalist, and socialist types of state among others. However, this conceptual typology is insufficient unless one can also explain the historical political development of each type of state. Clark and Dear emphasize that the question of form is thus directed "toward understanding how and why a particular state structure derives from a given social formation. In theory, a capitalist social formation should give rise to a distinctively capitalist state and an evolving social formation should be accompanied by concomitant changes in the state form."[64] The key problem, of course, is to identify how a specific structural form supplies the functional requirements of system maintenance during each stage of capitalist development. In this regard, the underlying hypothesis of form analysis is that

(H₅)   the processes of political development are located in the changing functional needs of capitalist societies at different stages of their economic and social development.

Structuralists have frequently suggested that historical variations in the functional structure of capitalist states can be analyzed along two axes. First, capitalist states tend to develop different *forms of intervention* in the economy, such as mercantilism, minimalism, and welfarism, with each emerging during different phases of capitalist development. Second, capitalist states demonstrate wide variations in the *forms of representation* that institutionalize the alliance between state and capital.

Structuralist theory embarked initially on a path blazed by Poulantzas, who argued that the analysis of state forms was not directly related to the historical study of political institutions. Poulantzas relied on a concept of "functional equivalence" to argue that different institutions could often fulfill the same function in various social formations. Thus, Poulantzas dismisses institutional studies as being important only "in so far as they elucidate the functions of the state."[65] From this perspective, the particular institution that executes a function is of secondary importance to the function that is being realized through a state institution. Consequently, it is no surprise that as late as 1987 Dunleavy and O'Leary could find few functionalist accounts of actual state institutions in the Marxist structuralist literature.[66]

The absence of such studies is related to the assumption that theoretically informed analyses of political institutions become possible in structuralism only to the extent that one can supply an a priori foundation for interpreting particular state forms.[67] Indeed, throughout the 1970s, Poulantzas maintained that the structural analysis of state forms was an a priori science which would allow theorists to deduce state forms from the functional requirements of capital accumulation that characterized each stage of capitalist development, namely, the phases of merchant, industrial, and state-finance capital.[68] The derivationist, or German capital logic, school emerged in the early 1970s partly as an attempt to operationalize that research agenda.[69] However, the derivationist hybrid, which is discussed in chapter 3, quickly exhausted itself and was largely abandoned by the early 1980s.

More fruitful efforts to theorize the forms of state intervention have emerged during the last decade in two similar schools of thought known as regulation theory (RT) and social structure of accumulation theory (SSAT).[70] These schools of thought have made considerable strides in translating structuralist concepts into midlevel abstractions that permit scholars' better integration of historical or institutional research with theoretical analysis. The RT and SSAT schools "seek to explain long-run patterns of capital accumulation by analyzing the relation between the capital accumulation process and a set of social institutions which affect that process."[71] The two schools have called attention to the fact that the historical process of capital accumulation can be sustained only to the extent that cultural values, forms of business organization, government policy, law, and educational curricula are compatible with the requirements of each phase in the accumulation process. The interconnected matrix of economic, social, and political institutions that support capital accumulation is called a regime of accumulation or a social structure of accumulation.

SSAT theorists have identified three social structures of accumulation (i.e., forms of intervention) in the United States in which each structural form is marked by the hegemonic ascendancy of a particular capitalist fraction. A competitive structure, in which merchant capital was ascendant, existed from 1815 to the mid-1890s. The competitive mode of regulation was centered on small enterprises utilizing a craft-based labor process that produced mainly for local markets. A corporate regime, centered in the hegemonic ascendancy of industrial capital, assumed dominance from the 1890s until the end of World War II. The corporate mode of regulation was characterized by the emergence of monopolistic industrial enterprises, standardized mass production, and the Taylorization of labor processes. Finally, from World War II to the present, the hegemony of finance capital has been institutionalized in a state-capitalist regime. The state-capitalist mode of regulation has been structured, first, on a partnership between government and monopoly capital and, second, on a series of "historic accords" or class compromises embodied in institutions such as routinized collective bargaining.

A key hypothesis of regulation theory is that, as the mode of accumulation changes (e.g., from competitive to corporate), noneconomic institutions which once supported the process of capital accumulation and class hegemony eventually become fetters on the process of capitalist development. An "accumulation crisis" is always the prelude to a transition from one social structure of accumulation to another. Thus, the RT and SSAT schools explain accumulation crises primarily as the result of emerging disjunctures between the changing structural requirements of capitalist accumulation and the organization or policies of supporting institutions, such as government and education. As a result, newly ascendant fractions of the capitalist class find that social institutions (e.g., the family), cultural orientations (e.g., consumerism), governmental institutions, and educational policies must all be reconstructed to catalyze and support a new wave of economic growth. Business leaders must therefore initiate movements to redesign cultural, political, and social institutions to sustain a new structure of accumulation.[72]

Similarly, particular regimes of accumulation require forms of state representation that institutionalize the political hegemony of the economically dominant capitalist fraction. A common feature of capitalist states is their tendency to institutionalize a hierarchical and horizontal distribution of state power (i.e., federalism and separation of powers). In the assessment of most structuralists,

(H₆)   the various levels and branches of the state apparatus institutionalize "differential access to the state apparatuses and differential opportunities to realise specific effects in the course of state intervention."[73]

State power is institutionalized asymmetrically through the state apparatus inasmuch as each level or branch of an apparatus constitutes the major power base of contending classes and class fractions within the state.[74] For example, competitive capital frequently discovers that decentralized and local forms of representation best serve its interests. One will often find that competitive capital has its strongest representation in the United States in state governments. On the other hand, finance capital often finds its strongest representation in the national executive branch. Consequently, different classes and class fractions will each favor a different form of representation that is identified with the way state power is distributed between levels and branches of the state apparatus.

Thus, if one concretely examines the process of policy formation within the state, policies appear to emerge as "the result of contradictions between, and within, the various state branches and apparatuses."[75] Consequently, Poulantzas infers that

(H₇)   the establishment of a state's policy is the result of class contradictions inscribed in the very structure of the state.[76]

Policy Analysis

Bob Jessop contends that structural forms of representation are designed for the systematic production of functionally "unequal and asymmetrical effects on the ability of different social forces to realise their interests through political action."[77] In this respect, the theoretical role of policy analysis is to test hypotheses concerning the functional relationship between state power and its effect on capital accumulation. Instrumentalist policy studies largely emphasize the class origins of policy initiatives and their organizational linkage to conscious class interests. To the extent that structuralism emphasizes the function of the state (as opposed to the composition of state or party elites), it identifies the capitalist content of state policies with their functional effect on the capital accumulation process. Hence, Goran Therborn notes that for structuralists

(H_8) "the class character of these policies may be seen in their direct effects upon the forces and relations of production, upon the ideological superstructure, and upon the state apparatus."[78]

For example, the graduated income tax was adopted with the initial intention of taxing individuals on the basis of their ability to pay and the later intention of providing a mechanism for directly redistributing income outside the marketplace. The social democratic objective of the graduated income tax was to finance universal public programs that would reallocate opportunities among classes for income and capital accumulation. Given the fact that the United States and other advanced capitalist societies have maintained nominally progressive tax rates for several decades, "one would expect not only some movement toward greater equality, but *significantly* greater equality."[79] However, despite the egalitarian intent, comparisons of before- and after-tax income, including the impact of government transfer payments, show that a nominally progressive tax schedule has had only a marginal redistributive effect on income allocations (see table 2.1).[80]

Similarly, the pathbreaking work of Samuel Bowles and Herbert Gintis on education policy found that, despite its rhetoric of equal opportunity and social mobility, the American educational system "has never been a potent force for economic equality." Quite the contrary, Bowles and Gintis's analysis demonstrates that "the association of income and occupational status with an individual's educational attainment is not due to measured mental skills" (i.e., IQ), but is more closely

Table 2.1. Money income of U.S. households: Percentage distribution, by quintile, and index of income concentration, 1986

	Lowest quintile	Second quintile	Third quintile	Fourth quintile	Highest quintile	Index of income concentration[a]
Income before taxes[b]	1.0	7.6	15.0	24.1	52.4	0.500
Income after taxes						
Federal income taxes	1.1	8.2	15.7	24.4	50.6	0.486
State income taxes	1.1	8.4	15.8	24.5	50.2	0.481
Social security taxes	1.1	8.4	15.8	24.4	50.3	0.483
After government transfers[c]	4.7	10.6	16.0	23.0	45.7	0.403

Source: U.S. Census Bureau, *Statistical Abstract of the United States, 1990* (Washington, D.C.: Government Printing Office, 1990), adapted from table 724, p. 449.

[a]This index is a statistical measure of income equality ranging from 0 to 1. A measure of 1 indicates perfect inequality (i.e., one person having all the income and the rest having none). A measure of 0 indicates perfect equality (i.e., all persons having equal shares of income).

[b]Includes all wages, salaries, capital gains, and health insurance benefits; excludes government transfer payments.

[c]Includes social security, railroad retirement, veterans payments, unemployment insurance, workmen's compensation, Medicare, school lunch subsidies, AFDC, supplemental security income, Medicaid, food stamps, rent subsidies, and other welfare payments.

associated with their original family background (i.e., class origins). The school and university systems do little to redistribute opportunities for future wealth or income among classes, but instead function "to perpetuate the social relationships of economic life . . . by facilitating a smooth integration of youth into the labor force."[81]

Thus, it comes as no surprise that structural analyses of wealth distribution consistently indicate that welfare state interventions do not have any demonstrable functional effect on the social structure. In fact, the distribution of wealth, particularly stock and bond holdings, has not changed significantly in the United States during the last seventy years (see table 2.2).[82] For structuralists, such examples are evidence that, despite the social democratic intent of tax-and-spend legislation, the functional effect of state policies has been to reproduce the existing class structure and to maintain an unequal distribution of income and opportunities.[83] Hence, Poulantzas concludes that even though state policy appears in the short term to be phenomenally incoherent and chaotic, particularly during the policy-formation process, a certain coherence arrives with the conclusion of the process.[84] The structural limitations of the state are quite clearly marked by its inability to supersede the functional constraints of the capitalist system.

Table 2.2. Personal wealth: Percentage of assets held by top 1 percent of adults in 1922, 1945, and 1972

Type of asset	1922	1945	1972
Corporate stock	61.5	61.7	62.7
U.S. government bonds	45.0	32.5	
State and local bonds	88.0	100.0	59.5 [a]
Other bonds	69.2	78.5	
Trusts	—	—	95.3
Cash, mortgages, notes	31.0	19.3	18.3
Real estate	18.0	11.1	15.0
Life insurance	35.3	17.3	7.1
Miscellaneous	23.2	21.4	12.6

Sources: For 1922 and 1945: Robert J. Lampman, *The Share of Top Wealth-Holders in National Wealth* (Princeton: Princeton University Press, 1962), p. 209. Reproduced by permission. For 1972: U.S. Bureau of the Census, *Statistical Abstract of the United States, 1984* (Washington, D.C.: Government Printing Office, 1984), table 795, p. 481.

[a] This 1972 figure is derived from a consolidation of U.S. government bonds, state and local bonds, and other bonds.

State and Revolution

The problems of defining a structuralist politics are best understood in terms of two dilemmas: the asymmetry of the state apparatus and the separation of state power from the state apparatus. Most structural theorists would argue that the existing state apparatus cannot simply be "seized" or captured by the working class as an instrument of transition because (1) the existing form of state power functions against noncapitalist interests, and (2) the state apparatus has no power, but merely channels the social power constituted in relations of production. The idea that forms of representation institutionalize asymmetrical distributions of political power suggests that working-class parties cannot establish their political dominance simply by seizing an existing state apparatus. As Poulantzas argues, the political implication of this perspective is that working-class interests cannot be advanced simply by a change in state personnel and state policies; the working class must structurally "*break, that is to say radically change,* the state apparatus."[85] Consequently, Jessop insists that "a principle aim of class struggle must be the reorganisation of the state apparatuses in order to redefine their accessibility and/or their instrumentality for various class forces."[86]

At a minimum, a successful working-class party will have to construct new forms of representation that asymmetrically institutionalize the power of working-class groups. However, as with social policy reform, a social-democratic strategy of evolutionary change is likely to trigger capital flight and disinvestment because such reforms threaten the dominance of the capitalist class. Once again, the probable outcome of social democratic reform initiatives is to trigger a renewed concern with business confidence, even among those groups which political reforms are designed to empower. Hence, Stephen Elkin points out that "regardless of their merits, the prospects of such reforms occurring are slim, not least because the very workings of the political economy that serve to prompt the concern for reform will substantially impede it."[87]

Consequently, structural analysis seems to imply the necessity of "smashing" the capitalist state and setting up a parallel, or "dual," system of state power through revolutionary activity. Nevertheless, Therborn notes that "the variance between state power and the state apparatus is limited by the fact that they express the class relations of the same society."[88] In other words, it is logically inconceivable that a socialist type of state can survive for long, even in a revolutionary context, so long as the means of production remain exclusively in private hands. One can surmise that such a scenario will produce economic chaos unless workers smash existing production relations at the factory level and simultaneously utilize the state to take direct control of the means of production.[89]

Criticisms and Unresolved Problems

There are many unresolved methodological problems with the structuralist approach to the state. The most basic problem is identifying the "functional needs" of a capitalist society. It is not at all clear how one can know with any certainty what functions are actually necessary to the continuation of a capitalist social formation. The orthodox response is to assume that Marx's *Capital* supplies an a priori answer to this question, but George Ross has rightly criticized this answer as a "Marxian leap of faith" that begs the question of how Marx came to know what functions are necessary to capitalist reproduction.[90] Moreover, the fact that Marx and Engels never produced a systematic study of the state makes such an assumption exceptionally problematic for political theory, even if one is inclined to accept such an answer.

Furthermore, the analytic and explanatory relationship between the concepts of function, form, and apparatus becomes increasingly tenuous when one moves away from abstract theorizing to the examination of

: institutions or policies. First, the analytic relationship be-
..... theoretical functions and historical institutions is complicated by
two factors: most apparatuses consist of several institutions, and most
institutions are multifunctional. For example, the concept of a state
ideological apparatus refers to an ideological function that is fulfilled
by many, often historically unrelated, institutions, such as the schools,
churches, mass media, army, and family. Thus, in order to understand
fully the ideological function as a state apparatus, one would have
to conduct comparative multi-institutional studies which demonstrate
that these institutions are a coherent "apparatus" directed by the state
fulfilling a common function. No such study yet exists.

On the other hand, when one examines specific institutions from
a structuralist standpoint, it is generally found that most institutions
simultaneously fulfill multiple functions. For example, schools both
realize a technicoeconomic function through manpower-training policies and fulfill an ideological function through curriculum policies that
promote political socialization to the existing economic and political
systems. Thus, schools could conceivably be understood as part of the
state's technicoeconomic apparatus or as part of its ideological apparatus. This observation is not necessarily a problem, although it com-
plicates the structuralists' conceptual scheme, because there is never a
unilinear relationship between functions, apparatuses, and institutions.
If one multiplies this problem across the wide number of apparatuses
and institutions that constitute the modern welfare state, the result
is a conceptual scheme which lacks the analytic rigor it first seems
to convey because of a confusing criss-cross of subapparatuses and
multiple-function institutions. Hence, in building a theory of the state,
the structural-functionalist jargon may do more to confuse historical
and empirical analysis than to organize it analytically.[91]

Establishing a precise explanatory relationship between state forms
and particular institutions is equally difficult. Comparative analyses of
late capitalist societies provide strong support for the thesis that welfare
states are the state form characteristic of all late capitalist societies. Yet,
when one compares the specific institutions and policies of different
welfare states, one finds a high degree of variability in the way institutions and policies fulfill the imputed functions of this state form.[92]
Hence, when structuralists have moved away from abstract theorizing
toward institutional and policy analysis, they have found it virtually impossible to make a reasonable case that specific institutions or policies
are required by the functional needs of particular capitalist societies.[93]
In fact, very different institutions are often found to fulfill the same

function in different countries. While the concept of "functional equivalence" creates a theoretical space for this variability, the concept does not explain the extensive institutional and policy variations that exist among different welfare states. More to the point, it is highly doubtful that a concept of function *can* explain the many institutional and policy differences between individual welfare states.

Consequently, critics have often argued that the concept of function is a theoretical black box that explains nothing because it purports to explain everything. Dunleavy and O'Leary point out that structuralists often incorrectly conclude that, because a particular policy achieves a given result, the policy or institution is functionally necessary to achieve that result. In other words, the structuralists' functional logic assumes that whatever occurs does so because it has to and because it is functional to the overall system. Thus, structuralism too frequently assumes that "whatever the state does is functional for the capitalist class in the long run, so the theory is immunized against any conflicting evidence."[94]

For this reason, most of the latest structuralist research has been designed to operationalize the approach empirically by "problemizing" many of its basic assumptions as provisional hypotheses. However, the results of such research have often done little to clarify the explanatory value of functionalist concepts. Quite the contrary, as one shifts to an explanation of the variation between welfare states, for example, it is difficult to escape the conclusion that specific policies and institutions exist because state managers in particular historical circumstances thought that they were necessary, somehow useful for their purposes, or because they were unable or unwilling to resist those who wanted such policies. Nevertheless, many structuralists have shown a peculiar reluctance to erode the functional determinism of structural theory by introducing the problems of historical agency into their framework. Dunleavy and O'Leary have suggested that the structuralists' discomfort with questions of historical agency stems from confusing "voluntarism (the notion that individuals have unconstrained choices) with methodological individualism (the notion that social phenomena should be explained through the intended and unintended consequences of human actors making choices within constrained feasible sets of options)."[95] One result of this confusion is that structuralists have increasingly welded rational choice models and game theory onto the structuralist approach in order to theoretically predetermine historical agency with the imputed structural constraints of rational action.[96]

Nevertheless, while structuralist assumptions have been increasingly problemized, empirical and historical analyses have raised some doubts about whether state policies always do function in the long-term interests of the capitalist class. For example, Jill Quadagno argues that the forms of representation institutionalized in the United States magnify the political power of local (small and landed) capital within the state so that compromise policies emerge which do not fully satisfy the needs of the capitalist class, but which do not overtly contradict the needs of any particular capitalist fraction.[97] Yet, if this is the case, it is not clear whether such compromises represent the interests of capital as a whole, an agglomeration of partial class interests, or in some cases merely afunctional policies. This interpretive ambiguity is only compounded when one introduces class struggle between labor and capital into the equation.

Similarly, Colin Crouch makes the empirical argument that finance capital has sometimes dominated particular state policies in Great Britain to the long-term detriment of capital as a whole.[98] Arguments of this type may pose a fundamental challenge to structuralist theory, or they may only raise the question of whether or not all policies and institutions are equally important to fulfilling the state's general maintenance function. It is conceivable that certain functional needs of capitalist accumulation could be left unmet, or that other needs be only partly fulfilled, without precipitating an accumulation crisis.

Finally, it is worth noting that the major structural mechanism proposed by Block and Lindblom assumes a logic of capitalist regulation that is both uniform and unilinear. The regulatory logic of capital flight and disinvestment assumes that all sectors of the capitalist economy will respond to state intervention and state spending in a uniform manner; that is, capitalists will uniformly oppose such measures with disinvestment and will uniformly respond to opposite measures with increased investment. The same regulatory logic also assumes a unilinear relationship between declining business confidence, its recognition by state elites, and the subsequent adoption of state policies that restore business confidence. However, there are several reasons to doubt whether this mechanism always functions properly or uniformly to discipline state policies.

First, what is ostensibly an "automatic" trigger mechanism assumes the existence of state planning and statistical apparatuses to monitor consumer confidence, business confidence, unemployment, investment rates, and productivity. The theory does not explain how or why such apparatuses emerge in the first place, but, more important, we should not necessarily assume that such apparatuses will always be accurate enough to function properly. Economic measurements such as unemployment are analytic constructs which frequently omit data that are potentially important to policy formation, and, hence, state elites may often respond on the basis of incomplete or misleading information. Unemployment statistics, for instance, do not include "discouraged workers" (i.e., the unemployed who have quit looking for jobs), and census data fail to report the homeless and minority populations adequately.[99]

Second, state elites may not be timely in their reactions to declining business confidence for political or ideological reasons. In 1988, Governor Michael Dukakis of Massachusetts persistently refused to deal forthrightly with a declining state economy (and an unbalanced state budget) for fear that it would jeopardize his chances of winning the upcoming presidential election. Likewise, President Bush and his political advisors continually downplayed the extent and depth of the 1991–1992 recession in order to avoid focusing public attention on a weak economy while leading up to a presidential election. Moreover, the Bush administration's ideological commitment to free-market economics led key officials to believe that the 1991 downturn in the business cycle would be a short-lived and self-correcting phenomenon. The crux is that neither administration responded in a timely manner to a deteriorating economic and fiscal situation.

Third, when state managers do take actions that explicitly respond to declining business confidence, not all capitalists recognize such policies as being in their best interests and, thus, may not respond uniformly in the manner expected by state elites. Finally, the notion that state elites will respond to declining business confidence and disinvestment by reducing state expenditures and taxes dismisses the possibility that state elites might actually counter disinvestment by restricting capital flight, by decisively increasing progressive income taxation, or by adopting policies of direct state investment in public or joint-venture enterprises. The point is that there are innumerable ways in which the market's trigger mechanism might malfunction or function differently from what Block originally anticipated.

The other side of Block's and Lindblom's trigger mechanism is the assumption that state elites who adopt lower taxes and reduce state expenditures will be rewarded by renewed investment and employment growth. The empirical foundation for this assumption is tenuous at best. For example, a chief economic argument for the 1981 Tax Reduction Act initiated by President Reagan was that if corporate taxes were lowered the affected corporations would reinvest their windfall in new capital equipment, product development, marketing, and technological innovation. Hence, proponents of the tax reduction claimed that it would reinvigorate our basic industries, boost worker productivity, improve our competitive position in international markets, and lead to more jobs. However, when the empirical relationship between business investment and corporate income tax rates was studied following the adoption of the Tax Reduction Act (from 1981 to 1984), the alleged causal nexus proved nonexistent. Among the 259 largest U.S. corporations during this time, 43 companies paid 33 percent or more of their profits in federal taxes. These forty-three corporations boosted investment by 21 percent and increased their work forces by 4 percent. By contrast, the forty-four companies that paid no federal corporate income taxes during this time reduced their investment by 4 percent and reduced their work forces by 6 percent.[100] In other words, high tax rates did not necessarily discourage investment, nor did low tax rates necessarily encourage investment.

Similarly, annual state-by-state surveys of the U.S. business climate typically emphasize low taxes, low rates of work-force unionization, and the absence of extensive business regulations. South Dakota nearly always ranks among the states with the most "favorable" business climate, while states such as California and Massachusetts rank comparatively poorly.[101] Yet, the actual patterns of investment, job growth, and per capita income indicate that capitalist enterprises do quite well in the latter group of states, and there is absolutely no evidence of massive capital flight from California and Massachusetts to South Dakota. The same pattern is reproduced on an international scale. Many nations with comparatively high taxes and high rates of work-force unionization, such as Sweden and Germany, have capitalist economies with low unemployment rates, high productivity growth, high wages, and high rates of investment when compared with the United States, despite the latter's relatively low-tax status and minimal work-force unionization.

Indeed, Block now acknowledges that the expected functioning of his major structural mechanism depends on accepting a neoconservative, or free-market, model of the business climate as an accurate description of what capitalists need from the state (i.e., to be left alone).[102] It is only plausible to assume that increased state expenditures or regulations will uniformly and universally undermine business confidence to the extent that one accepts a laissez-faire model of the capitalist economy. However, neoliberal theory[103] and the social structure of accumulation theory[104] both provide compelling alternative models of a favorable business climate.

These models suggest that public expenditures and state regulation can actually enhance business confidence by stabilizing the marketplace. Furthermore, state interventions can actually facilitate capitalist development by strengthening labor-market participation, by promoting the emergence of new industries, and by creating new opportunities for profitable investment. State investment in education and work-force retraining can act as a magnet that attracts capital investment in high-skills and high-wage industries. State environmental regulations have actually created new industries and opportunities for profit in waste management, recycling, and toxic waste disposal. Similarly, public enterprises in western Europe have often been at the cutting edge of national economic development and have stimulated increased private investment.[105] From this perspective, disinvestment in American industry and declining international competitiveness are not due to too much state intervention, but are the result of too little public investment and decaying social structures of accumulation. The implication of these competing models is to suggest that there are probably multiple logics of capital accumulation.

CHAPTER THREE

Between Neo-Marxism and Post-Marxism: The Derivationist Approach

The modern state, whatever its form, is an essentially capitalist machine; it is the state of the capitalists, the ideal collective body of all capitalists.
—*Engels*, Anti-Duhring, 1878

By the early 1970s, plain Marxists and neo-Marxists had lined up into competing schools of thought best symbolized by the infamous Miliband-Poulantzas debate.[1] It is clear in retrospect that the primary axis of early debate between instrumentalists and structuralists was a methodological dispute over whether agency or structure could better explain what is "capitalist" about the state and state policies. However, when the polemic between instrumentalists and structuralists degenerated into redundancy, Marxian theorists began looking for ways to move beyond this antinomy.

Moreover, despite the methodological antinomy between instrumentalism and structuralism, both approaches shared a common analytic postulate that was increasingly called into question during the 1970s. While adherents of the two approaches disagree about what mechanisms best explain the capitalist nature of the state, both sides agree that the state is able to implement the long-term interests of capitalists; that is, state policies succeed in reproducing the capitalist relations of production which allow capitalists to exploit the working classes. However, as the 1970s progressed, even the most developed welfare states seemed less able to deliver both economic growth and welfare services. The result was a crisis of the welfare state that is dramatically symbolized by the rollbacks of the Thatcher and Reagan era.

The Miliband-Poulantzas stalemate and the crisis of the welfare state defined the intellectual and political context in which the journal *Kapitalistate* first introduced derivationism to Anglo-American scholars. Although derivationism first emerged out of the West German student movement in 1969, by the time it appeared in the United States, most Marxian theorists were already engulfed by the instrumentalist-structuralist polemic. However, with the publication of *State and Capital* (1978), derivationism received a flurry of publicity when it was viewed briefly as a way to transcend the methodological antinomies of the Milband-Poulantzas debate. Likewise, for the first time, derivationism focused Marxist theory on the limitations imposed on the state by its relation to the process of capital accumulation. Consequently, derivationism also seemed initially to offer some hope of developing a more dynamic approach to the state which would explain the relationship between the state's historical development and the underlying contradictions of the capitalist mode of production.[2]

The Derivationist Method

The derivationist approach was tied closely to a specific reading of Marx's works that focused renewed attention on the methodological dialectic within Marx's political economy. On the one hand, the derivationists saw an underlying functionalist logic in Marx's *Capital* that ostensibly revealed "the development of capital in general" and that supplied the conceptual basis for explaining the historical development of particular capitalist societies. On the other hand, there is no question that Marx marshals an enormous amount of empirical and historical evidence in *Capital* to illustrate his central theses about the underlying tendencies of capitalist development.[3]

In many respects, instrumentalism emphasized the latter tendency, and structuralism emphasized the former tendency. However, derivationists were convinced that the dialectic between these two explanatory dimensions was mainly a question of how to relate the actual process of empirical research to a mode of logical presentation that was "analytically determined." Hence, the derivationists' key methodological objective was to put "Humpty Marx" back together again by deriving historical forms of the state from the underlying logic of capitalist development.

The primary methodological axiom of the derivationist approach is that the analysis of the relation between state and society must be deduced from contradictions inherent in the capitalist mode of production.[4] The rationale for this axiom is that if capitalism were in fact spontaneous, self-regulating, and self-sustaining as an economic system, then there would be no logical rationale for state action in relation to capital accumulation. Therefore, derivationists posit the state as a logically necessary instance of capitalist society that must perform for the capitalist class those tasks which it inherently cannot perform for itself.[5] These tasks, whatever their nature, define the general interests of the capitalist class.

In this respect, a major analytic objective of the derivationist approach was to give a conceptually more meaningful content to the idea of general and long-term interests than had been proposed by instrumentalist and structuralist theorists. Derivationists sought to construct a concept of general interests that was historically more concrete than the idea of "reproducing the relations of production" but that was also theoretically more meaningful than reducing the concept of general interests to whatever policies individual capitalists happened to favor at any point in time. Once constructed, such a concept would enable scholars to judge the success or failure of the state in realizing the general interests of the capitalist class.

The State Forms of Intervention

Accumulation Crisis

The most influential tendency within derivationism seeks to derive the state from the contradictory logic of capital accumulation.[6] The "capital logic" tendency in derivationism is most closely associated with the work of Elmer Altvater.[7] Altvater contends that the forms and functions of the state can be derived from the fact that capital appears and acts historically at the economic level only in particular units such as firms, industries, or sectors. However, the ability of these units to engage in profitable activities presupposes that certain general conditions necessary to capital accumulation are always present. Altvater identifies the general interests of the capitalist class with the provision of these general conditions.

Altvater identifies four general conditions that must obtain if capitalist production and, thereby, capital accumulation are to take place successfully. First, three general *political* conditions must be provided by the state if capitalism is to exist at all. Initially, the state must provide a general legal system that institutionalizes private property (capitalist relations of production) and markets (commodity circulation). Thus, the state must create and enforce a property and contract law that at least does not obstruct but that preferably facilitates regular market transactions and the separation of the worker from the means of production (i.e., the sanctity of private property). Next, because the process of capital accumulation rests on the exploitation of labor, the state must regulate the attendant conflict between labor and capital. In part the regulation of class struggle is conducted by the judicial apparatus, but it must also be supported domestically by police and ideological apparatuses. Likewise, the expansion of global markets and the guarantee of nationally based capital within foreign markets ultimately require a military apparatus. Finally, for capitalist production to take place profitably, one general *material* condition must always be provided to individual capitalists by the state. This material condition is infrastructure. Infrastructure consists of the material conditions that are necessary to all business activities but that cannot be produced directly by individual private businesses.

For Altvater, these four conditions constitute the "general maintenance function" of a capitalist state, and to the degree that a state successfully fulfills these conditions it realizes the general interests of the capitalist class. Thus, these conditions analytically define a general type of state that can be called capitalist. However, the form in which their attendant activities are organized and the specific policies through which their objectives are implemented develop on the historical foundation of capitalist development in individual social formations.

The capital logic model of political development rests on the following hypothesis:

(H$_1$)   as capitalism undergoes stages of development, the form in which the state must fulfill its role also changes.

Elmer Altvater, Claudia von Braunmuhl, Sol Picciotto, and Hugo Radice supply a corpus of works which identify four phases in the capital logic of state forms: (1) early capitalism, (2) competitive capitalism, (3) state capitalism, and (4) world capitalism.[8]

Altvater suggests the hypothesis that

(H$_2$)   in early capitalism the state's political function is the creation of the general prerequisites for free competition.[9]

In a general sense, early capitalism requires the abolition of any political conditions that obstruct its development and the establishment of new political conditions that facilitate the initial process of primitive accumulation. Consequently, Picciotto and Radice argue that

(H$_{2a}$)   the emergence of early capitalism is predicated on the construction of a strong central state that is capable of subduing precapitalist ruling classes.[10]

Likewise, the strong "absolutist state" characteristic of early capitalism is necessary to pursue the colonial and mercantile policies that are historically the economic foundations of primitive accumulation.[11] Finally, Altvater maintains that, to fulfill its positive functions, not only must the early capitalist state establish a general legal system within fixed territorial boundaries,

(H_{2b})   the early capitalist state must also institutionalize a separation of the political from the economic levels of society.

In feudalism, by comparison, the political function is one of unmediated force between competing landholders, and the feudal class structure is maintained through the direct application of force by individual landholders against their working classes (e.g., serfdom, corvée labor). On the other hand, capitalism presupposes the existence of a free market in both capital and labor as well as the impartial enforcement of market transactions (i.e., contract law). The state is in a position to enforce contracts impartially only to the degree that coercive force is separated from individual property-owners and to the degree that the state is not a direct participant in market competition. Altvater refers to this tendency in capitalist political development as "the autonomization" of the state.

Once the basic structures of a capitalist economy are set in motion, however, routine business activities require a new state form in order to maintain the general political conditions of capital accumulation. Altvater suggests that during competitive capitalism

(H_3)   the state assumes a background role that mainly involves policing and adjudicating market transactions.

During competitive capitalism, there is an observable historical tendency toward the escalation of overt class struggles between labor and capital. A repressive function is initially fulfilled directly by individual capitalists through firings, black lists, security guards, and company militias. However, as the organization of labor attains classwide proportions, the state must gradually take over these repressive activities. In order to police the labor market, the state's repressive apparatuses must be expanded and redeployed against labor on behalf of individual capitalists. Thus, paradoxically, the era of competitive laissez-faire capitalism results in the expansion of the state's domestic coercive apparatus (i.e., police, judiciary, intelligence).

Yet, successful capitalist development eventually sets in motion a new contradiction between the increasingly socialized forces of production and individual capitalist firms seeking profitable business opportunities. In a third phase of political development, the form of state capitalism is linked to state activities that provide the general material conditions of capital accumulation. Altvater argues that, because of the historical tendency for the rate of profit to fall, the state must assume greater direct responsibility for producing raw material and labor inputs to growth sectors of the private economy which can no longer be supplied profitably by individual firms. Thus, Altvater maintains that

(H₄)   activities which were once conducted profitably by individual firms must eventually be taken over by the state in order to sustain profitability in the private economy.

Hence, the continuation of profitable business enterprises requires a newly strengthened and more extensively interventionist state.

The logic of state capitalism is derived from the principle that some business enterprises or sectors produce infrastructural inputs for other business enterprises or sectors, for example, raw material extraction, the transportation of goods and materials, educated and skilled laborers. Yet, as capitalist development progresses, the provision of various infrastructural goods and services becomes unprofitable for individual private businesses. Altvater suggests that providing infrastructure can become unprofitable for any of five reasons:

1. The provision of infrastructure may require too large an initial capital investment for any one firm or consortium of private firms (e.g., railroads).
2. The time lag between initial investment and profit realization is too long or too uncertain (e.g., space exploration and satellite communications).
3. The product or service does not have a direct commodity character (e.g., public goods).
4. The market for a product or service is too small to be profitable (e.g., rural electrification and specialized pharmaceuticals).
5. There is a below-average rate of return in providing a particular good or service.

As the production of infrastructural prerequisites becomes unprofitable for private firms, an "infrastructure vacuum" is created that must be filled by the state. According to Altvater's model, infrastructure vacuums are most pronounced historically in spheres of production that involve the movement of goods and information (i.e., the transportation and communications sectors) and the provision of labor inputs (i.e., education and public health). Most important, over time the need for infrastructure can be filled only by the state because of its ability to engage in unprofitable production activities outside the marketplace. In this respect, Richard Scase observes that "the state is increasingly forced to 'underwrite' the costs of capitalist production by *direct* involvement in renewing and maintaining the forces of production, both in terms of various technological processes and in the reproduction of labor power." [12] However, as Altvater emphasizes, once the state takes over a sphere of unprofitable production, it is genuinely socialized and thus sets an objective limit to the operations of capitalist markets within a particular society.

Finally, according to Picciotto and Radice, the underlying logic of contemporary political development is driven by a contradictory "double movement" of state and global capitalism.[13] On the one hand, capitalist enterprises must increasingly rely on the state to provide the general political and material conditions of accumulation. As Claudia von Braunmuhl observes, the reproduction of capital remains nation-based insofar as key cost inputs are underwritten by the market interventions of a strong state apparatus.[14] Consequently, state boundaries still constitute a line of fragmentation and competition among capitalists operating in international markets. On the other hand, the accumulation process is increasingly centered in multinational and transnational enterprises that are creating unified global markets.[15] However, the development of a genuinely world capitalist system requires the elimination of all boundaries to the free movement of capital and labor. Thus, Picciotto and Radice hypothesize that

(H_5) the globalization of the accumulation process is resulting in a crisis of the state.

The crisis of the state involves both its historical form as a nation-state and its current functioning as a welfare state. First, the emergence of a truly global capitalist economy has strengthened the structural hegemony of international capital over individual states. This has occurred because

(H_{5a}) states must increasingly bargain with international capital for debt service and domestic investment so that nation-states must adopt policies favorable to transnational enterprises.

This "new" pattern of hegemony has long been evident in the Third World countries,[16] but it is also increasingly visible in the policies of the metropolitan capitalist nations.[17] Thus, states are experiencing a crisis of "sovereignty" in regard to economic policies and economic relations; that is, national boundaries are becoming more porous and indefensible when it comes to the movement of capital, labor, skills, and information.

Second, the rising hegemony of transnational capital means that

(H_{5b}) the state's domestic economic apparatus (function) becomes increasingly ineffective.

The crisis of the state's domestic economic apparatus can be observed mainly in two policy sectors. State attempts to defend national capital will generally fail in those sectors which have already been penetrated by "foreign" (i.e., international) capital. In addition, state-centered attempts to defend metropolitan workers against global wage compression and international cost reduction will also fail.

In this respect, the crisis of the state is derived from the need to remove nation-based obstacles that impede the development of a global capitalist system. However, the removal of these obstacles will not mitigate the continuing need for a political form that can provide the general political and material conditions of capitalist accumulation. Thus, Picciotto and Radice suggest that

(H_6) the crisis of the state can be resolved only through the creation of transnational federations and the creation of international development institutions.

Picciotto and Radice argue that transnational capital requires ever larger state units to perform the essential political and economic functions of capital accumulation. The primary limits to the scope of economic concentration and centralization are no longer organizational and geographic, but political, that is, the size of the home state.

Consequently, with the emergence of a world capitalist system, the nation-state will be forced to cede important functions to a new state form. The new state form will consist of transnational federations such as the European Economic Community,[18] international parastatals such as the World Bank and the International Monetary Fund, international cooperative councils such as the Group of 7 and the Organization of Economic Cooperation and Development, and, finally, multinational private policy groups such as the Trilateral Commission.[19] At the same time, the new state form will provide a framework in which to rationalize existing state structures by facilitating the coordination of functions between dominant capitalist states and by avoiding conflict between large blocs of multinational capital that are still nation-based. The "new

Table 3.1. Capital logic derivation of state forms

	Stage of capitalist development			
	Early capitalism	Competitive capitalism	State capitalism	World capitalism
Development of state functions				
General legal system	X			
Regulation of class struggle				
Police/ideology		X		
Military				X
Infrastructure			X	
State form of accumulation	mercantile	liberal	welfare	transnational

world order" will combine increased supranational cooperation among the dominant blocs of international capital and renewed militarization toward subordinate and dependent areas of exploitation.

Class Struggle

A second tendency within derivationism seeks to derive the state from the logic of class struggle.[20] The class struggle tendency among derivationists is best represented by the works of Joachim Hirsch and Heide Gerstenberger.[21] Hirsch contends that the starting point for a derivation of the state should be "the antagonism of wage-labor and capital" rather than the deficiencies of individual capitals as in Altvater. Consequently, Hirsch emphasizes the primacy of labor markets over other types of capitalist markets, because, above all else, capital must be able to purchase labor power in a competitive market in order to employ capital productively. Thus, the creation and maintenance of a free labor market is the essential condition of capital accumulation. However, in Marx's political economy, capitalist profits, rents, and interest are derived from surplus value, namely, the difference between what workers are paid and what workers produce. As a result, the capital accumulation process is based on an inherently antagonistic relationship between capitalists and workers.

In this respect, the process of capital accumulation requires a prior explanation of how capitalists are able to realize the labor of others as their own profits and to maintain market conditions that enable them to do so indefinitely. For, as Hirsch notes, the central paradox in deriving the state from class struggle is that appropriating surplus value and maintaining the cohesion of the social structure rarely "depend on direct relations of force or dependence between individual capitalists and workers, as in feudalism, nor do these conditions depend on the power and repressive force of ideology."[22] Quite the contrary, as Hirsch observes, workers "voluntarily" show up to sell their labor power in exchange for wages without direct compulsion and continue to do so even when they recognize that they are being exploited by the capitalist system.[23] For example, even members of the French Communist party show up daily to work for their wages, without the direct use of force and despite their ostensible liberation from bourgeois ideology.

It is precisely the "free" status of labor that distinguishes capitalism from other forms of surplus appropriation, such as slavery or serfdom. Thus, Hirsch surmises that the state, as a centralized monopoly of force, is necessary to deprive the working class of the instruments of violence. To the extent that capitalism presupposes the existence of free laborers, maintaining the process of exploitation "requires that direct producers be deprived of control over the physical means of force and that the latter be localized in a social instance" separated from the production process.[24] The separation of the political (i.e., force) from the economic level of society allows market forces exclusively to structure the relation between capital and labor while creating the ideological illusion of two equals meeting to negotiate a free contract. It is the underlying economic inequality between workers and capitalists that coerces the worker to accept less in wages than his or her labor produces for the capitalist during any given time.

However, maintaining the ideological structure of a free market also requires a real sacrifice on the part of capitalists. As in Altvater's derivation, the capitalist class must accede to an organized political force that is formally separated from individual capitalists and that can neutrally enforce contracts. For this reason, there is a necessary disjuncture between the state and the particular interests of individual capitalists. In other words, although the state creates the conditions necessary for capitalist accumulation, individual capitalists typically confront the state as though it were an antagonist, even when it is making possible the existence of the system as a whole.

Nevertheless, the capitalist class of a particular country also gains two additional advantages *if* it is willing to separate the political from the economic levels of society. First, by its very existence the nation-state creates the possibility of establishing territorially homogeneous markets. Second, as these markets are constructed, the centralization of force enables the state to secure its class interests externally on the world market. Thus, Hirsch concludes that the functions of the state are to deprive labor of the means of violence in the domestic sphere and to advance the interests of capitalists forcibly in international markets. Consequently, Hirsch contends that the forms of the state are primarily determined by its function as an "organization of domination."[25] According to Hirsch,

(H₇)   the state's development is driven by crises that emerge from domestic class struggles and international competition between capitalists.

Hirsch insists that because the exploitation of labor is an inherent contradiction in the accumulation process, class struggle never remains dormant indefinitely, but breaks out in periodic cycles or waves of conflict. What is important is that these cycles actually result in real gains for the working class, whether in the form of higher wages, better working conditions, shorter workdays, or tax-supported redistributive programs. This means that for Hirsch the tendency for the rate of profit to fall is a direct consequence of historical class struggles. Thus, with Hirsch's model, the timing, sequence, and severity of such crises are impossible to predict theoretically, but he hypothesizes that during each historical cycle of class struggle

(H₈)   the state implements countertendential policies designed to retard, offset, or counteract the tendency for the rate of profit to fall.

Hirsch argues that historically capitalists respond to the pressures of declining profitability in three ways. First, capitalists realize economies of scale and counteract the organization of workers by concentrating and centralizing capital. This response to class struggle is usually conceptualized in the transition from competitive to monopoly capital. Second, capitalists can expand enterprises beyond their national boundaries in search of new markets and lower costs. This response to declining profitability is designated as imperialism. Finally, capitalists can introduce new technologies that make labor more productive but that simultaneously increase the organic composition of capital. It is the rising organic composition of capital that catalyzes state-capitalist policies designed to subsidize input costs.

For Hirsch, the implementation of these countertendencies constitutes three theoretical "moments" in the development of a state's form. The first moment is constituted in the transition from a precapitalist political form to a capitalist state. This primarily involves the separation

of the political from the economic and the political imposition of a capitalist class structure, that is, free labor, obligation of contract, rights
in private property. A second moment of development ensues when
capitalists adopt strategic policies of capital concentration and imperialism. At a minimum, the state must remove domestic obstacles to the
concentration of capital and strengthen its external military capability.
Finally, in a third moment of political development, the state undertakes
activities to offset directly the growing costs and importance of technological innovation to the accumulation process. Moreover, in Hirsch's
model, the phases and activities of the capitalist state are cumulative in
their composition and do not represent discrete, discontinuous stages
of development.

Furthermore, it is important to note for methodological purposes
that Hirsch's conceptualization of state forms provides only an analytic "frame of reference within which the development of the concrete
state activities must be interpreted."[26] In Hirsch's explanatory model,
Marx's law of the tendency for the rate of profit to fall is not an
empirical economic concept. Instead, its logical status is to provide a
theoretical reference point that denotes "the objective basis of actual
class struggles."[27] It lays the foundation for a conceptually informed
understanding of historical processes, but at no point does it substitute for the detailed analysis of those processes. Consequently, Heide
Gerstenberger suggests that a derivationist approach can never do more
than propose a strategy for further research.[28]

Indeed, Gerstenberger proposes that any research informed by derivationist concepts should be guided by two methodological rules. The
first precept is that explanatory references to class struggle must have
"a decisive effect on the actual analytical approach" employed by scholars. Class struggles must be operationalized "in terms of their concrete
course and results" in order to explain historical functions of the state
in such a way as to understand, for example, family policy in France,
U.S. labor relations, or British health care policy.[29]

The second rule is to recognize that actual class struggles occur
within the framework of an already established political structure with
historically specific forms of intervention and representation. These
already existing state forms may open, shut off, repress, deflect, disorganize, or limit the effectiveness of particular class struggles. Nevertheless,
it is important to emphasize that it is one thing to arrive at a methodological conclusion of this sort, but it is quite another to act on that
conclusion in a research design.

The State-Capitalist Form of Intervention: The Welfare State

One of the only efforts to operationalize derivationist concepts, *The State in Western Europe*, was published in 1980 as a collection of essays edited by Richard Scase. The objective of these essays, authored by the likes of Bob Jessop, Pierre Birnbaum, Joachim Hirsch, and others, was to derive the form of "state-monopoly capitalism" (stamocap) from the tendency for the rate of profit to fall. From a comparison of eight European states, Scase concluded that it is possible to identify "a number of common trends in the development of national states" which constitute a specific form of intervention, that is, state-monopoly capitalism.[30] Scase identified state-capitalist intervention as having the following four tendencies:

1. increased administrative centralization of all state apparatuses;
2. socialization of the costs of maintaining and reproducing labor power, for example, education, housing, health, and welfare;
3. expansion of direct intervention in the production process instead of Keynesian macroeconomic policies, for example, low-interest loans, subsidies, public enterprises;
4. strengthening of the state's repressive apparatus (police and domestic intelligence capabilities) and the development of new forms of social control through educators, social workers, and health care crisis management.

However, beyond their relatively uncontroversial ability to establish the existence of this typological form, the essays in Scase's collection are more important for highlighting the methodological limits of the derivationist approach. As Joachim Hirsch predicted earlier, the law of the tendency for the rate of profit to fall cannot by itself explain the empirical course of political development in any particular society.

First, the authors found that state-capitalist policies are adopted and implemented "not as the result of the abstract logic of a given social structure . . . but only under the pressure of political movements and interests which, acting on this basis, actually succeed in pressing home their demands."[31] Thus, to explain the origins and implementation of individual policies, the authors had to analyze concrete political movements, actual class struggles, and conflicts between different sectors of the capitalist class. Second, these policy concretizations of state functions are determined more by the political context of accumulation crises than by their mere occurrence. The competing political movements concerned with a particular crisis like education, health care, or tariffs shape the actual content of individual policies.[32] In other words, one can derive the form but not the empirical content of state policies from the general functions of the state.[33]

Their "discovery" that policy content cannot be derived from the logic of state functions also demonstrated that explanations of individual state policies require the reconstruction of empirical class interests, especially those interests articulated by groups of politically organized capitalists and workers. The "empirical interests" articulated by capitalists can be conceptualized within the "general interests" rubric of Altvater and Hirsch. However, even when capitalists and state elites consciously recognize their general interests (analytically defined), actual policies often come up short in being able to realize fully or achieve these general interests.

In purview of such findings, Simon Clarke has argued that the concept of "the general interests of capital" should be discarded as a pure abstraction.[34] Scase offers the more constructive conclusion that the concept should be retained for analytic purposes, although on condition that empirical and historical analyses jettison the assumption that "there will always be a 'fit' between the functions of capital and those of the state; indeed, one of the shortcomings of the theory of 'derivation' is its under-estimation of the tensions and contradictions that exist in the relationship between capital and state."[35] In fact, Scase's conclusion served to reinforce Gerstenberger's earlier warning that, in spite of derivationist assumptions, it is conceivable that "actual state activity is not always the adequate expression of the interests of capital as a whole."[36]

Furthermore, a key assumption of both structuralist and derivationist theory is that, to realize the general interests of the capitalist class, the state must be relatively autonomous of particular groups of capitalists. However, the authors in Scase's collection found that individual states vary considerably in the degree to which they are autonomous of particular groups of capitalists.[37] Indeed, much as Hirsch had predicted, it was found that many states opt to secure the quite particular interests of dominant monopolies and monopoly groups because of their obvious importance in maintaining employment, work-force income, and state revenue. At the same time, as Gerstenberger observes, different business sectors are unevenly subject to the new global competition. As a result, external market pressures often impel state elites to favor multinational fractions of capital over purely domestic ones.

Yet, Hirsch argues that such policies may cause the state serious difficulties and conflicts in the long-run because they either fail to assure minimal conditions for the reproduction of capital as a whole or undermine strategies for keeping domestic class struggles latent.[38] In the former case, favoring dominant monopolies may be detrimental to the interests of capital as a whole when policies divert capital from potential growth sectors or impose additional costs on them. In the latter case, class struggle may be intensified, for example, by free-trade agreements that create downward pressure on domestic wages or by tax abatements that reduce revenues to support the welfare state.

Similarly, state apparatuses often institutionalize patterns of class representation, particularly democracy, that are inherently unfavorable to the general interests of the capitalist class. Hirsch suggests that to fulfill its general cohesion function, the state apparatus must be opened to increasingly divergent interests, including noncapitalist ones.[39] Thus, as Gerstenberger points out, formal democracy may constitute an inherent political limit on the ability of state elites to facilitate capital accumulation. Yet, once again, the authors in Scase's collection found wide variations in the extent to which nondominant classes are represented within state apparatuses.[40] It is important to note that representation of nondominant classes affects the content of state policies and the degree to which policies actually contribute to capital accumulation or act as a drag on the accumulation process. For example, Scase suggests that a strong representation of left-wing reformist parties is likely to intensify accumulation crises through class struggle, thus requiring even greater direct state intervention to counteract the effects of income redistribution.

Similarly, Scase's authors found that state elites' ability to realize the general interests of capital may be either limited or facilitated by the organization of the state apparatus. Scase equates state autonomy with the level of centralization in the state apparatus. Centralization is presumed to facilitate the realization of general interests for two reasons. First, centralization allows for greater coherence in the adoption and implementation of state policies. Second, centralization concentrates state power and thus gives key state elites a greater ability to assert state autonomy. However, Scase's comparative study of European states found wide variations in levels of state centralization. For example, Birnbaum found that France epitomizes the ideal of a highly centralized autonomous state with power concentrated in the executive branch. Thus, the French state was found to facilitate the adoption and implementation of an effective industrial policy.[41] On the other hand, Carlo Donolo described the Italian state apparatus as an "archipelago" of civil society that is deeply enmeshed in class divisions and unable to assert any political autonomy.[42]

Yet, aside from its importance as an empirical case study, Donolo's Italian example calls attention to a more far-reaching generalization. The need to administer an ever wider array of new functions tends to produce a steady diversification of the administrative and political apparatuses. In many instances, as noted above, the state's addition of these new functions also requires the apparatus to be opened up to a wider variety of class interests if the state is to mediate conflict successfully. Yet, as a consequence of these two developments, there is a simultaneous tendency for the state to lose its coherence and its autonomy. Thus, Hirsch concludes that state apparatuses are becoming in reality a "heterogeneous conglomerate of only loosely linked part-apparatuses."[43]

There are at least two significant implications to Hirsch's observation. An important theoretical implication is that, in trying to realize the general interests of the capitalist class, state elites construct a state apparatus that makes it systematically impossible to realize those interests. In fact, Gerstenberger contends that the constraints and contradictions within the state apparatus may eventuate in state policies that are amazingly unsystematic.[44] An equally important methodological implication is that, under the empirical conditions described by Hirsch and Gerstenberger, it becomes impossible to speak of *the* state apparatus. The concept of the state risks lapsing into misguided reification from the outset.

The Limits to the Welfare State

A central analytic insight of the derivationist analysis is its conclusion that the dual constraints of globalization and political democracy[45] may impose insurmountable and contradictory external limits on capitalist state policy. In this vein, Ian Gough's empirical analysis has demonstrated that welfare states do not necessarily pursue coherent or unified strategic policies. Rather, the institutions and policies of the welfare state are, in various combinations, both responses to the requirements of capital accumulation *and* real concessions designed to ameliorate class struggle. In fact, Gough finds that, depending upon the policy sector and apparatus, some policies (e.g., higher education) primarily facilitate capital accumulation, while others (e.g., public housing and social assistance) tend to undermine the coercive force of labor markets.[46]

Likewise, a fact that is often neglected or downplayed by Marxists is that public enterprises are socialized enterprises which erode the sphere of private property.

Consequently, Hirsch, Gerstenberger, and Picciotto and Radice, contend that the "mixed economy" is an unstable one and can be sustained only where state-capitalist interventions have promoted exceptionally high levels of private capital accumulation. However, Hirsch asserts that in the long run this condition will prove impossible to satisfy. Likewise, Gerstenberger maintains that as capitalism becomes more crisis-ridden, state elites will simply find that their options for resolving crises are exhausted or politically ineffective. Both suggest that it will become increasingly difficult for state elites to maintain the illusion of neutrality, because deepening accumulation crises will compel them to favor capital overtly at labor's expense.

Hugo and Radice echo this view by arguing that the globalization of accumulation processes will create new contradictions and new possibilities in the exploitation of labor. First, as free trade and transnational federations eliminate obstacles to the free movement of labor and capital, international capital will certainly strive to push down wages in the metropolises. At the same time, new waves of labor migration may well disorganize workers along ethnic, linguistic, religious, and other lines of division. Second, the international mobility of capital will increasingly encourage multinationals to bargain with state elites for the rollback of burdensome tax-supported state services and mandated benefits in exchange for domestic investment. Finally, and contrary to the expectations of most postindustrialists, the capital intensity of new technologies may actually decrease the market demand for skilled labor. According to Picciotto and Radice, should this occur the industrial proletariat will be largely supplanted by a massive lumpenproletariat.[47] Simply stated, the globalization of the accumulation process will create external pressures to dismantle the truly socialistic aspects of the welfare state. Yet, democratic patterns of class representation may facilitate domestic opposition to the more onerous demands of global accumulation. Thus, there are no guarantees that the requirements of capital accumulation will be fully realized or that the welfare state can successfully balance these contradictory demands. Indeed, the probability of at least partial failures of realization points to a second contradiction of the welfare state: the state never fully succeeds in rationalizing its domination of labor. Quite the contrary, the state institutionalizes contradictions between capitalists and between capital and labor within its apparatus and through its policies.

The Contradictions of Derivationism

Paradoxically, the major objection to derivationism is that it tends to remain ahistorical and nonempirical in its approach to the state. The derivationist approach sought to reunite Marx's capital logic with historical and empirical analysis, but most derivationists have been extremely short on history. Derivationism's failure to resolve this methodological antinomy stems partly from its assumption that the logic of capital accumulation entails a formal chronology of historical political development, namely, that logical categories subsume historiography in corresponding stages of political development.

However, as Holloway and Picciotto point out, there is always an internal methodological tension in the relation between logical derivation and historical analysis. On the one hand, a historical analysis of political development is always considered important, even crucial, to the derivationists. On the other hand, in actual practice the approach remains fundamentally analytic and ahistorical. For the most part, historical examples are cited casually as mere illustrations of their central hypotheses, but comparative history is never integrated into the process of theory-building itself. In the derivationists' research practice, "history is always something brought in from the outside as something external to the analysis."[48]

There are two methodological directions in which to resolve this antinomy. One option is to invert the methodological axis by deriving the logic of capital from its concrete historical development.[49] The work of Bernhard Blanke, Ulrich Jurgens, and Hans Kastendiek points in this direction.[50] Blanke, Jurgens, and Kastendiek emphasize that the contradictions of capital accumulation can at best "give only the *general points of departure* for the development of 'functions' of the process of reproduction . . . The question of how this formation takes place in detail, how it is transposed into structure, institution and process of the state, can no longer be answered by form analysis. It would have to be made the subject of historical analysis."[51]

However, the underdevelopment of Marxist economic history has posed a major obstacle to developing a historical concept of capital accumulation. Until this failing is rectified, the concept of capital accumulation will remain an overly abstract and sometimes scholastic point of departure for analyses of the state. Fortunately, the American social structure of accumulation theorists and the French regulationists have made significant strides toward filling this analytic lacuna.

Even so, Gerstenberger has extended this critique by arguing that any "attempt to break through the limitations of previous state analysis would introduce on the analytical horizon factors whose analysis Marxists have hitherto left exclusively to political science." Gerstenberger's conclusion is derived from the finding that policy content and its administrative implementation are affected by national patterns of class representation and the organizational capacities of a particular state apparatus. Hence, any further advance in understanding the possibilities and limits of state policy will occur on the terrain of political history and institutional analysis. Yet, as Gerstenberger also observes, political history assigns analytical significance to particular institutions which, at the same time, are the result of previous class struggles in a society and which cannot, therefore, be derived a priori.[52] As a result, Gerstenberger concludes that the very enterprise of constructing *a theory* of the capitalist state is still premature. Instead, Gerstenberger argues that "only after an extensive process of historical research—which has hardly begun yet—will a systematic construction of *theories* be possible."[53]

On the other hand, a second option for resolving the methodological antinomy between capital logic and political chronology is anticipated by Holloway and Picciotto. The second option often seeks to evade the hard work of elaborating "the actual historical struggles which have mediated and formulated the development of the contradictions of the capital relation."[54] In fact, there has been a temptation among many Post-Marxists "to short-circuit this process" with continuing appeals to functionalist categories or with the claim that further conceptual analyses are required before historiography can prove theoretically useful.

Consequently, the tensions within derivationism have tended to spiral off in the two contradictory methodological directions of historiography and conceptual analysis. Moreover, as Marxian strategies have once again diverged along the methodological axis, the analytic axis has also shifted from a consideration of conjunctural to disjunctural relations between state and capital. The convergence of these two sets of antinomies now largely constitutes the most recent work in Post-Marxist political theory: systems analysis and organizational realism.

CHAPTER FOUR

Post-Marxism I: The Systems-Analytic Approach

The laboring population therefore produces, along with the accumulation of capital produced by it, the means by which itself is made relatively superfluous, is turned into a relative surplus population; and it does this to an always increasing extent.

—*Marx*, Capital, *1867*

The politics of advanced capitalist societies has been destabilized during the last two decades by a cumulative series of economic, political, and cultural crises.[1] These crises have led a growing number of Marxian theorists to suggest that systematic and insurmountable limitations are imposed on state policy by the developing contradictions of the capital accumulation process.[2] Hence, it can no longer be assumed that the state will succeed in maintaining the capital accumulation process or in resolving the underlying conflicts generated by that process. Indeed, a key thesis of recent post-Marxist theory is that, regardless of efforts by state elites, the state will become increasingly ineffective at sustaining capital accumulation or in mediating the conflicts generated by the attendant disintegration of capitalist societies.

Hence, unlike earlier approaches to the state, such as instrumentalism or structuralism, the theoretical objective of post-Marxist analyses is to develop a theory of the capitalist state that can identify the limits of its policy-making capacities.[3] Thus, a key departure from Marxist and neo-Marxist theories is its emphasis on being able to conceptualize, anticipate, and explain the crisis tendencies of late capitalist societies, unlike the other two theories' emphasis on being able to describe state maintenance and stabilization mechanisms.[4] The systems-analytic approach to the state seeks to establish these limits mainly by identifying specific examples of policy breakdown, particularly those instances where state policy fails either to maintain capital accumulation or to restabilize social order among disaffected subordinate classes.

96

The Methodology of Systems Analysis

In the view of leading post-Marxist theorists such as Claus Offe, Jurgen Habermas, and Andre Gorz, late capitalism is best conceptualized as a system. The capitalist system, in this view, is actually a matrix of three interrelated but relatively autonomous subsystems: the economic system, the political system, and the socialization system. The most important institutions associated with the economic subsystem are the relations of production between classes in the workplace and relations of exchange between buyers and sellers in the marketplace. The socialization subsystem, from which individuals derive normative values, includes the family, educational institutions, religion, and culture. Finally, in late capitalism, the political subsystem consists primarily of those institutions and policies that constitute the welfare state.

What is important, though each subsystem encompasses concretely identifiable institutions, is that the system as a whole is posited as an ontological entity—real in itself—which produces consequences through institutions, but which is therefore never reducible to institutions. Offe maintains, for example, that the capitalist system is a "superordinate level of *mechanisms that generate 'events.'*"[5] However, the superordinate "reality" of this system is observable empirically only when those mechanisms which fulfill a maintenance function fail to suppress the underlying "contradictions" of the capitalist mode of production. A contradiction, according to Offe, "is the tendency inherent within a specific mode of production to destroy those very preconditions on which its survival depends."[6] Consequently, the historical development of a contradiction must inevitably culminate in some crisis event that makes the contradiction perceptible as a crisis.[7]

Therefore, in a systems-analytic approach to the state, the methodological point of departure is not "the forms, procedures, rules and instruments of state activity [i.e., institutions]," but "hypothetical notions about the functional connection between state activity and the structural problems of a (capitalist) social formation."[8] The objective in studying state activity, as in structuralism, is to explain state policies by analytic reference to their substantive functions.[9] Yet, taking that approach a step further, post-Marxist systems analysis aims to understand the increasing failure of state activities in terms of the developing contradictions within the capitalist system.[10]

Systemic Power and the Labor Market

According to Habermas, the relative dominance of the economic sub-system in capitalist society is what generates the contradictory dynamics of development within the overall system.[11] Claus Offe specifies this dynamic in the structure of capitalist labor markets, where the exchange of commodities between equals (labor power for wages) must coexist with an unequal distribution of property (relations of production). Offe emphasizes that capitalist labor markets can exist only to the extent that workers are propertyless in two senses: "Labor can neither *be* the property of another nor *possess* property."[12]

In the first instance, labor markets are possible only to the extent that labor is free and mobile and, thus, available for sale on the market in exchange for wages. Yet, as Offe also observes, the rise of a market in labor power is not necessarily the natural outcome of liberating labor from precapitalist forms of bondage such as serfdom or slavery.[13] A second and more coercive condition for the existence of labor markets is that workers cannot control property, and thus cannot control their own chances of securing an existence outside of the labor market. Wages offer the inducement, but a propertyless condition imposes the necessity of an individual's entry into the labor market.

Thus, the asymmetrical structure of the capitalist labor market establishes an unequal bargaining position between laborers and capitalists. Quite simply, capitalists are always in a position to outwait workers and to strike a more favorable bargain in the negotiation of wage contracts, because they own the means of production. In this respect, labor markets constitute "the most significant feature of capitalist social structures," because they are the "power-generating mode of interaction that leads to a relatively stable and consistent matrix of social power" within capitalist societies.[14]

However, Offe contends that an economic subsystem organized by the labor market is continually threatened by potential disintegration to the extent that labor power is *not* really a commodity.[15] Labor power is a "fictive commodity" in the sense that one cannot physically separate it from the laborer or, therefore, unequivocally transfer rights to it in the process of exchange. Labor power and the laborer are in fact inseparable. As a result, any extended reproduction of the economic subsystem requires the uninterrupted support of a socialization subsystem and the persistent intervention of the political subsystem. A labor market can operate smoothly only to the extent that socialization mechanisms sustain a normative structure in which it is legitimate to view labor power as if it were a commodity. Yet, the labor market itself does not provide such mechanisms but instead generates class conflict.

Therefore, the political system must increasingly support the socialization subsystem and supply the coercion and inducements necessary to maintain the asymmetry of labor-market exchanges. Thus, drawing on the earlier work of Joachim Hirsch, Offe emphasizes that the state must actively intervene in the economy and society initially to constitute and subsequently to maintain the labor market.[16] Offe refers to these interventions as "social policy." The operational objective of social policy is to establish "a state strategy for incorporating labor power into the wage labor relation."[17] By contributing to the constitution of the working class, particular configurations of social policy (i.e., state forms) make the appropriation of surplus value possible at each stage of capitalist development.[18]

State social policy can fulfill a maintenance function in various ways at different stages of capitalist development. It can, for example, remove traditional protections that buffer the coercive powers of the labor market, such as the British Speedhamland system. The state can utilize its coercive apparatus to force workers directly back into the labor market by breaking strikes or using troops to carry out emergency nationalizations. On the other hand, particularly with the rise of political democracy, state social policy has utilized inducements designed to increase the rewards (e.g., social security) and reduce the risks (e.g., workmen's compensation) of labor-market participation, and to adopt policies that facilitate the extended reproduction of labor power through state subsidies (e.g., public education, health care, housing). This matrix of social-policy inducements is particularly characteristic of late capitalism and is the empirical reference for Offe's concept of the welfare state (see figure 4.1).[19]

Contradictions of the Welfare State

In systems analysis, the methodological criterion for conceptualizing what is "capitalist" about the welfare state is to specify the ways in which the state is functionally related to and dependent upon the capital accumulation process.[20] Therefore, at a general level, the methodological strategy of systems analysis differs little from that of the structuralists and derivationists. However, Offe has specified this functional relation in terms of four analytic principles: the principles of exclusion, maintenance, dependency, and legitimation.[21]

POLITICAL SUBSYSTEM   SOCIALIZATION SUBSYSTEM

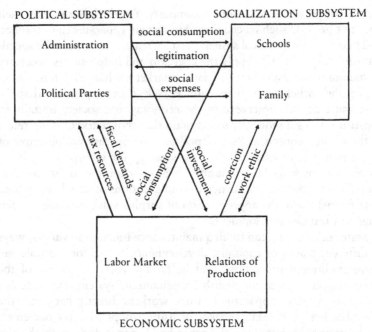

ECONOMIC SUBSYSTEM

Figure 4.1. Systems-analytic model of late capitalism

The principle of exclusion refers to the separation of property owner-ship and political authority in capitalist societies. The private ownership of property in a capitalist society requires that economic decisions be made exclusively by those who own or directly manage productive as-sets. Thus, the separation of economic decision-making from political authority means that "the state has no authority *to order production* or *to control* it."[22] The functional result is that the state cannot com-mand economic performance; the state can only induce investment and employment by offering incentives to those who control productive as-sets.[23] To adopt social policies that exceed this "systemic boundary" would entail a type of state that by definition is noncapitalist. In this sense, the principle of exclusion functions as a "selective mechanism" at the structural level to screen out social policies that are incompatible with the private ownership of productive assets.

However, the principle of exclusion merely entails the rejection of policies that are functionally incompatible with the structural founda-tions of a capitalist economy, namely, private property and labor-market participation. Consequently, Offe infers that a maintenance principle must also operate to insure that the state has not only the authority but also the mandate to create and sustain inducements to private accumulation.[24] This mandate can be consistently realized only if further selective mechanisms function within the state apparatus to produce the required social policies systematically.[25] First, to fulfill its maintenance function, *coordinative mechanisms* within the state apparatus must insure that state policies possess the requisite rationality, that is, that state policies will in fact induce optimum levels of investment and employment. State personnel must be able to recognize and select the general interests of the capitalist class amid the competition of special interests. Likewise, the state apparatus must be sufficient for the purpose of implementing and administering maintenance policies. Second, *repressive mechanisms* within the state apparatus must function simultaneously so as to filter out any noncapitalist policies which have not effectively been negated at the structural level.

However, by themselves, the exclusion and maintenance principles do not explain why the state must promote private accumulation or how the state is prevented from exceeding its capitalist boundary constraints. The operation of these two constraints is functionally linked to the principle of dependency. The dependency principle is that the decision-making power and policy capabilities of the state are always dependent upon the success and continuity of the accumulation process. This is most immediately evident in the state's dependence on its capacity to raise tax revenues. The modern state's dependence on tax revenues means that every interest which the state and state personnel "may have in their own stability and development can only be pursued if it is in accordance with the imperative of maintaining accumulation." Moreover, "this fundamental dependency upon accumulation also functions as a selective principle upon state policies," for to violate the logic of accumulation would simultaneously weaken or undermine all state capacities. Thus, a concern for the continuity of private accumulation is "incorporated in the pursuit of interests and policies that, considered by themselves, may have little or nothing to do with accumulation."[26]

Finally, in a political democracy, the capitalist state must also be legitimate. According to Offe, a capitalist state which sustains an exploitative accumulation process can achieve legitimacy only by deploying concealment and ideological mechanisms. Concealment mechanisms, such as administrative secrecy, facilitate the adoption and implementation of maintenance policies outside the sphere of class struggle and special-interest competition. The state's ideological mechanisms convey the image that its power is organized to pursue the general interests of society as a whole, even though it functions in a specific relationship to capitalist accumulation.[27] Consequently, a capitalist state must sustain and yet conceal a structural disjuncture between its democratic form and its capitalist functions.[28]

The capitalist state must respond to contradictions in the capitalist mode of production with social policies that are compatible with these four principles and are, therefore, sufficiently "rational" to maintain private capital accumulation. The question for Offe, however, is whether the state can do so systematically without violating the logic of its own boundary constraints. The basic dilemma, in Offe's view, is that the state must protect the capital–wage labor relation "from the social conditions it produces without being able to alter the status of this relationship as the dominant relationship" in capitalist society.[29] Thus, he observes, a number of political contradictions have accompanied the development of the welfare state.

The initial dynamic of these contradictions resides in the maintenance principle. In effecting the state's role as the "ideal collective capitalist," state policies must in principle represent the interests of the capitalist class as a whole. However, precisely because " 'capital as a whole' exists only in an ideal sense, i.e., is incapable of articulating and perceiving a common and unified class interest, it requires special guidance and supervision by a fully differentiated political-administrative system."[30] In other words, to execute the maintenance principle, the state is systematically compelled to violate the exclusion principle.

On this point, Offe's systems analysis explicitly accepts Elmer Altvater's thesis that individual capitalists cannot themselves produce the general political and material conditions necessary for profitable business activities. Thus, maintaining the accumulation process requires the state first to articulate and then to enforce the general interests of the capitalist class against the narrow and empirically divergent interests of individual capitalists or business sectors. Second, the ability to execute these general interests through social policy requires that a certain amount of surplus value (taxes) be allocated for the maintenance of the state and state personnel. Taxes are an appropriation of value that is no longer available for capital investment or for private distribution as profits, interests, or rent. Consequently, on both fronts, individual capitalists confront the state as a source of constant annoyance that is parasitic, wasteful, and expropriative in its interventions.[31]

However, as the derivationists have already demonstrated, capitalism's maintenance as a total system requires greater and greater direct intervention over time into the economic and socialization subsystems. The tendency for the rate of profit to fall requires the state to socialize more and more of the costs of production, while the attendant increases in class struggle require the development of an ever more extensive state ideological apparatus. When maintenance policies of this type are executed to their fullest extent such interventions establish a technocratic strategy for managing crises. However, the state's ability to pursue a pure technocratic strategy is systematically obstructed, because (1) such a strategy would violate the exclusion principle, and (2) the state's overt intervention directly on behalf of capital would also violate the legitimation principle (i.e., the state's democratic form). The latter boundary violation then sets in motion an internal contradiction between the democratic form and capitalist functions of the state.

On the other hand, the state can neither rely on nor create a democratic strategy for transcending the exclusion principle by reconstituting the economic subsystem (e.g., as social or economic democracy). Mobilizing the latter option would violate the maintenance principle. For example, the state is prevented from significantly increasing revenues either by nationalizing directly productive activities or by introducing a highly progressive tax system. Either option would produce a decline in business confidence and, hence, trigger an investment strike. An investment strike, as the structuralists have demonstrated, finally invokes the dependency principle (because of declining state revenues), which then realigns the functioning of the state with capital.[32] To counter declining private investment, the state must then offer new inducements and incentives to private investors.

However, an important feature distinguishing post-Marxist systems analysis from similar structuralist analyses is the realization that welfare states actually fail to function at precisely those moments when most needed and that these system failures result in genuinely contradictory outcomes.[33] On the one hand, the welfare state's financial capacity to provide social insurance is dependent on the level of employment and income (e.g., social security and unemployment taxes). The higher the rates of employment and income, the greater the welfare state's capacity to deliver income supports that are needed by fewer and fewer people. Yet, the volume of the welfare state's social insurance demands is determined by the amount of income and employment needs that remain unsatisfied by the labor market because of either unemployment or low wages. Consequently, the more the welfare state is needed owing to the shrinking employment opportunities offered by the economy, the less capable the welfare state becomes of satisfying these needs.

As already noted, the antipodal policy options under this scenario are either to increase tax rates progressively or to reduce legal entitlements. The first option encounters the boundary constraints of capital flight;

the latter option erodes the state's democratic legitimacy and thus invokes the boundary constraints of the legitimation principle. Consequently, Offe concludes: "If state policy is to be adequate, however, it is forced to rely on means which either violate the dominant capital relation or undermine the functional requirements—the legitimacy and administrative competence—of state regulation itself."[34]

Furthermore, as state policy is increasingly buffeted between fulfilling the contradictory requirements of accumulation and legitimation, there is a twofold impact throughout the capitalist system. First, state policies become "opportunistic" (i.e., nonstrategic) short-term responses that are neither predictable nor coherent in their objective. The result is a political subsystem which increasingly operates at a suboptimum level in fulfilling both its maintenance and legitimation functions. Moreover, these suboptimal policy outputs feed back into the socialization and economic subsystems as suboptimal policy inputs. Consequently, these subsystems generate cumulatively less and less normative loyalty and economic growth for the political system. The cumulative impact of suboptimal social policy is that organized capitalism is steadily disorganized by the very subsystem most responsible for maintaining the system's functional integration. A second impact is that the organization of the state apparatus is rent between the contradictory imperatives of legitimation (i.e., social democracy) and accumulation (i.e., technocracy). As a result, the state apparatus steadily disintegrates into uncoordinated and mutually contradictory policy networks.

Crisis Tendencies of the Welfare State

It should be emphasized that Offe's crisis scenario is derived by deducing the hypothetical consequences of a general pattern of capitalist development. Yet, it remains a hypothesis which, in his own view, "clearly requires more empirical evidence to be plausible."[35] Moreover, analytically informed policy histories guided by this heuristic framework are still virtually nonexistent. Nevertheless, some important attempts have been made to sketch the possible crisis tendencies immanent within this framework.

Jurgen Habermas has supplied the most comprehensive and analytically coherent typology of potential crisis conditions within the late capitalist system.[36] Habermas notes that for systems-analytic theory "crises arise when the structure of a social system allows fewer possibilities for problem solving than are necessary to the continued existence of the system. In this sense, crises are seen as persistent disturbances of *system integration*."[37] The important difference between a crisis and a mere problem is that crises ultimately cannot be resolved within the system's boundaries because they are generated by structurally inherent system imperatives that are mutually incompatible, that is, contradictory in the Marxian sense.

Habermas suggests that crises of capitalism may be generated potentially from within any of its three subsystems. However, all systems analysts agree that the underlying economic crisis of capitalism has been largely displaced into the state through state-capitalist and welfare policies. Thus, economic crisis tendencies are now more likely to culminate in a *fiscal crisis* of the state than in a full-scale economic collapse on the magnitude of the Great Depression.[38] Similarly, the contradictory strains between accumulation and legitimation also generate two additional crisis tendencies from within the political system. First, opportunistic social policies, along with the disintegration of state apparatuses, suggest the possibility of a *rationality crisis,* in which the state apparatus is increasingly unable to generate the requisite system outputs in the form of economic growth. Second, a *legitimation crisis* occurs when the state can no longer create normative loyalties among the mass population by concealing its capitalist functions with administrative secrecy and democratic symbols. Finally, "output deficits" in the other two subsystems become input deficits for the socialization system in the form of declining resources and symbols. Consequently, a *motivation crisis* may be generated, which undermines people's willingness to participate in capitalist labor markets or to accept the policy boundaries imposed by the capitalist system.[39]

The Fiscal Crisis of the State

Although James O'Connor's work *The Fiscal Crisis of the State* was not directly influenced by post-Marxist theory, Offe has frequently cited it to illustrate the kind of empirical policy research entailed by the systems-analytic approach.[40] O'Connor starts from the shared analytic premise that contemporary capitalist states must try to fulfill an accumulation function and a legitimation function simultaneously. As previously defined, the accumulation function both authorizes and mandates the state to maintain or create conditions in which profitable business activities can take place.[41] At the same time, the state must try to win the loyalty of the classes that are exploited economically by the capitalist accumulation process. Thus, O'Connor agrees with Offe that the two functions are in principle mutually contradictory.

O'Connor's thesis, like that of Altvater and Offe, is that the welfare state largely represents a socialization of the costs of production in the monopoly sector. O'Connor argues that increases in state spending are now the basis for continuing growth in the monopoly sector, because its profitability is heavily dependent on state outlays for physical and human infrastructure. At the same time, to insure its legitimacy, the state must meet the escalating material demands of those who suffer the costs of economic growth through unemployment, injury and disability, industrial health care problems, and environmental and urban damage. Thus, there is simultaneous political pressure to increase state expenditures for items such as social insurance, social welfare, housing, education, and health care.

O'Connor conceptualizes state expenditures as either social capital outlays or social expenses. Social capital outlays consist of those state expenditures that are required to maintain or induce profitable business activities (i.e., capital accumulation). Social capital outlays can take the form of social investments or social consumption. Social investments consist of projects and services that increase labor productivity and, hence, business profitability. *Social investments* occur mainly through expenditures on physical infrastructure, such as industrial parks, interstate highways, airports, scientific research and development, and communications systems. Social consumption consists of projects and services that lower the cost of labor inputs to private business. *Social consumption* occurs through expenditures on items such as social insurance, education, housing, and health care. What is important is that by sustaining or accelerating economic growth, social capital expenditures are at least indirectly productive and may also provide expansion opportunities for private firms (e.g., highway construction, health care providers, etc.). On the other hand, social expenses consist of state expenditures on projects and services that are not even indirectly productive, but that are necessary to maintain social and political order (i.e., legitimacy). The best examples of social expenses are the welfare system and defense outlays.

It is important to note, as does O'Connor, that many state expenditures are simultaneously social capital outlays necessary to maintain monopoly accumulation and social expenses designed to maintain legitimacy.[42] Thus, O'Connor's empirical classification of state expenditures as either social capital outlays or social expenses is at best impressionistic and is designed "more to illustrate a line of theoretical argument than to verify in any systematic way a set of hypotheses."[43] Yet, equally important, this classification leads O'Connor to conclude that as state expenditures rise a "structural gap" develops between the expenditures necessary to maintain accumulation and legitimacy on the one hand and the revenues available to finance those expenditures on the other.

O'Connor emphasizes that, while social capital outlays increase the total surplus available in society, "increases in the surplus tend to be monopolized by capital and labor in the monopoly industries" through high profits and high wages.[44] Thus, the monopoly sector and organized labor will resist the appropriation of additional surpluses (taxes) to finance social expenses. Meanwhile, those outside the monopoly sector (competitive business and nonunionized workers) will vigorously oppose taxes, since they are not direct beneficiaries of either the social capital outlays or social expenses. Consequently, tax constraints and a rising need for state expenditures inexhorably generate a fiscal crisis that is empirically observable as a long-term structural gap between state expenditures and state revenues, that is, as a persistent operating deficit. The extent to which deficit financing can defer this crisis is not analytically certain, although recent political history suggests that it cannot be carried on indefinitely. Financial receivership in New York City and Yonkers, as well as the near bankruptcy of Cleveland during the 1970s, has made the fiscal crisis most evident in the local state. However, the spectre of statewide bankruptcy and financial receivership finally surfaced at the state level during the 1991 Massachusetts fiscal crisis.[45]

Crises of Rationality and Legitimation

Habermas, Offe, and O'Connor each suggest in various ways that surmounting the contradiction between accumulation and legitimation is also obstructed by systemic limitations on state rationality. First, Offe points out that state elites are not the beneficiaries of marginal cost curves which allow them to calculate rationally the optimal expenditures on social capital. Therefore, it is certainly conceivable that a state might produce more infrastructure than is necessary to support capital accumulation, at which point the surplus social capital outlays become social expenses. A state might also underallocate for social capital, in which case it would fail to support capital accumulation at optimum levels. Yet, these "rationality deficits" become evident only after the fact when their effects become visible as a crisis.[46]

Second, Offe calls attention to a potential contradiction between the democratic legitimacy and capitalist functions of the state administrative apparatus. In modern states, the legitimacy of state policy inheres in formal rules and procedures whose observation by political authorities obligates citizens to comply with the state's laws and decisions. However, Offe makes the important observation that the legitimating status of formal rules and procedures is linked to an assumption that their application and observation by state officials will systematically result in functional consequences that contribute to the common and individual welfare. Thus, the legitimacy of legitimating procedures does not inhere in the rules themselves, but resides over the long term in common expectations about their functional effectiveness.[47]

The result is that state administrative agencies may choose between two potentially competing sources of rationality: rationality may inhere in the strict observation of formal bureaucratic procedure (legitimation), or it may inhere in functional effectiveness (accumulation).[48] However, to the extent that these two criteria diverge, state administrative agencies must choose between maintaining short-term formal legal legitimacy and long-term functional effectiveness (or vice versa). Indeed, Offe and Habermas suggest the hypothesis that a historically increasing discrepancy between the two criteria of rationality is gradually yielding a dichotomy in welfare-state administrative policy. The result is a type of state administration that constantly oscillates between the two sides of this dilemma but does not resolve the dilemma itself. Moreover, the state cannot resolve the dilemma within its current systemic constraints, because the wholesale pursuit of either strategy risks either a legitimation deficit or an accumulation failure.[49]

Again, one must emphasize that Offe's and Habermas's hypothesis on the possibility of rationality crisis is nonempirical in the sense that neither examines the actual rules that govern action in specific bureaucracies. Thus, they can demonstrate only a hypothetical divergence between the two criteria of administrative rationality. However, O'Connor's empirical analysis does suggest that state rationality deficits systematically exacerbate fiscal crises, which one can observe in three ways. First, there is a great deal of waste in state expenditures, mainly because of duplication and overlap in the provision of state services and in the administration of state infrastructure projects. Second, some state policies won by particular groups conflict with one another and cancel each other out in terms of their functional policy effects, for example, a progressive income tax that is cumulatively nullified by loopholes, allowances, exemptions, and incentives.[50] Finally, some state projects and services are mutually contradictory in their policy effects, for example, making expenditures on cancer research while subsidizing tobacco farming. In brief, O'Connor concludes: ". . . the accumulation of social capital and social expenses is a highly irrational process."[51]

Motivation Crisis

The logical outcome of fiscal and rationality crises would seem to be an "implosion" of the welfare state. Either the welfare state will fail to satisfy the requirements of capital accumulation, or its legitimacy will be jeopardized by policies that are necessary to maintain capital accumulation. Equally important, however, is the claim by systems analysts, such as Gorz, Offe, and Habermas, that capitalist development also generates "cultural contradictions" in the socialization subsystem.[52] Habermas points out that as market relations expand throughout a society traditional, or "natural," bonds such as family, church, and apprenticeship are increasingly ruptured by labor-market mobility and individualized competition.[53] These "cultural gaps" are filled historically by state institutions such as schools and family-support programs. Thus, output deficits in the economic and political subsystems may lead to input deficits in the socialization subsystem because of an insufficient allocation of resources and services. Consequently, the crisis feedback loop is closed and cumulatively exacerbated while the socialization subsystem turns out insufficiently skilled workers that are also unhealthy, unmotivated, and anomic.

On the other hand, when the administrative distribution of cultural inputs is sufficient, the welfare state tends to generate value changes that also result in motivational output deficits. First, insofar as state policies generate enough growth to offset social expenses, the welfare state's redistributive policies unhinge income from direct labor-market participation. Second, the political allocation of economic values creates distribution-based entitlement groupings such as students, pensioners, and "welfare mothers," as opposed to production-based classes. Thus, state social expenditures facilitate the emergence of cultural identities that are detached from labor-market participation and economic productiveness.[54] The cultural output deficit can be observed sociologically in individuals that are increasingly motivated by the non-workplace-centered, nonproductivist normative values of a "postmaterialist" culture.[55]

Post-Marxist Politics as a Logic of Disintegration

The labor market can function as a power-generating system only to the extent that it organizes individuals within its matrix of social relations. However, post-Marxist systems analysts have suggested that the structural contradictions of late capitalism are eroding the labor market's power-generating capacities. For analysts such as Joachim Hirsch, Andre Gorz, Alain Touraine, and Claus Offe the erosion of the labor market's systemic power is deduced from the contradictory implications of postindustrialism.[56] The post-Marxist, postindustrial thesis draws on Marx's observation in *Grundrisse* that, at a certain point in the development of production, science and technology become qualitative forces of production that can increasingly generate value independent of human labor (e.g., through automation).[57]

Since the objective of investing in constant capital is to facilitate increases in productivity and, therefore, in the rate of exploitation, value-generating technology emerges as the "postindustrial" culmination of the rising organic composition of capital. The derivationists pursued the implications of this concept only in terms of its relation to the tendency for the rate of profit to fall and the attendant need for state interventions to fill infrastructure gaps. However, post-Marxist systems analysts have complemented the derivationist analysis by drawing out its hypothetical implications for the emergence of a growing surplus population.[58] The surplus population of a capitalist society consists of those individuals who are nonproductive in the sense that they no longer directly create surplus value (i.e., profits, rents, and interest).

In this respect, an additional long-term contradiction of the rising organic composition of capital is the ability of capitalist economies to generate economic growth and capital accumulation without any corresponding growth in employment. Indeed, paradoxically, the labor market's capacity to absorb the individuals who depend on it for wages and salaries is shrinking primarily because of increases in productivity.[59] Hence, for the first time in capitalist societies, systems analysts envision a developing employment crisis that is not related to a short-term cyclical downturn or to falling rates of investment. Quite the contrary, investment in growth-generating, productivity-enhancing technologies is resulting in the structural disintegration of capitalist labor markets.

Thus, a central hypothetical projection of post-Marxist systems analysis is that

(H₁)   labor markets in many countries are starting "to exhibit a declining absorption potential, thus removing or excluding increasing numbers of potential workers from direct and full-time contact with the supposedly central power mechanism of capitalist society." [60]

The new pattern of postindustrial development has three structural consequences of importance to post-Marxist systems analysis.[61] First, reduced market demand for labor power is creating a long-term tendency toward rising structural unemployment. Second, the same forces are yielding institutionalized patterns of structural underemployment in the form of casual labor markets, part-time work, and migratory labor. Third, there is an increasing tendency for individuals to get locked into peripheral labor markets in an emerging low-wage, no-benefits, part-time service sector.[62] Thus, contrary to the expectations of neoconservative postindustrialists, post-Marxists do not envision a tertiary service sector based in a professional middle-class, but rather a peripheral labor market that is neoproletarian if not quasi lumpen-proletarian.[63] As a result, post-Marxists have been virtually unanimous in predicting the political displacement of the classical Marxian proletariat by a postindustrial population that is economically and socially marginal to the labor market. Gorz refers to this surplus population as a new "servile class," which is defined structurally more by its status as a *non*working class that lacks institutionalized participation in capitalist labor markets.

The macrosociological result of postindustrialism's contradictory development is a new pattern of class divisions structured as an advanced postindustrial economic core and a marginalized periphery. The economic core of postindustrial capitalism consists mainly of monopoly-sector capitalists, its professional-technical elite, and largely unionized, high-wage, skilled workers. As already noted, the state's economic policies are designed to promote the continued development of this sector. However, for that reason, the state's social expenses simultaneously increase because the sociological side effect is a marginal sector of unskilled workers (neoproletariat), an underemployed servile class, and burgeoning structural unemployment.

Claus Offe deduces a further hypothesis from this pattern of development:

(H$_2$)   "The movement of capital systematically, cumulatively, and irreversibly produces social phenomena and structural elements which are functionally of no value for the continuation of capitalist development."[64]

For Offe and other post-Marxist systems analysts, late capitalist development is marked by a centrifugal tendency; the structural contraction of the labor market systematically throws off afunctional social tailings. These labor-market tailings consist of the chronically unemployed, underemployed, and unemployable; youth that are socially and culturally displaced; a growing class of pensioners with burgeoning health care demands; a servile class with growing social welfare requirements; and ever more state workers to fill the escalating demand for infrastructure and social welfare services.

Offe and Gorz particularly emphasize that the growth of a surplus population places exponentially more pressure on state social policy, because the "new social groups" lay outside the logic of labor commodification; that is, their redistributive demands are not linked to labor-market participation but directly to social need.[65] Consequently, Offe suggests that

(H$_3$)   the new social groups are impediments, threats, and "ballast" to capitalist development, because their members do not contribute to the process of surplus-value creation.[66]

One implication of this hypothesis is that at some point the welfare state will have to shed its sociological ballast in order to maintain capital accumulation at optimal levels.[67] Hinrichs, Offe, and Wiesenthal point out that adopting such policies would entail "a downward redefinition of the welfare state's legal entitlements and the claims granted by it, most of all the claims of those groups that are least well organized and hence least likely to engage in collective conflict."[68] Yet, for this reason, most post-Marxists envision the new social groups as the systemic agents of a countermovement for postindustrial socialism.[69] In line with this projection, Offe infers an additional hypothesis:

(H$_4$)   The new social groups "contain the seeds of non-capitalist organizational forms."[70]

Offe has articulated one of the most lucid versions of new social movement theory by suggesting that the politics of postindustrial capitalism is structured by two competing paradigms. A Keynesian paradigm is anchored in the distributional issues of labor-market participation, and a new social movement paradigm is rooted in the social values of "decommodified" groups which have been marginalized by the disintegration of labor markets. According to Offe, the political paradigm of the Keynesian welfare state stands on four legs: capitalism, class compromise, distributional interests, and party representation. The central pillar of the Keynesian welfare state is the willingness of organized labor to concede the exclusion principle, namely, that investment decisions are the prerogative of private managers and owners whose chief operating criterion is profitability (i.e., capitalism). However, in exchange for this acceptance, the welfare state institutionalizes mechanisms for negotiating income distribution and for guaranteeing income security. Thus, collective bargaining and social insurance become the centerpieces of the Keynesian class compromise. What is important for Offe is that this historic accord is possible only to the extent that political issues are defined by distributional conflicts over market allocations and, therefore, by actors whose identities are defined by their relative positions within the labor market. Finally, the welfare state is able to manage conflict precisely because macrodistributional issues are settled by party competition within a constitutional framework.

On the other hand, Offe contends that the new social groups are not amenable to Keynesian distributional criteria, because they operate within a paradigm of noninstitutional politics. First, the new social movements advance claims that are "anticapitalist" and "nonproductivist," because they call attention to the destructive side effects of continued economic expansion, for example, ecological destruction, public health disasters, urban decay, unemployment, poverty, and discrimination. Second, the new social groups define conflicts in terms of entitlement values and social rights that are nonnegotiable principles. Moreover, Offe suggests that the new social groups can articulate their claims only in this form, because, unlike organized labor, they are not structurally positioned to bargain. In the first place, they have nothing tangible to offer in exchange for concessions (e.g., the unemployed), and, second, their forms of organization typically preclude leader-negotiated compacts that are binding on the membership. The reason for the latter situation is that new social movements do not employ an organizational principle of mobilization as trade unions do with their horizontal (member/nonmember) and vertical (leader/rank and file) patterns of differentiation. Instead, their patterns of organization tend to rely on an amorphous, ad hoc, and transient floating membership which assembles only for mass demonstrations and similar activities.

Finally, post-Marxist new social movement theory persistently emphasizes that the actors within these groups do not rely for their political self-identity on the established ideological spectrum (left–right), which defines positions in relation to distributional issues. Nor therefore do the actors define their collective identities in terms of related market-based positions, that is, lower, middle, working, or capitalist class. Instead, their decommodification makes possible a reclassification of political space in terms of a multiplicity of divergent identities, such as gender, age, race, locality, and life-style. In each case, entitlement claims and social rights are advanced from social locations that have been uncoupled from class positions and labor-market participation.[71]

Some Contradictions of Systems Analysis

The systems-analytic approach, particularly in the form developed by Offe and Habermas, is now widely acknowledged as having made a decisive contribution to the theory of the state. Its most important contribution certainly lies in having jettisoned the assumption that the state must always function to preserve the general interests of the capitalist class.[72] Yet, despite its conceptual advance over previous approaches, the systems-analytic framework also poses a number of unanswered methodological questions while making some historical claims that seem less and less tenable in the 1990s.

First, as Habermas and Offe both concede, if the methodological strength of systems analysis is the rigor of its axiomatic methodology, the ability to operationalize systems analysis is simultaneously hindered by numerous conceptual ambiguities. For example, the rigor of Habermas's crisis theorems is somewhat illusory when attempts are made to assign an empirical meaning to the important concept of input and output deficits. The tendencies toward systemic crisis are deduced axiomatically from the concept of a closed system. Hence, if one postulates the suboptimal performance of a particular subsystem (e.g., the economy), this implies an input deficit for the other subsystems that rely on its output for their optimal performance. The result is that suboptimal performances by a subsystem result in output deficits that become input deficits, and so on through the system until performance failures cumulate in a systemwide implosion.

However, as Habermas acknowledges, output and input deficits can be measured empirically only against the "requisite quantities" necessary to sustain an optimal performance within each subsystem and by the overall capitalist system. The difficulty in operationalizing systems analysis empirically becomes immediately evident when Habermas defines the concept of requisite quantities as including the financial, rationality, legitimation, and motivation inputs and outputs necessary to sustain the optimal performance of a capitalist system. Moreover, the concept of requisite quantities includes not only the amount but also the quality and timing of resource and symbolic inputs and outputs. Yet, the fact is that scholars do not know what type, amount, quality, or timing of resource allocations is necessary to the actual survival of particular institutional networks; nor can we specify with any empirical precision when serious problems in resource allocations become crises in the systems-analytic sense. Thus, short of a complete system implosion, it is virtually impossible to know definitively whether social problems are genuinely systemic contradictions or merely difficult policy dilemmas. Finally, it is even conceivable that "suboptimal" performances are quite typical of any system and that, consequently, performance deficits have no important effect on the long-term viability of capitalist systems.

On many occasions, Habermas and Offe have both sought to circumvent this difficulty with circular methodological appeals. Habermas suggests that systems analysis with all its attendant concepts serves only an "analytic purpose," and Offe often proclaims that his "aim is to propose a heuristic perspective."[73] Paradoxically, the usefulness of an analytic or heuristic perspective is typically judged by its capacity to direct and catalyze empirical or historical research. Up to this point, systems analysis has yielded a healthy crop of "Analytic Marxists," but it has produced very little in the way of systems-theoretic policy research. Indeed, Habermas is not altogether convinced that this state of affairs can be surmounted: "Whether performances of the subsystems can be adequately operationalized and isolated and the critical need for system performances adequately specified is another question. This task may be difficult to solve for pragmatic reasons."[74] Habermas insists that problems of operationalization are not insurmountable in principle, though the strong possibility remains that they may be impossible to solve in practice. Offe also explicitly sets aside "the serious difficulties" associated with the operationalization and empirical measurement of systems-analytic concepts.[75]

However, Offe has addressed this problem indirectly by suggesting that policy studies, particularly policy history, can provide the methodological tools for demonstrating what particular processes are necessary to the capitalist system. Offe is convinced that a systems analysis guided by historical materialism will be able to overcome operational problems with comparative ease, because historical materialism proceeds from the idea that the functional imperatives of a social system are registered and established in class struggles.[76] In other words, from a systems-analytic standpoint, whenever and wherever one can observe overt class conflict, there is an input-output deficit in the system. The capitalist system is functioning at an optimal level when the class conflicts that register structural contradictions are latent and quiescent.[77] In this manner, systems analysis and policy history jointly provide a critique of the capitalist state's regulatory capacities.[78]

Yet, even assuming that a transition from systems analysis to analytic policy studies was undertaken, such activities may only shift the conceptual ambiguities in systems analysis to another level of explanation. A major reason for advancing this criticism is the continuing ambiguity in Offe's concept of the state. Offe's formulation of the concept in his 1975 essay, entitled "The Theory of the Capitalist State and the Problem of Policy Formation," remains one of the most compelling in the literature. His relational definition of the state avoids the dogmatic functionalism of thinkers like Poulantzas and yet rises above the atheoretical *ex post* descriptions prevalent in the new institutionalism discussed in the next chapter.[79] Yet, at the same time, there remain serious ambiguities in this concept which point toward the need for incorporating historical political institutions into the theoretical analysis.

In fact, in more recent formulations Offe concedes that it is "both possible and meaningful to define more precisely the concept of the 'capitalist state.'"[80] Nevertheless, while Offe has a great deal to say about what the state is not (e.g., it is not reducible to state institutions) and about the functional effects of the state, Offe has very little to say about the state itself. Offe never specifies the meaning of the state concept beyond identifying it with nonempirical functional relations or subsequently with its empirical reappearance in the policy effects of those relations. At a minimum, this renders the concept of state selective mechanisms "so general and broad, that it rather seems to be an empty concept."[81] What is missing are the context in which selective mechanisms operate, a specification of the mechanisms themselves, and the units (institutions) of selection.

Unless this lacuna is plugged by some type of middle-range institutional theory, then, as in structuralism, there is nothing in Offe's framework that can be peculiarly identified as state power. Instead, social power is generated exclusively in the economic subsystem by labor-market relations and relations of production. Social power appears as political power only through the transmission of systemic effects that are eventually registered empirically as social policies. The state, as such, remains a black box of systemic conversion processes and abstract selective mechanisms. Gold, Lo, and Wright have pointed out that Offe is acutely aware of the methodological problems involved in studying the state so long as it is understood mainly in terms of axiomatic principles.[82] Indeed, Offe has frequently attempted to surmount this difficulty in various ways.

One option available in Offe's corpus is to identify the state with one or another of its two causal antinomies, that is, to identify the state with systems-functional relations or to dissolve the state into the disparate policy networks that constitute its empirically observable effects. Offe has often been inclined to pursue the former option, for example, claiming that the "state is characterized by constitutional and organizational structures" which define the patterns of "organizational linking or mutual insulation of the three 'subsystems.'"[83] The state, if one adopts this approach, is posited as a system of relationships that are not directly knowable, but which can be inferred to exist through observation of their effects in policies. Similarly, Offe has identified the state with "functions, their consequences and the contending interests within the state." Yet, from this perspective, the point of departure in systems analysis will necessarily remain "hypothetical notions about the functional connection between state activity and the structural problems of a (capitalist) social formation."[84]

In other instances, Offe has suggested the even more abstract proposition that the state, instead of being a system of functional relationships, is the pattern of functional relationships between subsystems that are constituted and organized by the state. Hence, rather than functioning as a selective mechanism, "the state protects and sanctions . . . a set of institutions and social *relationships* necessary for the domination of the capitalist class."[85] However, this approach clearly pushes the state further back into an analytic a priori which is antecedent to even the functional relationships that it allegedly sanctions. At this point, we are undoubtedly stalking "the Idea of the State, as propagated largely in hazy German metaphysics."[86]

On the other hand, it is possible to specify empirically a concept of the capitalist state by referring to observable policy networks. However, Offe has not taken this option seriously, partly because the systems-analytic framework posits social policy as an effect of social power that is mediated by political conversion processes and selective mechanisms. Thus, to define the capitalist state as its policies would result in the methodological paradox of policy effects without proximate causes.

Hence, in an important methodological polemic, Offe has acknowledged that "any sophisticated functionalist" must recognize that "the
function of an institution or a pattern of behavior is not, by itself, a
sufficient cause for the existence of the institution or pattern in question." [87] Instead, the systems-analytic framework supplies an "analytic
technique" for understanding the function of institutions and policies,
but one cannot explain the genesis of institutions and policies on the
basis of imputed functions alone.

Offe comes closest to resolving this methodological dilemma of systems analysis by suggesting that the concept of a capitalist state "describes an institutional form of political power which is guided by"
the dual functional requisites of capital accumulation and democratic
legitimation.[88] However, in proceeding along these lines, Offe's and
Habermas's frameworks generate yet another internal paradox; namely,
the analytic separation of democratic form from capitalist content in
liberal democracies prevents them from pursuing this option seriously.
As noted earlier, Offe contends that "there is a dual determination of
the political power of the capitalist state: the institutional *form* of this
state is determined through the rules of democratic and representative
government, while the material *content* of state power is conditioned
by the continuous requirements of the accumulation process." [89]

A necessary implication of this hard separation is that the capitalist
class content of state policies is real but that its democratic form is
illusory. As noted earlier, the state's selective mechanisms are presumed
to work automatically to screen out class interests that are logically
incompatible with the maintenance and exclusion principles. Consequently, the state's democratic form functions to legitimate the state in
relation to the underlying population while, in principle, it necessarily
denies that population any substantive input into state policy if it is to
function as a *capitalist* state. In a quite telling statement, Offe even concedes that his view of legitimacy "comes fairly close to a reformulation
of the Marxian concept of ideology." [90] The political forms of liberal
democracy are regarded by Offe as symbolic illusions which conceal
the real class character of the state.

The separation of state and economy (i.e., the exclusion and dependency principles) further reinforces the antinomy between the state's
democratic form and its capitalist function. For Offe, in particular,
the dependency principle does not merely condition the behavior of
state managers, it rigorously determines the institutional self-interest of
political elites to such an extent that state managers are only "basically
interested in promoting those political conditions most conducive to

private accumulation." [91] This means that state managers and the political institutions which they occupy are merely vacuums through which functional imperatives are automatically implemented. Offe quite explicitly reinforces this critical interpretation by referring to political institutions as the "instruments of state policy" and as the "political and administrative means" of channeling social power.[92]

This bifurcated concept of the state poses an explanatory dilemma for a systems-analytic approach precisely because input-output deficits can be identified and studied only in class struggles. In other words, it is *social actors* engaged in class struggle that make the imperatives of the social system both imperative and contradictory.[93] Thus, as Offe observes at one point, the historical development of state institutions and the implementation of social policy is impelled (i.e., caused) by "the organizational strength of the working class, which raises and enforces appropriate *demands* on the state." Indeed, a causal explanation of the welfare state "presupposes that the system of political institutions is constituted so that it actually concedes the demands of working-class organizations" in some form. Only then can these demands be "refracted and mediated through the internal structures of the political system" and converted into policies which are less than optimal because of their noncapitalist content.[94] In this vein, Offe offers the insight that state institutions must be compatible with the "systemic requirements" of accumulation and, thereby, enable state elites to pursue "functional" administrative strategies in response to class demands.[95] Thus ultimately, in conceptualizing the contradictions of the welfare state, Offe must continually refer (if rather obscurely) to "the state's efforts at political innovation," to the problem of "social policy development," to the "strategic calculations" and "strategies of rationalization" pursued by state elites.[96]

It is at this point that systems analysis confronts its inherent limitations: a series of methodological constraints that Offe has quite openly acknowledged.[97] First, the concept of strategic decision-making presupposes that state officials and corporate elites are making strategic decisions. Indeed, it is impossible to explain the possibility of functionally equivalent institutions, policies, and strategies without a historical concept of strategic decision-making.[98] Second, the systems-analytic concepts of selective mechanisms and input-output deficits suggest that historical, institutional forms impose real limitations and restrictions on administrative strategies.[99] Third, systems analysis always assumes a historically indeterminate level of class conflict as the structural basis for the political contradictions of capitalism. Consequently, there is a great deal of historical and institutional contingency that systems analysis must account for in its explanatory framework.[100]

In an important sense, however, the axiomatic method employed by systems analysts continues to obstruct the transition from system to agency and from logic to history. One result is a powerful methodological temptation to "rationalize" political and administrative actions by reconceptualizing the role of state elites and class mobilization within the rational choice models of a purely Analytic Marxism.[101] Thus, for example, even where Offe finds it necessary to explain social policies as the outcome of "political *decision-making within the state apparatus*," he is inclined to dismiss decision-making as theoretically insignificant, because "the space of possible decisions is determined by societal forces."[102]

Offe's rationale for this claim depends on whether his methodological approach can be dissolved into historical categories. Offe claims "that the systems-theoretical approach is an adequate tool of analysis because it corresponds to the way the managers of the system conceive it."[103] Certainly, corporate liberal theorists would not disagree with Offe, because their work offers considerable historical support for this claim.[104] However, shifting the explanatory weight of systems analysis onto its dominance as an elite decision-making framework shifts the location of its power-generating capacities from the economic subsystem to the ideological subsystem; that is, the power-generating capacities of "the capitalist system" reside in its persuasive force as an ideology of corporate and state elites.

The Historical Challenge of the 1990s

There is no doubt that among contemporary scholars systems analysis is regaining a transideological appeal that seemed unthinkable only a decade ago.[105] Yet, paradoxically, just as systems analysis seems poised to make a methodological comeback, many of the historical claims deduced from its axioms seem less and less tenable. The most important historical challenges concern the contradictions of the welfare state and the emerging role of the new social movements. In retrospect, it now seems that systems analysts have persistently overestimated the crisis potential of contradictions within the welfare state. Foremost among these miscalculations has been the tendency among systems analysts to underestimate continually the state's capacity to reduce its social expenses.[106] On this point, the crisis projections deduced by systems analysts have missed the mark in at least four ways.

First, the welfare state has shown a remarkable capacity both to capitalize and to rationalize its social expenses through corporate liberal reform agendas. James O'Connor argues that corporate liberal reform movements are attempts to restore the fragile balance between accumulation and legitimation by converting unproductive social expenses to productive social capital.[107] For example, the provision of equal educational opportunity may be necessary to maintain the state's democratic legitimacy in late capitalism, but in itself education may also be an unproductive social expense. However, to the extent that corporate liberal initiatives successfully link educational curricula and scientific research to corporate demands for manpower training and scientific infrastructure, schools and universities become social capital outlays.[108] Consequently, the greater the extent to which welfare-state services can be integrated with corporate markets, the more those state expenditures can be moved from the social debit to the social asset column of the state's expenditure ledger.

Similarly, as James Weinstein has admirably demonstrated, corporate liberal initiatives nearly always entail rationalization movements. Certainly, in the United States, government rationalization movements have sought explicitly to systematize social policy networks, to restore administrative coherence, and to upgrade the technical capacities of key personnel.[109] The conclusion, as Roger King observes, is that systems crisis theory has severely underestimated the ability of politicians and state administrators to overcome apparent structural deficiencies in policy and administration.[110]

Second, it now seems reasonable to conclude that many of the production costs which were socialized in the post–World War II period were socialized more as a consequence of political objectives, whether social-democratic or statist, than because of any functional needs to subsidize capital accumulation. At a minimum, one must acknowledge that the state's rising social capital expenditures apparently exceeded the system's actual needs by the 1980s. Moreover, to the extent that direct socializations of productive assets established a socialist or statist obstacle to private accumulation, social capital investments became surplus expenditures that could be scaled down through privatization.

Third, like most Marxian theorists, systems analysts have misconceptualized the normative basis of legitimacy and the functional importance of legitimacy to the capitalist state. Systems analysts, along with Marxists of nearly every type, have greatly overestimated the extent to which normative loyalty to the state is functionally linked with its tangible resource allocations (i.e., social capital, social expenses). As a result, projections that a legitimation crisis would be precipitated by any dramatic rollback of social welfare expenses have been thoroughly confounded by the Reagan-Thatcher duo. The fact is that systems analysts failed to anticipate or to understand the degree to which normative loyalty is attached to political myths, national symbols, and rituals of participation which in principle are unrelated to fiscal considerations.[111] Hence, crisis theory failed dramatically in not being able to anticipate the way that neoconservatives have redefined the rules of legitimacy by invoking symbolic myths that explicitly discount the state's responsibility for economic growth, individual well-being, and distributive justice.

Furthermore, Theda Skocpol intimates that the very concept of legitimacy is rendered questionable by the prolonged survival of such blatantly repressive and domestically illegitimate capitalist regimes as that of South Africa.[112] Skocpol provides a historical and comparative reminder that the capitalist state may not need legitimacy but only acquiescence, and this can be achieved efficiently through repression, fear, and neglect. As a result, both the basis and the importance of legitimacy must be reassessed, particularly because neither organized labor nor the new social movements have effectively prevented the privatization of state industries and services or the rollback of social expenses.[113]

Finally, the overestimation of the legitimation costs that would accrue from a rollback of the welfare state is intimately tied to the concept of a closed system. The tendency to conceptualize capitalist social formations as closed national systems resulted in downgrading "external disturbances" to "accidental" events of little theoretical significance. Hence, those systems analysts who concentrated on the dynamics of late capitalist societies, such as Offe and Habermas, were unable to anticipate the immense structural leverage that capital would achieve over labor and the state through globalization and international capital mobility.[114] The threat of international relocation has provided multinational capitalists with enormous leverage to exert downward pressure on wages and social expenses by fleeing the high wage–high tax metropoles, thus utilizing the power-generating capacities of an international labor market to render the metropolitan working classes more dependent on capital for access to national or local labor markets.[115] Over the long run, it is entirely possible that any legitimation deficits stemming from globalization and welfare rollbacks will give way to popular acquiescence and a heightened sense of dependency.

In summary, the welfare state has shown a much greater capacity to shed its fiscal and administrative ballast than was expected by systems-analytic crisis theory. As a result, the rise of the New Right has challenged many of our preconceptions about what is functionally necessary to the late capitalist state and about the long-term historical tendencies of future capitalist development. For, as Simon Clarke observes, the New Right has been successful at scaling back the welfare state "without any regard for the supposed necessity of this or that aspect of the state, and without any consideration of the supposed contradiction between the 'accumulation' and 'legitimation' functions of the state." [116]

In this regard, a far more controversial aspect of systems analysis concerns its projections about the future role of the new social movements. Once again, the axiomatic foundation of systems analysis has often resulted in speculative deductions that must be challenged from an empirical and historical perspective. First, post-Marxists systematically exaggerate the "noncapitalist" character of the new social movements. In fact, most of the new social movements in the United States articulate distributional interests associated with ascriptive inequities in the labor market, for example, affirmative action in the case of ethnic minorities, and comparable worth and day care in the case of women. The "empirically real" new social movements actually tend to draw their members from labor-market participants who are seeking to eliminate ascriptive irrationalities in the system through organized interest group activities. Furthermore, as the new social groups succeed in achieving these objectives there is mounting evidence that the movements and the consciousness of their participants is reshaped by the imperatives of labor competition. [117]

Consequently, Carl Boggs's comparative analysis of the new social movements finds that "they are just as vulnerable to a range of co-optative and integrative pressures as their social-democratic, reformist precursors." [118] Therefore, Boggs concludes that it is no more possible to predict whether the new social groups will become genuinely radicalized than it was to project the revolutionary character of working-class struggles, which Marx attempted in the nineteenth century. The unfortunate truth is that post-Marxists tend to ontologize the far fringes of the new social movements, often consisting of leftist intellectuals, by placing these outer tendencies at the center of their theoretically constructed ideal types.

However, at the other end of the spectrum, sociological tailings are being cast off in ever-increasing numbers by the developing structures of the postindustrial labor market. These are the underskilled and underemployed servile class, along with the chronically unemployed castoffs that Gorz calls the neoproletariat. Gorz and Habermas are justifiably ambivalent about the potential of these new social groups, precisely because their marginal attachment to the labor market excludes them from participating in the central power-generating mechanism of a capitalist society.

Their displacement from the labor market excludes the neoproletariat and the servile class from access to its social power in the sense that they have nothing of economic value (i.e., labor power) to bargain with or to exchange for concessions.[119] As underemployed, unemployed, or unproductive labor, the neoproletariat and the servile class are an utterly surplus population in the vilest sense of the concept. The key, as Habermas observes, is that the pauperization of these groups no longer coincides with economic exploitation in the technical Marxian sense, because the system no longer depends on their labor for the creation of surplus value. Thus, these groups cannot gain any structural leverage by collectively withdrawing their labor from the marketplace, and, for the same reason, capital incurs no direct costs from their repression because of lost productivity. Consequently, Habermas concludes that unless these groups "are connected with protest potential from other sectors of society no conflicts arising from such underprivilege can really overturn the system—they can only provoke sharp reactions incompatible with formal democracy." [120]

There is good reason to believe that the postindustrial neoproletariat and servile class are more likely to be an underclass that can be easily suppressed, neglected, and contained through coercion and violence. Joachim Hirsch offers the ominous prognosis that, as the contradictions of the welfare state intensify and the illusion of class neutrality collapses, state elites will more readily resort to the use of overt violence as a means of waging class warfare.[121] In addition, their ability to repress social conflict successfully has been enhanced by a state apparatus with new capacities for internal police actions, paramilitary assaults, counterterrorist units, domestic surveillance, disinformation, and political infiltration.[122] There is no reason to believe that postindustrial societies will not continue to disintegrate, to become more segmented between a privileged core and a dependent periphery, and consequently sink deeper into violence, injustice, and fear.[123]

CHAPTER FIVE

Post-Marxism II: The Organizational Realist Approach

Taxes are the source of life for the bureaucracy, the army . . . for the whole apparatus of the executive power. Strong government and heavy taxes are identical.

—*Marx*, Eighteenth Brumaire, *1852*

During the last decade, state theorists influenced by the new institutionalism[1] have elucidated a second post-Marxist approach to the state called organizational realism.[2] Organizational realism conceptualizes the state as an organization that attempts "to extend coercive control and political authority over particular territories and the people residing within them."[3] A fundamental thesis of organizational realism is that in pursuing this political objective state managers are self-interested maximizers whose main interest is to enhance their own institutional power, prestige, and wealth. Thus, organizational realists view states not only as decision-making organizations but also as autonomous organizational actors that must be considered real historical subjects in relation to social classes.[4]

The methodological objective of this approach thus far has been to utilize institutional research and policy analysis as vehicles for developing middle-range issues and hypotheses that have been deemed inaccessible to "grand theories" of the state, such as those considered in earlier chapters.[5] Consequently, organizational realism starts from the polemical assumption that preexisting theories of the state are useful only for generating research questions, analytical concepts, and causal hypotheses about possible relationships between the state and capitalist society.[6] Therefore, the aim of this research strategy has been to focus on the theoretically limited task of constructing empirical generalizations by using comparative historical case studies of policy formation and state institutional development.

The Possible Autonomy of the State

The proponents of organizational realism are a diverse set of scholars with wide-ranging substantive concerns, but they nevertheless share the theoretical goal of establishing the "possible autonomy of the state" in capitalist societies.[7] Theda Skocpol articulates this thesis succinctly by pointing out: "The fatal shortcoming of all marxist theorizing (so far) about the role of the state is that nowhere is the *possibility* admitted that the state organizations and elites might under certain circumstances act *against* the long-run economic interests of a dominant class, or act to create a new mode of production."[8]

From this perspective, Skocpol contends that neo-Marxists' inability to conceptualize policy realization failures, social-democratic political and economic reform, or even successful revolution stems from the prevailing assumption that the state is either nothing more than an instrument of business dominance or is merely "*an arena* in which conflicts over basic social and economic interests are fought out."[9] As a result, Skocpol maintains, there is a continuing tendency for Marxian theorists to conclude that state policies simply reflect a preexisting balance of social power between and within classes that is established in class conflicts outside the state. Consequently, Marxian approaches to policy analysis are "society-centered" theories which presume that the origins and effects of public policy must always reflect the interests of the capitalist class, and, to the extent of that reflection, policy reproduces the dominance of that class.[10] Intrinsic to an organizational approach, on the other hand, is its methodological refusal "to treat states as if they were mere analytic aspects of abstractly conceived modes of production, or even political aspects of concrete class relations and struggles. Rather it insists that states are actual organizations controlling (or attempting to control) territories and people."[11]

Moreover, insofar as organizational realists are engaged in exploring the possible autonomy of the state, they are seeking to develop empirical and historical research which challenges the assumption that states will always act in the interests of a dominant class. In fact, Skocpol concludes that, if the state were always acting to secure the political dominance of a ruling class, it would not even be worth bothering to talk about the state. Unless the state formulates goals that are at least nominally independent of immediate class interests, "there is little need to talk about states as important actors" in the class struggle.[12] Therefore, a meaningful theory of the state must be able to incorporate methodologically some element of autonomy, that is, the contingent possibility of historical and policy disjunctures between state and capital.

This possibility rests on a concept of the state that grants it an independent source of power as the historical and empirical basis for state autonomy. State autonomy is theoretically possible only if one can locate at least a minimal degree of state power within the state apparatus that is analytically independent of the class power constituted in relations of production. In this vein, Skocpol argues that "the administrative and coercive organizations [of the state] are the basis of state power as such."[13] In this respect, Skocpol concludes, the state properly conceived is "a set of administrative, policing, and military organizations headed, and more or less well coordinated by, an executive authority."[14]

However, Skocpol explicitly cautions that the extent to which states actually are autonomous, and to what effect, varies from case to case. A primary methodological stricture of organizational realism is "that the actual extent and consequences of state autonomy can only be analyzed and explained in terms specific to particular types of sociopolitical systems and to particular sets of historical international relations."[15] It should be emphasized in this respect that Skocpol formulates the autonomy of the state only as a limited and hypothetical proposition to be tested against comparative case studies. Case studies are selected to demonstrate that in *some* cases, which are contingently and specifically delineated, the state does act autonomously, that is, against or beyond the interests of the dominant capitalist class.[16] Beyond the mere cumulation of such instances, however, the aim of comparative and case study research is to develop some empirical generalizations about the factors and conditions which are most likely to result in an actual exercise of the state's potential autonomy.

Skocpol suggests that in a general sense these factors reside in the uniquely political tasks that are performed by all states: resource extraction, administrative capacity, and coercive control.[17] First, and fundamentally, states must extract resources from society (i.e., tax) in order to deploy those resources toward creating and supporting the coercive and administrative organizations which are the basis of state power. This means that "state organizations necessarily compete to some extent with the dominant class(es) in appropriating resources from the economy and society." The coercive and administrative organizations themselves are normally oriented toward performing two tasks: the maintenance of internal order and political-military competition with other actual or potential states. Therefore, state policies are formulated by state elites with the primary goal of achieving these two aims effectively and efficiently. Skocpol observes that in pursuing such goals "states usually do function to preserve existing economic and class structures, for that is normally the smoothest way to enforce order."[18]

Gianfranco Poggi suggests in this context that the development of a special historical relationship between capitalism and the modern state is best explained as a "convergence of interests" between "two autonomous forces, neither of which was originally and inescapably dominant over the other" in Western history. Organizational realists consistently emphasize that state-building and political development have been largely motivated by the territorial designs of state elites, the requirements of policing and administering an expanding territory, and by the necessities of competing with other states in an international system. Thus, Poggi maintains that capitalist development has been synchronous and functionally correlated with modern state development only insofar as commerce has created a new tax base for expanding states and because an industrial base has been viewed as increasingly advantageous to the state's own war-making capacity. Hence, Poggi concludes that, as one moves further into the modern era, states "must to some extent preserve and/or foster the requirements of continuing capital accumulation" in order for state elites to achieve their own political objectives.[19]

However, Fred Block and Theda Skocpol contend that "exceptional periods" of domestic or international crisis may compel state elites to implement social policies, economic reforms, and institutional changes that concede subordinate class demands and/or violate the interests of those classes which benefit from the existing economic arrangements within a state's jurisdiction. Hence, in principle, the political objective of restoring internal order may at times be served best by social and economic policies that respond to the demands of working classes, even though such policies are opposed by the economically dominant classes.[20] Depending upon the circumstances, Skocpol notes, "these concessions may be at the expense of the interests of the dominant class, but not contrary to the state's own interests in controlling the population and collecting taxes and military recruits."[21] Likewise, a state's involvement in an international network of states provides another basis for potential autonomy from the capitalist class. Skocpol suggests that "international military pressures and opportunities can prompt state rulers to attempt policies that conflict with, and even in extreme cases contradict, the fundamental interests of a dominant class."[22] The imperatives of war-making create exceptional needs for additional tax resources, for industrial production that can be coordinated and directed by state elites, and for the maintenance of mass loyalty. The result is that state elites may be tempted under the pressures of warfare to exceed normal tax constraints or even to seize direct control of privately owned production facilities.

It should again be emphasized that those instances in which a state is most likely to act against the interests of a dominant class are normally the result of rare crisis situations in which state elites conclude that they must do so in order to achieve basic political goals, that is, domestic order and national defense. Within this conceptual framework, Skocpol thus derives two general hypotheses about the conditions in which state elites are most likely to assert their autonomy against a dominant class:

(H_1)   "The basic need to maintain control and order may spur *state-initiated* reforms."

(H_2)   "The linkage of states into transnational structures and into international flows of communication may encourage leading *state officials* to pursue transformative strategies even in the face of indifference or resistance from politically weighty social forces."[23]

As a corollary to these hypotheses, Skocpol and Block both suggest that major institutional and policy reforms are more likely to occur when these conditions reach crisis proportions—in a word, during times of domestic rebellion or as the result of involvement in international warfare. However, for Skocpol, the mere presence of one or both of these conditions, although necessary, is not sufficient to compel state elites to act autonomously or against the interests of a dominant class. State elites must also have the collective psychological will and the organizational capacity to assert their potential autonomy when the opportunity or necessity arises. Consequently, Skocpol offers this further hypothesis:

(H_3)   The state is most likely to assert its potential autonomy when it consists of organizationally coherent collectivities of state officials.

Furthermore, there is a greater likelihood that state elites will constitute coherent collectivities when

(H_{3a})   state elites are collectivities of *career* officials;

(H_{3b})   career officials are "relatively insulated from ties to currently dominant socioeconomic interests."[24]

Thus, Skocpol finds that, with specific reference to capitalist societies, Ellen Kay Trimberger's definition of an autonomous state elite is persuasive: ". . . a bureaucratic state apparatus, or a segment of it, can be said to be relatively autonomous when those who hold high civil and/or military posts satisfy two conditions: (1) they are not recruited from the dominant landed, commercial, or industrial classes; and (2) they do not form close personal and economic ties with those classes after their elevation to high office."[25]

Moreover, Skocpol adds to Trimberger's definition of autonomy a third hypothetical condition derived from the work of Alfred Stepan,[26] namely:

(H$_{3c}$)   Career officials must have "a unified sense of ideological purpose about the possibility and desirability of using state intervention."[27]

Therefore, the empirical reference for an autonomous state is one in which the leading elites are career officials who are recruited from the ranks of nondominant classes, who refrain from close personal or economic ties to the dominant class after their elevation to high office, and who develop a sense of ideological purpose which legitimates the desirability of using the state to act against the dominant class. This complex pathology of state autonomy is clearly not exemplary of the normal operations of any state, including capitalist states. As a result, even Skocpol concedes that instances of an entire state asserting its autonomy as represented by reformist coups and revolutions from above are "extraordinary instances of state autonomy" that cannot be considered typical of any state at any time.[28] Indeed, Skocpol is willing to agree that state autonomy should not be considered "a fixed structural feature of any governmental system."[29] The much more likely scenarios— and even these are rather limited in scope, time, and location—"are more circumscribed instances of state autonomy" as illustrated "in the histories of public policy making in liberal democratic, constitutional polities, such as Britain, Sweden, and the United States."[30]

Strong States and Weak States

Because the pure concept of state autonomy is circumscribed in its applicability, organizational realists have attempted to generalize its theoretical usefulness in terms of two other ideas: (1) a strong state–weak state spectrum of analysis, and (2) the uneven development of state organizations. First, capacities for state autonomy are *generally* limited by the overall strength or weakness of a state's institutional design. Second, the segmented and uneven organizational development of modern state apparatuses also places *specific* limits on the potential for state autonomy in particular policy areas.

The strong state concept utilized by most organizational realists has actually been formulated most clearly by Stephen Skowronek. Skowronek measures the political development (i.e., strength) of states across three dimensions of descending importance: "the *organizational orientations* of government, the *procedural routines* that tie institutions together within a given organizational scheme, and the *intellectual talents* employed in government."[31] The organizational orientation of a state is determined by the degree to which four organizational qualities characterize its institutional apparatus:

1. The *concentration* of authority at the national center of government
2. The *penetration* of institutional controls from the governmental center throughout the territory
3. The *centralization* of authority within the national government
4. The *specialization* of institutional tasks and individual roles within the government.[32]

The greater the degree to which a state institutionalizes these four characteristics, the stronger its organizational orientation. Within a particular organizational orientation, a state's procedural dimension consists of the way in which actions by state officials and the policies of various agencies are coordinated between and within institutions. Skowronek observes that "stable, valued, and recurring modes of behavior within and among institutions are needed to lend governmental operations coherence and effectiveness." Consequently, the actual governing potential "within any given organizational scheme will be found in the working rules developed to guide the actions of those in office."[33] These working rules, and career officials' collective identification with them, potentially form the basis for a degree of internal coherence and unity of action by state elites.

Finally, the state is not only an arrangement of institutions and procedures; it is also an intellectual enterprise which draws upon the empirically irreducible skills of state officials to formulate policy goals and to administer, implement, and enforce those goals. Consequently, "the intellectual talent available in government for problem solving and innovation is critical to the capacities of a state to maintain itself over time."[34] This is essentially a problem of integrating intellectuals and technical experts into the state's institutional network and policy-formation process.

The configuration of institutional development postulated along these three dimensions may be taken as the ideal type of a strong state.[35] The more closely a state approximates these developmental ideals, the greater the general presumption that the state can act autonomously at home and abroad by establishing and pursuing political goals independent of dominant classes. A weak state by contrast is one in which the apparatus of state power is more decentralized, fragmented, and tied down by nonexpert patronage linkages to dominant social interests which restrict its range of actions, often in contradictory ways.[36] Therefore, one of organizational realism's central hypotheses is that:

(H$_4$)   strong states are more able to act autonomously against the interests of a dominant class if the hypothetical conditions discussed above are also met.

On the other hand,

(H$_5$)   a weak state is presumed to be less able to act against the interests of a dominant class, even if state elites should will it.

In this vein, Skocpol argues that in capitalist societies the strength or weakness of a state's institutional design will "powerfully shape and limit state interventions in the economy."[37] However, Skocpol also warns that a state's capacity to intervene autonomously against or on behalf of dominant social interests must always be analyzed concretely in terms of a historically "relational approach." A state's actual strength cannot be measured solely in terms of its conformity to the ideal type of a strong state. This is because the historical (as opposed to the analytic) answers to whether a specific state can act autonomously "lie not only in features of states themselves, but also in the balances of states' resources and situational advantages compared with those of nonstate actors."[38]

A state's centralized institutional coherence, its ability to draw on autonomous technical expertise, its ability to generate revenue, and its ability ultimately to maintain a monopoly on disciplined professional violence (i.e., police, army) are meaningful analytic concepts only in relation to the degree, lesser or greater, that nonstate actors (e.g., class-based organizations) possess the same capacities. A nominally weak state confronting weakly organized social actors may well possess the same actual capacities for intervention as a strong state confronting well-organized classes.[39] Thus, as Skocpol readily concedes, organizational realism constitutes at best a highly indeterminate "conceptual frame of reference." [40] However, beyond this general observation, Peter Evans, Dietrich Rueschemeyer, and Theda Skocpol conclude from their survey of the new institutionalist research that organizational realists, therefore, should not (and in fact do not) actually spend much time "debating whether states in general are autonomous." [41] The general conclusion of research thus far is that the strong state–weak state antinomy at best represents an analytic spectrum along which all states are "relatively autonomous" in degrees that can be specified only against relational comparative measures.

In these terms, organizational realists are more or less agreed that Sweden and the United States represent the two poles of the strong state–weak state antinomy among the advanced capitalist welfare states.[42] Skocpol argues, for instance, that during the economic crisis of the 1930s the United States failed to secure a genuine social-democratic breakthrough in welfare state policies.[43] Moreover, Skocpol observes that the United States is "a polity in which virtually all scholars agree that there is less structural basis for such autonomy than in any other modern liberal capitalist regime." [44] On the other hand, most of the Nordic and many of the western European nations with strong state histories did achieve social-democratic policy breakthroughs in varying degrees.[45]

Thus, by comparison, Margaret Weir and Theda Skocpol find that "Sweden aimed to become—and very largely succeeded in achieving—a full-employment economy with high levels of public income allocation for social purposes." Moreover, welfare policies were designed to promote widespread social equality. On the other hand, the U.S. welfare state was constructed around an economic growth strategy which left class inequality and the private control of investment largely intact. This strategy has been pursued through "the use of tax cuts and modest levels of automatic (as opposed to discretionary) public spending to stabilize the economy." [46] Furthermore, any U.S. welfare policies that could be construed as social democratic have been subordinated to business concerns with maintaining low inflation and low taxes. Weir and Skocpol contend that the different levels of social-democratic breakthrough can for the most part be explained by the relative positions of the United States and Sweden along the strong state–weak state spectrum.

It is against this background that Skocpol's and others' recent work on the New Deal is explicitly presented as a limited research agenda

designed only to illustrate "that autonomous state contributions to domestic policy making can occur within a 'weak state.'" It should not be
understood as a general defense of the autonomy of the state, because
Skocpol's own work finds that "autonomous state contributions hap-
pen in specific policy areas at given historical moments" and "are not
generally discernible across all policy areas" in any state.[47] In fact, one
of Skocpol's most vaunted achievements, in her own words, amounts to
nothing more than having "found a *part* of the early-twentieth-century
U.S. national government that allowed official expertise to function in a
restricted policy area" (i.e., the U.S. Department of Agriculture).[48] Similarly, in their more expansive study of U.S. social policies, Weir, Orloff,
and Skocpol find that the types of strong state agencies which they
consider appropriate to initiating and administering social policy are
"typically *isolated islands* of expertise within local, state, and federal
governments." Thus, they conclude that only "*some* islands of administrative expertise in American federal democracy became capable of
expanding or improving the social programs under their aegis, when
political opportunities for reform and innovation opened up."[49] The
obverse implication, of course, is that in most cases, most of the time,
states in capitalist society have not acted autonomously of the capitalist class.

Such findings suggest that "one of the most important facts about
the power of a state may be its *unevenness* across policy areas."[50] In
other words, patterns of centralization, elite recruitment, bureaucratic
expertise, and ideological orientation may vary widely between policy
sectors and even across subsectors.[51] Indeed, Evans, Rueschemeyer, and
Skocpol's survey of the new institutionalist research shows "that states
are not likely to be equally capable of intervening in different areas
of socioeconomic life" because of the "unevenness of a state's existing
capacities, either at one moment or over time."[52] Moreover, since this
unevenness may be the most important structural feature of a state's
ability to meet challenges, the utility of deriving a state's capacity from
some generalized concept of overall state strength is increasingly doubtful. In fact, Evans and his colleagues conclude that "telling variations
in state structures and capacities often occur among states that appear
to belong to the same broad type."[53]

An example which Skocpol and Finegold use to illustrate this point
is their comparison of the policy failure of the National Industrial
Recovery Act (NIRA) with the relative success of the Agricultural Adjustment Act (AAA) (both passed by the U.S. Congress in 1933). In this
instance, the authors conclude that the "most decisive" factor in the

AAA's success was the existence of a professional cadre of agricultural policy experts which had been built up in the U.S. Department of Agriculture over several decades. According to Skocpol and Finegold, these experts "were willing to make policy *for,* rather than just *with,* the farmers and their organizations." Moreover, their professional expertise coupled with previous career experience and the existence of clear departmental procedures "had given them a concrete sense of what could (and could not) be done with available governmental means."[54] Thus, a cohesive cadre of agricultural policy experts was able to devise policies related to institutional capacities that were unknown to the major social actors while screening out policies which they knew were beyond the capacities of the department or that seemed technically unsound.

The result was that technocratic state elites had the expertise to formulate an interventionist agricultural strategy during the Great Depression that went beyond the immediate demands of farmers, but was also linked to the concrete institutional capacities of the implementing agency. Furthermore, Skocpol and Finegold argue, the "agricultural experts, their ideas, and the administrative means they could use to implement the ideas *all* were products of a long process of institution building whose roots go back to the Civil War, when the U.S. Department of Agriculture was chartered and the Morrill Act was passed."[55] In other words, seven decades of previous political development had created the political will and the institutional ability to intervene successfully. In this respect, Skocpol and Finegold also challenge the social-democratic model by claiming that the Great Depression and the demands of farmers merely provided the occasion for new policy departures, but were not a promixate influence on policy content. The authors maintain that the actual contents of workable policies tended to come from government administrators and the initiatives of other expert elites, not from the presence or absence of mobilized class demands.[56]

As opposed to agricultural policy, however, the U.S. state had no developmental history in the area of industrial planning. There were no currently existing administrative means for developing or implementing an industrial policy. Consequently, there was no cadre of autonomous state policy experts capable of drawing on decades of previous institutional learning. Instead, the NIRA mandate had to create a new administrative agency (the National Recovery Administration) and had to rely on the leadership and talents of self-interested business leaders and parochial trade union officials. As a result, Skocpol and Finegold conclude, "the National Recovery Administration failed in its mission of coordinating industrial production under the aegis of public supervision, and the apparent opportunity offered by the National Industrial Recovery Act's extraordinary peacetime grant of economic authority to the U.S. government was lost."[57]

The Problem of Theory in Organizational Realism

As a methodological project, organizational realism has successfully shifted neo-Marxist and post-Marxist research "away from abstract conceptual disputes toward meeting the challenge of explaining actual historical developments."[58] However, it has also been philosophically naive in assuming that historical or empirical research alone would be sufficient to resolve or circumvent the grand scale theoretical and conceptual disputes that often seem to paralyze Marxian theory. The mounting of a joint polemical counterattack against Skocpol by corporate liberals (instrumentalists) and structuralists provides an excellent illustration of this methodological dilemma in relation to a specific issue. G. William Domhoff, Theda Skocpol, and Jill S. Quadagno recently engaged in a three-way polemic concerning the origins of the Social Security Act of 1935, legislation that is widely regarded as a cornerstone of the U.S. welfare state.[59] As such, similar disputes over the class origins and economic content of the legislation have come to occupy a prominent role in arbitrating the claims of competing Marxist theories of the state.[60]

Skocpol contends that an explanation of the U.S. Social Security Act must focus on the role of "social science professionals and other 'experts' as a sociopolitical force partially autonomous from both business and labor."[61] From this perspective, Skocpol accuses both instrumentalists (e.g., Domhoff) and structuralists (e.g., Quadagno) of exaggerating big business's influence on the legislation, especially within the executive branch of government. On the other hand, Domhoff argues that "business leaders were far more important in the formulation of the Social Security Act than Skocpol is willing to admit."[62] Quadagno, although generally sympathetic to Domhoff's analysis, suggests that corporate liberal theory "underestimates" the influence of nonmonopoly power blocs (local businessmen) which were based in the Congress, particularly in the House of Representatives.[63]

All three authors have developed their claims in terms of concrete historical analyses of the Social Security legislation. Thus, each is convinced that the others would have to accept his or her conclusions, if only they would confront "the facts." In the simplest terms, all three authors agree that the initial thrust for Social Security came primarily from the American Association for Labor Legislation (AALL). The AALL and a few other policy groups successfully lobbied President Roosevelt to support a national proposal for unemployment insurance and old-age pensions. A specific proposal was developed in the executive branch and submitted to Congress. Congress eventually passed the legislation, but substantially altered the unemployment compensation provisions so as to keep its administration at the state level and also to allow variations in compensation levels from state to state.

Domhoff thus correctly points out that there are substantial points of similarity between all three authors at the purely descriptive level in their "common emphasis on the AALL and its experts, the conservative role of Congress, and the lack of national-level pressure from organized labor."[64] Furthermore, all three authors agree "that no plan for social insurance got anywhere until the Great Depression overwhelmed company programs [e.g., pensions] and local relief programs, generating strong pressures for unemployment insurance and old-age payments" throughout the country.[65] However, what does this tell one theoretically about the nature of the state in capitalist society? The answer hinges on prior assumptions about how to understand the role of political organizations.

For instance, a major issue in locating the "class content" of the Social Security legislation turns on how to interpret the social role of the AALL. The AALL was a policy group which recruited its members primarily from among corporate leaders and intellectuals (i.e., government policy experts and academics). Its work was largely financed by contributions from wealthy individuals, corporations, and corporate-sponsored foundations. However, as Domhoff notes, "what corporate-liberal theory sees as a classic corporate reform group, Skocpol sees as an organization of experts."[66]

Clearly, the debate hinges on how to interpret the *organizational relationship* between the corporate leaders and the policy experts within the AALL. The theoretical implications of the AALL's role in developing the content of the legislation are substantially different depending upon how one conceptualizes the relationship between corporate officials and intellectuals (i.e., policy experts). Domhoff argues that "big-business leaders and *their* experts in policy groups were very important in shaping key aspects of the legislation" through the executive branch. Domhoff suggests further that "most of this influence happened through the AALL and the BAC [Business Advisory Council], but experts from the

Rockefellers' [note the possessive] Industrial Relations Counselors . . . joined with experts from the AALL to play leading roles."[67] Quadagno's "Poulantzian" analysis is not substantially different from Domhoff's on this point.

Fred Block objects to corporate liberal conceptualizations of this sort, because, in his view, many political actors can be linked to the financial support of foundations or wealthy individuals in one way or another. Hence, the key theoretical issue for Block is whether or not corporate liberal theorists can demonstrate not merely whether a particular policy initiative has the support of a few prominent business leaders, but also whether these individuals actually represent business organizations that have some kind of widespread business support.[68] However, Alvin Gouldner has pointed out that the dilemma involved in responding to such an objection is that, "for the most part, classes themselves do not enter into active political struggle; the active participants in political struggle are usually organizations, parties, associations, vanguards." Consequently, except in the rarest instances (e.g., revolutions, general strikes), classes as such are not political actors, but are "cache areas in which these organizations mobilize, recruit, and conscript support and in whose name they legitimate their struggle."[69] Hence, the plausibility of Domhoff's and Quadagno's class analyses is theoretically dependent on a willingness to accept the idea that political organizations "represent" classes and class fractions and that such representatives are capable of class-conscious action. For instrumentalists, the theoretical concept of class representation is rooted in the empirical analysis of power structures. Class membership, financial support, and other institutional linkages tie the political organization (e.g., the AALL) predominantly to corporate class interests. For Quadagno, a similar theoretical linkage is presupposed as part of a structural class analysis.[70]

Skocpol, on the other hand, refuses to draw that linkage, because she presupposes a different concept of social structure and class action, particularly in the American case. Skocpol's concept of the U.S. social structure presupposes, for reasons that are left unexplained, that both industrial workers and capitalists inherently "lack the political capacity to pursue classwide interests in national politics." Consequently, Skocpol makes the analytic assumption that one cannot view corporate officials in the AALL and other groups as "representatives of the capitalist class or of entire sectors of business."[71] Hence, as Michael Goldfield observes in a similar context, Skocpol simply dismisses "claims of the historic corporate influence over various reformers" and asserts instead that liberal reformers and reform organizations (e.g., the AALL) "had independent reform agendas that were neither influenced nor coincident with those of major capitalists."[72]

Thus, Skocpol's judgement about the theoretical implications of the AALL's role differs from those of instrumentalists and structuralists, because she starts out from a premise that analytically severs active political organizations from class structure. Skocpol can therefore comfortably assert that middle-class professionals are not in most cases "witting or unwitting tools of business interests." Skocpol instead persistently builds into her empirical analyses a theoretical presumption that contributions by policy experts are generally autonomous. Hence, Skocpol and other organizational realists, in the execution of their research projects, have continually violated their original methodological premises. What Skocpol and others originally set out to prove, they have since come to assume. As a result, when challenged by what Goldfield calls the "extensive and impressive" evidence marshaled by corporate liberal theorists, Skocpol has attempted to bolster and disguise this assumption by dismissing class-conscious business leaders in America in a rather cavalier manner as mavericks.[73]

Consequently, when it comes time to interpret the process of policy formation that took place within the executive branch of government, corporate liberalism views the same political actors (i.e., AALL, BAC) as representatives of big business, while Skocpol sees them as organizations of autonomous intellectuals and policy experts. This is not a behavioral dispute over who the major actors were, but an intractable theoretical dispute over how to interpret the meaning of organizational actors in relation to social classes. Skocpol denies that big business played any significant role in shaping U.S. Social Security legislation, not because she is unaware of its presence in the policy-formation process, but because she interprets their role to be unimportant on the basis of prior analytic considerations.

Skocpol can thus argue that government officials were the central figures in shaping the legislation and, given her emphasis on their autonomy, is led to highlight those instances in which the preferences of corporate leaders "were ignored, overridden, or simply did not matter."[74] Once armed with these examples of relative autonomy, Skocpol can infer that, when the preferences of corporate leaders and policy intellectuals did coincide, it was only incidentally and contingently related to the process of policy formation. Coming at the same issue from different analytic assumptions, Domhoff and Quadagno place these preference conjunctures at the center of their analyses.

Similarly, once the issue moves to Congress, the same kinds of analytic disputes lead to competing interpretations of the amendments to
the unemployment provisions. Skocpol sees the unemployment amendments as a move by political conservatives, primarily southerners, to
protect states' rights that were largely unrelated to the class content
of the Social Security legislation. The changes to unemployment are
explained as the result of institutional patterns of local representation
that were autonomously institutionalized in the Congress. Skocpol and
Amenta's analysis of this phase in the legislation is designed to illustrate that "one cannot account for the influence of Southern agricultural
interests in the New Deal by examining only their class interests or economic weight in the national economy. Their leverage was registered
through an electoral structure that disenfranchised blacks, and through
a Congressionally centered and federally rooted policymaking process
that allowed key committee chairmen from 'safe' districts to arbitrate
many legislative details and outcomes." [75]
    In other words, the constitutional structure of local district repre-
sentation combined with congressional seniority rules, party alignment,
and southern voter-registration restrictions magnified the political capacities of southern landlords at the national legislative level. Thus,
Skocpol and Amenta argue, "it makes little theoretical sense to collapse the state into class relations or interests." Instead, one must view
policy outcomes primarily as the consequence of an "*intersection* of
state structures and social relations." [76] Yet, as Quadagno points out,
this claim is not incompatible with Poulantzian structuralism.
    First, Poulantzas and the structurally influenced derivationists both
point to the relative autonomy of the state as the basis for explaining the
existence of partial disjuncutures between public policy and dominant
class interests. For structuralist theory, politics in a capitalist society
is the effort by labor to create policy disjunctures between state and
capital and by capital to close disjunctures between various fractions
of capital. Poulantzas actually emphasizes that one must look at the
specific forms of the state because "each state branch or apparatus and
each of their respective sections and levels . . . frequently constitutes the
power-base and favoured representative of a particular fraction or bloc"
of the contending classes in a capitalist society. [77] As a result, Skocpol's
analysis is theoretically consistent with Poulantzas's observation that
"*the establishment of the State's policy must be seen as the result of the
class contradictions inscribed in the very structure of the State.*" [78]
    Second, as Quadagno points out in a more specific manner, Skocpol's
analysis of the southern role in Social Security does not make a case

for the general autonomy of the state. Quadagno finds that the "local interests" institutionalized in Congress have an underlying "economic dimension." According to Quadagno, the corporate liberals' lack of congressional success on an unemployment program reflected that institution's segmented class linkages to nonmonopoly capital and to southern landlords. Quadagno thus points to the same scenario as exemplifying the way in which "economic power" is "translated into political power through the direct intervention of corporate liberals and through a hierarchical structure of the state, which allows competing factions to petition state managers for direct agendas in social policy." [79] Quadagno's Poulantzian analysis is only marginally distinguished from Domhoff's power-structure analysis on the grounds that "corporate liberalism underestimates the weight other [nonmonopoly] power blocs carry." [80] Consequently, it is not at all clear to what degree organizational realism actually offers a conceptual or an empirical challenge to existing Marxist and neo-Marxist theories.

However, even if one accepts Skocpol's interpretation of the original Social Security legislation, subsequent analyses of the program's historical development raise fundamental problems about organizational realism's key explanatory concept (i.e., state strength). In a recent follow-up to their earlier research, Weir, Orloff, and Skocpol note that once the Social Security Act was adopted "further social policy innovations were often generated from 'within the state' itself." [81] These authors observe that the U.S. Social Security program was subsequently "expanded to encompass virtually the entire wage and salaried population, and was also extended into related programmatic areas such as disability insurance and medicare for the elderly." What is both important and consistent with organizational realism is their argument that "these developments were primarily propelled by the Social Security administrators themselves, as they adroitly deployed bureaucratic resources to manage public and expert opinion, to sooth congressional committees, and to prepare new legislative proposals for passage at opportune political conjunctures." [82]

The explanatory paradox in accepting this scenario is that Weir, Orloff, and Skocpol now conclude that the Social Security Administration was enormously effective despite being a weak state organization with very little bureaucratic capacity or technical expertise. The agency has pursued an effective social policy, not because it developed a reservoir of internal policy expertise or a large professional bureaucracy, but because the design of the Social Security program involves "nothing more than collecting taxes from employers, keeping updated individual records, and putting a check in the mail."[83] In other words, Social Security was effective in achieving its policy objectives because its programmatic design required only weak administrative capacities and virtually no technical capacity for direct social intervention. If this analytic narrative is correct, then the development of the U.S. Social Security Administration suggests a serious flaw in organizational realism's analytic framework, because it unhinges the assumed linkage between a strong state and an autonomous or effective state. More to the point, if a weak state can be as effective as a strong state, and be so on the scale of the U.S. Social Security program, then one must certainly question the utility of the strong state–weak state dichotomy.

The theoretical implications of Skocpol and Finegold's persuasive comparison of the Agricultural Adjustment Act (AAA) and National Industrial Recovery Act (NIRA) are equally ambiguous. First, in the study alluded to above, Skocpol and Finegold failed to mention Finegold's earlier study in which he found that, despite loud cries for state intervention from farmers during the 1920s and the willingness of government agricultural officials to intervene at that time, big business successfully vetoed interventionist measures throughout the decade.[84] After 1929, however, the intensification of the U.S. agricultural depression when coupled with a general economic downturn "proved an economic danger to big business as well, since the continued weakness of rural purchasing power served as a barrier to industrial recovery."[85] Only then did political avenues open up for government experts to launch an interventionist agricultural policy. Finegold thus concludes separately from Skocpol that the negative veto power of big business insured that the AAA "addressed the problem of farmer prosperity without challenging the position of the dominant class interests within agriculture."[86] Therefore, even in this case, it is a highly problematic venture to establish historically to what degree the U.S. state acted autonomously of the negative structural constraints of capital. In fact, the exercise of a negative veto by big business is compatible with either a structuralist or a sophisticated instrumentalist approach to agricultural policy.

At the same time, George E. Paulsen has also recently suggested that the NRA was "doomed from its inception," though for reasons different from those offered by Skocpol and Finegold.[87] Although the program did eventually bog down in administrative confusion, as Skocpol and Finegold contend, according to Paulsen its failure was more deeply rooted in the NRA's inability to secure the cooperation of big business. Paulsen's study finds that once businessmen understood "that the prohibitions against unfair trade practices would be stringently enforced . . . business leaders lost all interest in the voluntary agreements and NRA-supervised cooperative self-regulation."[88] Consequently, one can again argue from either a structuralist or instrumentalist perspective that big business support was crucial (if only indirectly) to the success of the AAA and damned to failure the initiatives of the NRA.

Furthermore, regarding the AAA, even if one accepts the idea that policy experts acted autonomously, Skocpol and Finegold's theoretical conclusions about the meaning of that autonomy are suspect. Skocpol and Finegold's theoretical conclusions about the meaning of that autonomy are suspect. Skocpol and Finegold's case for USDA autonomy is based on the observation that the programs initiated by government policy experts went beyond the immediate demands of commercial farmers, not against them. In other words, as Paul Cammack notes in a recent review, "during the phase of recognizable state autonomy the efforts of the state were directed wholeheartedly to furthering the interest of the capitalist class concerned," that is, large commercial farmers.[89] If anything, therefore, the USDA's autonomy is more plausibly an instance of the state acting as an "ideal collective capitalist." In fact, Skocpol and Finegold suggest this conclusion themselves in one passage where they observe that the USDA "proved much more successful in organizing commercial farmers for their own collective good than did the NRA at organizing industrial capitalists."[90] Moreover, as Cammack further points out, "this much-vaunted phase lasted in any case only for a couple of years, whereupon the commercial farmers took it [i.e., the USDA] over."[91]

Consequently, it is not clear where one goes with these or similar case studies in terms of a theory of the state. The new institutionalist research does seem to demonstrate that formal processes institutionalized in the state must be taken into account as part of any Marxian theorizing about the state.[92] In that respect, it is a useful conceptual and methodological corrective to the continuing prevalence of analytic and deductive strategies. However, it is still far from clear that one should completely abandon theorizing on a grand scale as demanded by organizational realists. Indeed, the difficulties of trying to sort out what proportion of a particular piece of legislation can be explained by business-dominance variables as opposed to state-centered or class-struggle variables are far from being solved.[93] Block has even suggested skeptically that "the closer the debate comes to actual empirical case studies, the more sterile and less informative it becomes."[94]

Furthermore, the entire effort to sort out state-level and society-level variables is ultimately somewhat arbitrary, because, as Block notes further, "state and society are interdependent and interpenetrate in a multitude of different ways."[95] Yet, the concept of an autonomous state depends to a considerable degree on the ability to distinguish analytically between the state and civil society, that is, between state actors and class actors. Bob Jessop has pointed out critically that in order to be constituted as an autonomous organization, the state must exhibit clear frontiers or boundaries between itself and other institutional orders.[96] However, there are any number of political (or politicized) private institutions "located on the uncertain boundary between society and the state." Although this condition has always prevailed to some extent, many would argue that the boundaries of the state in late capitalism have become increasingly blurred by the proliferation of parastatal organizations such as public enterprises and by extrastatal political institutions such as parties, interest groups, and professional associations, by a mass media that relies increasingly on "government sources," by foundations and other service agencies that implement state policies, and by corporate planning organizations that formulate state policies. On this point, Timothy Mitchell has insightfully argued that the distinction between state and society is not an intrinsic organizational boundary, but is in one sense an artificial conceptual line that is "drawn *within* an unbroken network of institutional mechanisms through which a certain social and political order is maintained."[97] Furthermore, these boundaries are created simultaneously as an effect of political struggle and by our theoretical discourses about the state.

In addition, by relinquishing the idea that there are firm external boundaries to the state, it becomes possible to resolve the paradox of a weak state pursuing effective social policies as in the case of the U.S. Social Security program. Rather than viewing state strength merely as the ability to exert coercive powers *against* particular classes, it should be recognized that state organizations may enhance their capacities for effective action by working cooperatively *with* key private organizations in civil society.[98] The effect of such a strategy is to greatly enhance state capacities *de facto* without actually penetrating civil society and despite an otherwise weak institutional design. Thus, by acting to mobilize and coordinate private associations, the state can enhance its infrastructural capacities and its policy effectiveness by drawing on the personnel, expertise, financial resources, and communicative networks of existing organizations.[99]

Finally, the ambiguity in the boundaries of the state concept is compounded by the analytic requirement that, for political authority to achieve stateness, there must be a relative unity to the apparatuses exercising that authority within the boundaries of what we call the state.[100] However, as a result of its internal development and expansion during the twentieth century, Poggi argues that it is now "totally unrealistic . . . to conceive the state as making up *an* organization," as suggested in the definitions profered by Skocpol, Skowronek, and others.[101] In fact, their emphasis on the unevenness of state development suggests a research agenda in which it is possible to talk about organizations that wield state powers, but in which one cannot any longer talk realistically about *the* state or *a* state.

Quite the contrary, as Poggi observes, examining only the state's administrative apparatus makes it painfully evident that the state is now a vast, diverse, and complex organizational matrix consisting of largely independent units. These independent units of authority (e.g., agencies and bureaus) are often strongly insulated from effective central control, routinely engage in competition among themselves, and frequently form coalitions with one another in order to evade and resist higher-level guidance. There is a marked tendency for the state's diverse organizations to seek and to establish a growing distance between themselves as units of authority and any ostensible unitary center.[102] At the same time, as has frequently been mentioned in the text, individual state organizations often establish close, privileged relationships with organized social interests, or, conversely, these same administrative units become bridgeheads for organized social interests within the state apparatus. When these two tendencies emerge in tandem (i.e., when the state's individual organizations separate from their center and link to organized interests), there is a resulting tendency for "contemporary state structures to regress toward political arrangements similar to those preceding the emergence or the maturity of the state."[103] This emerging political arrangement might best be described in terms reminiscent of the fragmented political authority in feudalism, in which there are no boundaries between political authority and civil society and where the units of authority have limited coherence and no central coordination. We could well be witnessing the disintegration of the state as a form of institutionalized political authority, at least as it has heretofore been understood in the modern era.

CHAPTER SIX

The Antinomies of Marxist Political Theory

The inability of any one approach to carve out a dominant position effectively in contemporary critical theory establishes an insurmountable end point for this text. It is my contention that critical theory should be viewed as a matrix of logical antinomies yielding five distinct approaches to the state: instrumentalism, structural functionalism, derivationism, systems analysis, and organizational realism. Moreover, as I have attempted to illustrate in previous chapters, this typological matrix can be grounded in a comparative analysis of explanatory logics while reproducing more accurately the historical development of critical theory.[1]

The five theoretical approaches constituting this typology can be viewed for comparative purposes as occupying specific points along an analytic and a methodological axis. The analytic axis of Marxian political theory rests on its stipulation that the object of inquiry is a conceptual understanding of the state-capital relation. The existence of a theoretical nexus between the state and the capitalist class has typically been a controlling axiom in Marxian political theory. The hypothesized relationship between state and capital is posited as the basis for a theory of the state insofar as this relationship infuses state policies and institutions with a capitalist "class content." Thus, the state-capital relation is approached as the theoretical basis for a state that broadly serves the interests of the capitalist class. However, given this axiom, critical theories of the state diverge in their answers to two complementary questions: (1) How does the state realize the interests of the capitalist class? (2) Why does the state serve the interests of the capitalist class?[2]

As a general proposition, the answer to the first question is fairly simple. The state realizes class interests through public policies and through specific institutional arrangements of the state apparatus. Where the state succeeds in realizing capitalist-class interests, there is a *conjuncture* between state and capital.[3] Where the state fails to realize the interests of the capitalist class, there is a *disjuncture* in the state-capital relation. Figure 6.1 posits the policy antinomies of a conjunctural and disjunctural state as the logical end points of an analytic axis.

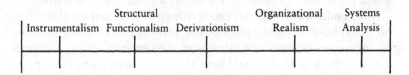

Figure 6.1. Theories of the state arranged on a state-capital axis

The five theories of the state identified earlier are positioned on this axis on the basis of their hypothetical assumptions about how well the state actually achieves the policy conjunctures necessary to maintain capitalist society. Hence, instrumentalist theory is positioned at a point on the analytic axis that is fundamentally conjunctural, that is, as a hypothetical position which argues that the general interests of the capitalist class are realized by the state. Systems-analytic theory is positioned at a point on the analytic axis that is fundamentally disjunctural, that is, as a position in which the state systematically fails to realize the general interests of the capitalist class. Derivationist theory occupies an ambiguous and unstable midpoint that emphasizes the problem of partial realization failures.

The problem of why the state serves or fails to serve the interests of the capitalist class is the point at which the analytic axis of Marxian theories intersects the methodological axis of social scientific research. The methodological axis not only specifies why the state realizes the interests of the capitalist class; in doing so, it also specifies the kind of theoretical and empirical research that is necessary to support particular explanations of the state-capital relation. Yet, Anthony Giddens observes that contemporary social science methodology has typically ben polarized between the antinomies of "action" and "structure."[4] Marxian explanations of the state-capital relation are no exception to this general rule, but are similarly grounded in competing logics of action and structure.[5]

Action theories involve a form of explanation that refers to continuous flows of conduct attributable to historical subjects. In the case of critical theory, the most important historical subjects (or actors) are hypothesized to be "classes" and "state elites." Classes and state elites, by their stream of actual or contemplated conduct, are said to "cause" events such as policy conjunctures and disjunctures.[6] Moreover, as Giddens notes, since action must always refer to the individual or collective activities of an identifiable agent, action can be fully elucidated only within historically located modes of activity, for example, within this or that particular capitalist society during a particular time frame.[7]

As a result, action theories necessarily emphasize empirical and historical explanations of the state-capital relation. Furthermore, since the reconstruction of particular streams of class or state action presumes that the identified agents could have acted otherwise at any given point in time, state-capital relations are always hypothesized as logically indeterminate and empirically or historically contingent. This means that even where a hypothesized relationship between state and capital is "verified" through policy or institutional research, such instances offer only particular cases of that relationship.[8]

Therefore, the logic of social action must rely on an inductive process of theory-building. Theory construction takes place primarily through the accumulation of case studies of public policy and institutional behavior that are designed to test particular hypotheses. The historical analysis of case studies in a particular country enables the theorist to establish a continuous flow of conduct by that country's active classes and state elites. In this manner, the theorist can identify historical *patterns* of class action in particular capitalist states. Patterns of class action that establish a relationship between classes and state elites are called political processes. Finally, the comparative analysis of political processes across capitalist societies offers the potential, though by no means the certainty, that one may develop a theory of the state in capitalist society.[9] The inductive process of theory-building proceeds from the formulation of hypotheses to policy and institutional case studies, to empirical generalizations about political processes, and finally to the possible development of theory.[10]

Consequently, the notion of a theory of the state in capitalist society is an important outcome of this methodological approach to the state. The logic of any explanation that relies on historical class action from the outset precludes any possibility for a theory of the capitalist state, namely, a state that of necessity must be capitalist in its class content. Instead, explanations are restricted to the reconstruction of a state-capital relation in which class agency is viewed as an "external" cause acting on the state to produce public policies.[11]

On the other hand, some Marxian analyses rely on the structural properties of social systems to explain the state-capital relation.[12] Social systems involve regularized relations of interdependence between individuals or groups, and as recurrent social practices, they exist independently of individuals and the particular historical subjects who are involved in those practices at any particular time or place. For example, nineteenth-century Great Britain and twentieth-century America are both capitalist social systems. Our ability to make this judgement is based on the assumption that the capitalist character of the system resides not in the particular groups and individuals living at that time (i.e., its historical subjects), but in certain recurrent social relationships between groups and individuals that are common to both societies. These social relationships are called structures or systems.

To the degree that structures persist across time and space despite the birth and death of particular historical subjects, they are viewed as properties of social systems that can be known independently of any historical subject. Indeed, Alex Callinicos points out that "social relations often involve regularities which occur with the agents involved in them not understanding, or even necessarily even being aware of them." [13] Thus, the logic of structural explanation is not geared toward the historical actions of empirically specifiable agents. Rather, it is the persistence of social relationships (i.e., structures) that define and distinguish different forms of social systems. Thus, these social forms must be produced and reproduced across time and space in order to maintain a particular social system. The maintenance and reproduction of these social relationships are therefore conceptualized as systemic or structural "needs" that "cause" the recurrent interaction of historical subjects. [14] Thus, as Giddens points out, in structural explanations "the state is not defined just in terms of what it does, or how it operates, but in terms of how what it does contributes to the 'needs of the system.' " [15] The interpretations of the state that are built around this conception purport to explain the state's activities through their functional indispensability or usefulness to the continued existence of the capitalist system.

A structural, or systems, explanatory logic typically leads to a deductive or analytic process of theory-building. One begins with a theoretical concept of the capitalist system defined in terms of the essential structural properties which make the system capitalist. This concept has typically been constructed through a reading of the Marxian classics. [16] Moreover, in the context of such a reading, deductive theory-construction is rooted in the assumption that certain social relationships (i.e., systemic needs) must be fulfilled in order for a system to remain a capitalist system. [17] Moreover, a further assumption is often made that all (or at least most) structures exist to fulfill some systemic need, and thus one explains such structures (e.g., the state or public policies) in terms of their objective effects in meeting these needs. Consequently, the way in which the state objectively fulfills this role is internally de-

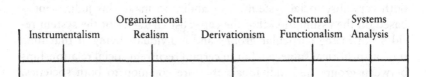

Figure 6.2. Theories of the state arranged on a methodological axis

termined by its role within the reproduction of the overall capitalist system. The state must necessarily be a capitalist state in order to fulfill its role within the system.

The five theoretical approaches to the state identified earlier are positioned on a methodological axis in figure 6.2. Instrumentalism and organizational realism occupy points on the methodological axis which tend toward an explanatory logic of action. Structural functionalism and systems analysis occupy points on the methodological axis which tend toward an explanatory logic of structure. Derivationism again occupies an ambiguous midpoint on the axis.

The analytic and methodological axes of critical theory intersect in the problem of specifying what kind of research is necessary to demonstrate (i.e., prove) which particular state-capital nexus is posited by a particular approach. The intersection of these axes yields a matrix of four distinct approaches and one hybrid (derivationism), which are defined in relation to the set of antinomies defining the end points of each axis (see figure 6.3).[18] *The ambiguity of the terrain staked out between these end points supplies the essential controversies of the Marxian paradigm.* In this respect, the Marxian paradigm of state research should be understood as an analytic constellation[19] that is not reducible to any particular set of conclusions; nor can it be identified with any single methodological approach. Instead, one must acknowledge that as a paradigm "Marxism is a complex and contradictory body of theories whose meaning is contested by a diversity of political currents."[20]

Toward an End to Metatheory

The conclusion of this analysis stands in sharp contrast with the recent efforts to construct a grand synthesis of state theory. The antinomies at the core of Marxist political theory establish an inherently disjunc-

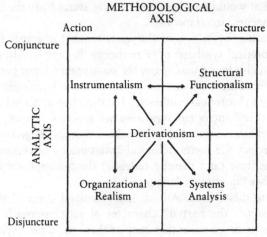

Figure 6.3. Logics of explanation

tural and pluralistic epistemological formation. Thus, although the instrumentalist and structuralist approaches are frequently in agreement along the analytic axis (i.e., they agree that the state is in conjuncture with capital), adherents of the two approaches strongly disagree on the methodological standpoint necessary to explain that conjuncture (see figure 6.3). As a result, they also strongly disagree about the logic of explanation, the type of evidence necessary to test hypotheses, and ultimately even about what counts as an "adequate" theory of the state. Conversely, the instrumentalist and organizational approaches generally agree on the logic of explanation, on what types of evidence are necessary to test hypotheses, and on the process of theory construction, but adherents of the two approaches sharply disagree along the analytic axis about whether or not "the facts" actually support a theoretical conclusion in regard to whether the state is in conjuncture (instrumentalism) or disjuncture (organizational realism) with capital.

Thus, when one adopts various positions within the matrix in figure 6.3, one finds that for every point of unity between two approaches, there is a point of disunity along some other axis. This paradigmatic structure is best described as complementary dissociation. The Marxian approaches *in toto* enable us to examine states and state policies from competing standpoints, including a consideration of the possibility that modern states might not actually be capitalist states. However, the central antinomies that separate each approach from its competitors make it impossible to achieve an epistemological vantage point within the matrix that would enable one to analyze states from the perspective of all approaches simultaneously.

Consequently, in one of the most notable attempts to establish a metatheoretical synthesis of state theory, Robert R. Alford and Roger Friedland also found that "*from the standpoint of each perspective*" one always encounters either an analytic or a methodological obstacle to achieving a theoretical synthesis.[21] For this reason, Alford and Friedland caution that "attempted syntheses are typically illusory," because in order to maintain their own internal consistency alleged syntheses must silently reject the methodological assumptions of certain approaches or reconstitute (and thereby redefine) the assumptions of competing approaches "in another language." [22]

Despite this caveat, Alford and Friedland contend that a critical awareness of "the partial" character of each approach establishes a privileged vantage point that enables them to "offer a synthetic framework for a more comprehensive theory of the state." [23] The synthetic framework developed by Alford and Friedland emulates earlier, if less elaborate, formulations by Steven Lukes and Fred Block.[24] All the authors follow a similar strategy designed to eliminate the antinomies of state theory by reconceptualizing them as separate "home domains" (Alford and Friedland), "dimensions" (Lukes), or "levels" (Block) of power. These three levels order the competing approaches hierarchically by each supplying a successively broader context in which to understand the operations of state power. Alford and Friedland refer to the home domains of each approach, and in order of their importance, as the situational, structural, and systemic forms of power.[25]

Thus, the instrumentalist approach, which they claim (incorrectly) focuses only on processes of individual decision-making, is best able to explain the concrete "political behavior of individuals and groups and the influence their interactions have on government decision-making." Organizational realism ostensibly conceptualizes a structural dimension of state power that best explains "single-state organizations, or interorganizational networks seen as constituting the state." Finally, structural functionalism and systems analysis conceptualize the macrosocial relations between capital and labor and between both classes and the state.[26]

Drawing on this framework, Alford and Friedland suggest that most disagreements between adherents of the competing approaches result primarily from exporting an approach from its home domain into other domains where a different approach is more suitable. However, as Alford and Friedland are well aware, the analytic success of such a strategy depends on the assumption that each home domain (or level of analysis) has its own potential autonomy from the other home domains. If this assumption is accepted, a successful synthesis must not only be able to understand each home domain (approach) in its own terms (and complementary dissociation is sufficient for this purpose), it must also be able to articulate a theoretical relationship between each home domain.[27] Alford and Friedland are admittedly unable to articulate the theses necessary to bridge the analytic space between their home domains or between the different levels of analysis.[28] Similarly, Alford and Friedland's strategy altogether fails to bridge the methodological antinomy, because they must concede that Marxian approaches are structured by a "division of labor between functional [i.e., structural] and political [i.e., action] approaches."[29]

In light of these shortcomings, it is necessary to emphasize that Alford and Friedland do not consider their multidimensional analytic framework a comprehensive or synthetic theory of the state. Instead, a careful reading of Alford and Friedland's analysis indicates that their "main concern is to develop a synthetic framework *out of which a new theory of the state can be constructed,*" but they never claim to have developed such a theory.[30] The most important obstacle to completing this metatheoretical agenda, as noted, is that, once the levels of analysis have been identified and described, it is still necessary to connect theoretically the different levels with each other and to explain their interrelationships in determining state power and state policy. However, it is Alford and Friedland's conclusion that to establish such connections, the state "must be charted historically and comparatively."[31]

Although pursuing a somewhat different strategy, Bob Jessop has made an equally ambitious attempt to synthesize the Marxian literature on state theory. Jessop's initial work in this direction concludes by articulating five methodological principles to be used as substantive criteria in evaluating the comparative adequacy of the competing Marxian approaches. Jessop's five methodological guidelines are reproduced in column 1 of table 6.1. Jessop concludes that in relation to these criteria no existing approach is wholly adequate for an explanation of the capitalist state. Thus, in conjunction with his methodological criteria, Jessop goes on to propose four analytic research guidelines that should be followed in his anticipated effort to construct "an adequate theoretical account of the state in capitalist society."[32] Jessop's four analytic guidelines are reproduced in column 2 of table 6.1.

These guidelines ostensibly "imply a 'relational' approach to the analysis of the state apparatus and state power" which, according to

Jessop, both draws on and supersedes (i.e., synthesizes) the insights of previous approaches.[33] In his most recent work, *State Theory*, Jessop elaborates his "strategic-relational approach" at greater length and juxtaposes it to the existing approaches with the aim of demonstrating its comparative and comprehensive analytic superiority. Jessop articulates his alleged synthesis of the literature in the form of six general theses about the modern state. Jessop's six theses are intended to "complement and build on the theoretical guidelines" established earlier. The six theses are reproduced in column 3 of table 6.1.

Despite his claims to the contrary, Jessop's theses are far from being original, because they often merely restate some basic tenets of Poulantzian structuralism, albeit without the functionalist verbiage (especially theses 1, 5, 6). Therefore, it is no accident that the theses fail to provide a genuine synthesis. For example, Jessop's fifth thesis reads: "... as an institutional ensemble the state does not (and cannot) exercise power: it is not a real subject."[34] Yet, this assertion, instead of being synthetic, is at the very heart of the methodological antinomy which separates structuralism from organizational realism and instrumentalism. Similarly, the debate over whether or not the state can (or does) ever act as an independent subject is the central analytic antinomy which separates organizational realism from instrumentalism. In this particular case, Jessop's fifth thesis cannot be regarded as synthetic, precisely because its claim is part of what structures the entire debate within state theory.

Furthermore, it is difficult to regard Jessop's theses as having any synthetic power, because they sometimes articulate claims that stand in sharp contradiction to one another. For example, it is neither logically nor historically possible to regard the state *simultaneously* as an "institutional ensemble with its own modes of calculation" (thesis 4) and as an institutional ensemble that "does not (and cannot) exercise power" (thesis 5). In the first case, the state must be viewed as a subject (which contradicts thesis 5), and in the second case the state is merely a Poulantzian arena of class struggle (in which case thesis 4 is rendered irrelevant).

Consequently, it is again important to note that Jessop's six theses do not constitute a synthesis of state theory, but instead serve merely "to bring out the more general implications of the strategic-relational approach." Jessop suggests that the most important implication of this "adequate" approach is that "research on the state should proceed in tandem with more general theoretical and empirical work on the structuration of social relations." Jessop elaborates this idea with the

Table 6.1. A metatheoretical conceptualization of the state

Methodological principles	Analytic research guidelines	General theses
A Marxist analysis of the state is adequate to the extent that 1. it is founded on the specific qualities of capitalism as a mode of production and also allows for the effects of the articulation of the CMP [capitalist mode of production] with other relations of social and/or private labor. 2. it attributes a central role in the process of capital accumulation to interaction among class forces. 3. it establishes the relations between the political and economic features of society without reducing one to the other or treating them as totally independent and autonomous. 4. it allows for historical and national differences in the forms and functions of the state in capitalist social formations. 5. it allows not only for the influence of class forces rooted in and/or relevant to non-capitalist production relations, but also for that of non-class forces.	1. The state is a set of institutions that cannot, *qua* institutional ensemble, exercise power. 2. Political forces do not exist independent of the state: they are shaped in part through its forms of representation, its internal structure, and its forms of intervention. 3. State power is a complex social relation that reflects the changing balance of social forces in a determinate conjuncture. 4. State power is capitalist to the extent that it creates, maintains, or restores the conditions required for capital accumulation in a given situation.	1. An adequate account of the state can only be developed as part of a theory of society. 2. Modern societies are so complex and differentiated that no subsystem could be structurally determinate in the last instance nor could any one organization form the apex of a singular hierarchy of command whose rule extends everywhere. 3. The state is the supreme embodiment of this paradox. It is the state that is responsible in the last instance for managing the interdependence of all subsystems. 4. The state must be analyzed both as a complex institutional ensemble with its own modes of calculation and operational procedures and as a site of political practices which seek to deploy its various institutions and capacities for specific purposes. 5. As an institutional ensemble the state does not (and cannot) exercise power: it is not a real subject. 6. The state's structural powers or capacities and their realization cannot be understood by focusing on the state alone—even assuming one could precisely define its institutional boundaries.

Sources: Of the methodological principles: Jessop, *The Capitalist State*, p. 221; of the analytic research guidelines: Jessop, *The Capitalist State*, pp. 220–28; of the general theses: Jessop, *State Theory*, pp. 365–67.

observation that Marxist state theorists need to focus their research "on the connections between state power and class domination."[35] That such generalities add to state theory is dubious, since the attempt to establish, explain, and clarify the state-capital relation theoretically is again the very basis of the entire debate within Marxist state theory. It is a bit silly to think that a mere restatement of that objective can provide the basis for a theoretical synthesis or, even less ambitiously, for a merely adequate theory of the state.

Finally, David Held and Joel Krieger have also surveyed the literature with the goal of laying the foundations for a "fruitful synthesis" of state theory. Held and Kreiger conclude their analysis by articulating eight propositions that are intended to synthesize "the most salient contributions of state theory to date, and indicate a direction for future investigations." However, as with Jessop and as with Alford and Friedland, Held and Krieger find that their eight propositions merely point out the need for more "comparative and historical analysis of state activity in parliamentary capitalist democracies."[36] In this respect, their conclusion does not differ substantially from Martin Carnoy's synthetic inference that scholars should undertake "specific historical analyses [of the state] within a set of universalistic 'rules.'"[37] The implication of such findings is that competing approaches may enable scholars to conduct theoretically informed analyses of states, but it is unlikely that anyone will be able to develop *a* theory of *the* state, or even *a* theory of *the capitalist* state.

The sparse results of the more notable attempts to generate a synthesis of state theory would seem to bear out the expectation that such efforts will not succeed in realizing their objective. Quite the contrary, the conceptual apparatus available to the Marxian paradigm and the methodological approaches to which the paradigm is wedded make it highly unlikely at this point that there can be any further theoretical discoveries of a revolutionary nature. Quite simply, all the cards have been dealt, and this is as good as the hand will get, because the conceptual and methodological antinomies of Marxism establish a bounded matrix of plural, but finite, theoretical options.

The idea that there are finite heuristic possibilities available to a paradigm is certainly inherent in Thomas Kuhn's definition of the concept. Kuhn points out that a paradigm is embraced by scholars, not because it finally solves all the problems that it poses, but because it offers a compelling "promise of success discoverable in selected and still incomplete examples" of its application.[38] Thus, once the research options generated by a particular paradigm have been clarified, "normal-scientific research is directed to the articulation of those phenomena and theories that the paradigm already supplies."[39] Kuhn refers to the research activities entailed in the normalization of a scientific paradigm as "fact-gathering."[40]

If there is any indicator of the normalizing tendencies running through contemporary critical theory, it is that the one consensus (as opposed to synthesis) among theorists of the state is the recognized need for more extensive fact-gathering. Indeed, the single common conclusion of the metatheoreticians is the call for more comparative empirical and historical research. Kuhn observes that by shifting research and investigation toward fact-gathering a normalization of science enables scholars to investigate particular phenomena, in this case the state, "in a detail and depth that would otherwise be unimaginable."[41] It is already the case that much of the more interesting work being done on the state is no longer abstract or conceptual in its orientation, but is theoretically informed fact-gathering. Thus, to suggest that the Marxian paradigm may have exhausted its available theoretical options is to imply merely that the types of state research and the paradigmatic level at which research takes place is shifting toward fact-gathering. In all likelihood this means that future theoretical confrontations will be fought as sporadic skirmishes in a phase of theory construction that Kuhn describes as "mopping-up operations." In this respect, my analysis points to a historical period in which Marxian political theory is entering an extended phase of "normal science" restricted by the conceptual and methodological boundaries established by its paradigmatic matrix.

Notes
Sources Consulted
Index

Notes

Introduction

1. For the best comprehensive treatments, see Patrick Dunleavy and Brendan O'Leary, *Theories of the State* (New York: Macmillan, 1987); Roger King, *The State in Modern Society* (Chatham, N.J.: Chatham House Publishers, 1986); Robert R. Alford and Roger Friedland, *Powers of Theory: Capitalism, the State, and Democracy* (Cambridge: Cambridge University Press, 1985).

2. Cf. Bob Jessop, *State Theory: Putting Capitalist States in Their Place* (Cambridge: Polity Press, 1990); idem, *The Capitalist State: Marxist Theories and Methods* (New York: New York University Press, 1982); Martin Carnoy, *The State and Political Theory* (Princeton: Princeton University Press, 1984).

3. I have assumed only that readers should have read selected Marxian texts of the type that any undergraduate would encounter in a course on the history of political thought, introduction to social theory, or the history of economic thought; see, for example, Robert C. Tucker, ed., *The Marx-Engels Reader*, 2nd edition (New York: W. W. Norton, 1978).

4. Stephen Bornstein, David Held, and Joel Krieger (eds., *The State in Capitalist Europe: A Casebook* [Boston: George Allen and Unwin, 1984], p. vii) complain correctly that "the literature on the state remains difficult and mystifying, obscured by an arcane specialists' jargon."

5. See Jessop, *The Capitalist State*, pp. 1–31; also, Jean-Claude Girardin, "On the Marxist Theory of the State," *Politics and Society* 5, no. 1 (1973): 193–223.

6. Bob Jessop, "Recent Theories of the Capitalist State," *Cambridge Journal of Economics* 1 (1977), p. 354: ". . . the same is true of other classical Marxist theorists, such as Engels, Lenin, Trotsky and Gramsci."

7. The best recent effort is Hal Draper, *Karl Marx's Theory of Revolution*, Vol. 1 (New York: Monthly Review Press, 1977).

8. The order of the chapters in this text closely parallels the historical development of state theory as outlined in Fred Block, *Revising State Theory* (Philadelphia: Temple University Press, 1987), chap. 1.

9. Ian Gough, *The Political Economy of the Welfare State* (London: Macmillan Press, Ltd., 1979), pp. 1–5.

10. Saundra K. Schneider, "The Sequential Development of Social Programs in the Eighteen Welfare States," *Comparative Social Research* 5 (1982), p. 195.

11. Ibid., pp. 209–13.

12. John Logue, "The Welfare State: Victim of Its Success," in Stephen R.

Graubard, ed., *The State* (New York: W. W. Norton, 1979), pp. 71–72.

13. Arthur L. Stinchcombe, "The Functional Theory of Social Insurance," *Politics and Society* 14, no. 4 (1985), pp. 423–24.

14. Tom B. Bottomore, *Classes in Modern Society* (New York: Vintage Books, 1966), chap. 3.

15. Logue, "The Welfare State," p. 77.

16. Max Weber, "The Quantitative Development of Administrative Tasks," in Hans H. Gerth and C. Wright Mills, eds., *From Max Weber: Essays in Sociology* (New York: Oxford University Press, 1946), pp. 209–11.

17. Weber, "Qualitative Changes of Administrative Tasks," in Gerth and Mills, *From Max Weber*, pp. 212–14.

18. Gough, *Political Economy of the Welfare State*, p. 1.

19. For example, Richard Bernstein, *Beyond Objectivism and Relativism* (Philadelphia: University of Pennsylvania Press, 1983).

20. Max Weber, *The Methodology of the Social Sciences* (New York: Free Press, 1949).

21. Alford and Friedland, *Powers of Theory*, p. 398.

22. Mark E. Warren, "What Is Political Theory/Philosophy?" *PS: Political Science and Politics* 22 (September 1989), p. 607.

23. Karl Mannheim, *Ideology and Utopia* (New York: Harcourt, Brace, Jovanovich, 1936).

24. W. B. Gallie, "Essentially Contested Concepts," *Proceedings of the Aristotelian Society* 56 (1955–1956): 167–98.

25. Russell L. Hanson, *The Democratic Imagination in America* (Princeton: Princeton University Press, 1985), pp. 29–30.

26. Edward W. Lehman, "The Theory of the State versus the State of Theory," *American Sociological Review* 53 (December 1988): 807–23.

27. Theda Skocpol, "The Dead End of Metatheory: Review of *Powers of Theory: Capitalism, the State, and Democracy*, by Robert R. Alford and Roger Friedland," *Contemporary Sociology* 16 (1987): 10–12.

28. John Gray, "On the Contestability of Social and Political Concepts," *Political Theory* 5, no. 3 (August 1977), p. 333; Alford and Friedland (*Powers of Theory*, p. xiii) agree that "each perspective has immediate ideological and political implications" which cannot, existentially, be separated from its central assumptions. Nevertheless, in the attempt to advance their methatheoretical project, Alford and Friedland ignore this fact and, instead, "purposely focus mainly upon the analytic potential of each" perspective.

29. Robert Grafstein, "A Realist Foundation for Essentially Contested Political Concepts," *Western Political Quarterly* 41 (March 1988), p. 26.

30. Georg Lukács, *History and Class Consciousness* (Cambridge, Mass.: M.I.T. Press, 1971), p. 1.

31. Eduard Bernstein, *Evolutionary Socialism* (New York: Schocken Books, 1961), chap. 1. This claim stands in sharp contrast to much of the structuralist literature, for example, Erik Olin Wright, *Class, Crisis and the State* (London: New Left Books, 1978), chap. 1.

32. Cf. Alex Callinicos, *Making History: Agency, Structure and Change in Social Theory* (Ithaca: Cornell University Press, 1988).

33. Paul Roth, *Meaning and Method in the Social Sciences: A Case for Methodological Pluralism* (Ithaca: Cornell University Press, 1987).

34. Brian Fay, *Social Theory and Political Practice* (London: George Allen and Unwin, 1975), p. 41. First italics are mine; second italics are in the original quote.

35. Claus Offe, *Contradictions of the Welfare State* (Cambridge, Mass.: M.I.T. Press, 1984), p. 254.

36. Alford and Friedland, *Powers of Theory*, p. 286.

Chapter 1. Plain Marxism: The Instrumentalist Approach

1. The term "plain marxism" was introduced by C. Wright Mills, *The Marxists* (New York: Dell, 1962), p. 98, as a self-description. It has been applied more recently to scholars such as G. William Domhoff, Gabriel Kolko, Ralph Miliband, and Maurice Zeitlin. See G. William Domhoff, *The Power Elite and the State* (New York: Aldine de Gruyter, 1990), p. 14; and Maurice Zeitlin, *The Large Corporation and Contemporary Classes* (New Brunswick: Rutgers University Press, 1989), p. 47, for recent uses of the term. The term is used here to describe scholars employing the method of power structure research.

2. Paul Sweezy, *The Theory of Capitalist Development* (New York: Monthly Review Press, 1942), p. 243.

3. G. William Domhoff, *Who Really Rules?* (New Brunswick: Transaction, 1978), chap. 4.

4. Robert A. Dahl, *Polyarchy* (New Haven: Yale University Press, 1971), pp. 82ff.

5. The reader is referred to Steven Lukes, *Power: A Radical View* (London: Macmillan Press, Ltd., 1974), for a lucid treatment of the problem. Lukes suggests that "an attribution of the exercise of power involves, among other things, the double claim that A acts (or fails to act) in a certain way and that B does what he would not otherwise do" as a consequence of A's act (or failure to act) (p. 41).

6. The classic model for reputational analysis is Floyd Hunter, *Community Power Structure* (Chapel Hill: University of North Carolina Press, 1953).

7. G. William Domhoff, *The Higher Circles: The Governing Class in America* (New York: Vintage Books, 1970), pp. 9–32.

8. Domhoff has repeatedly emphasized that the *methodology* of power structure research "is beholden to no theory about the dynamics of history or the structure of society or the future of man"; *Who Rules America?* (Englewood Cliffs, N.J.: Prentice-Hall, 1967), p. 2. Indeed, its recent intellectual history as a social science methodology is tied more closely to the works of Max Weber than directly to Marx, see Domhoff, *Who Really Rules?* pp. 140–45.

9. See Robert A. Dahl, *Who Governs? Democracy and Power in an Ameri-*

164   Notes to Pages 15–18

can City (New Haven: Yale University Press, 1961), for an example of pluralist power structure research.

10. Karl Marx, *Capital*, Vol. 1, trans. Samuel Moore and Edward Aveling (New York: Modern Library, 1906), pp. 81–161, 671–710, respectively.

11. For example, see Karl Polanyi, *The Great Transformation* (Boston: Beacon Press, 1949).

12. Robert A. Dahl, *A Preface to Economic Democracy* (New Haven: Yale University Press, 1985), pp. 54–55.

13. Marx's summary of the General Law is: "With the increasing mass of wealth which functions as capital, accumulation increases the concentration of wealth in the hands of individual capitalists." *Capital*, Vol. 1, p. 685.

14. Ralph Miliband, *The State in Capitalist Society* (New York: Basic Books, 1969), p. 23.

15. David A. Gold, Clarence Y. H. Lo, and Erik Olin Wright, "Recent Developments in Marxist Theories of the Capitalist State, Part I," *Monthly Review* 27, no. 5 (October 1975), p. 32.

16. Miliband, *State in Capitalist Society*, p. 23.

17. G. William Domhoff, *Who Rules America?* p. 4; cf. Robert A. Dahl, "A Critique of the Ruling Elite Model," *American Political Science Review* 52 (1958): 463–69.

18. Gardiner C. Means, *The Structure of the American Economy* (Washington, D.C.: GPO, 1939); Edward S. Mason, *Economic Concentration and the Monopoly Problem* (New York: Atheneum, 1964), chap. 1; Richard C. Edwards, Michael Reich, and Thomas E. Weisskopf, eds., *The Capitalist System*, 2nd edition (Englewood Cliffs, N.J.: Prentice-Hall, 1978), chap. 4.

19. Paul A. Baran and Paul M. Sweezy, *Monopoly Capital: An Essay on the American Economic and Social Order* (New York: Monthly Review Press, 1966).

20. Beth Mintz, "United States of America," in Tom Bottomore and Robert J. Brym, eds., *The Capitalist Class: An International Study* (Washington Square, N.Y.: New York University Press, 1989), p. 208. I have dispensed with the obligatory rejoinder to the managerial thesis. It is now well established that its theoretical claims were never anything but a "pseudofact." For evidence, I refer readers to Maurice Zeitlin, "Corporate Ownership and Control: The Large Corporation and the Capitalist Class," *American Journal of Sociology* 79, no. 5 (1974): 1073–119. Likewise, see the excellent summary of the literature by Michael Useem, *The Inner Circle: Large Corporations and the Rise of Business Political Activity in the U.S. and U.K.* (Oxford: Oxford University Press, 1984), pp. 29–33.

21. G. William Domhoff, *The Powers That Be: Processes of Ruling Class Domination in America* (New York: Vintage Books, 1979), p. 4.

22. See Miliband, *State in Capitalist Society*, pp. 15–19, for a more detailed analytic summary of U.S. class structure.

23. Grant McConnell, *Private Power and American Democracy* (New York: Alfred A. Knopf, 1966).

24. Mintz, "United States of America," p. 207.

25. Baran and Sweezy, *Monopoly Capital*, p. 17. There is an extensive sociological literature on interlocking directorates. For state-of-the-art research see Gene Johnson and Beth Mintz, eds., *Networks of Power: Organizational Actors at the National, Corporate, and Community Levels* (New York: Aldine, 1988); Beth Mintz and Michael Schwartz, *The Power Structure of American Business* (Chicago: University of Chicago Press, 1985).

26. Mintz, "United States of America," p. 214.

27. Frans Stokman, Rolf Ziegler, and John Scott, eds., *Networks of Corporate Power* (Cambridge: Polity Press, 1984); Mark Mizruchi, *The American Corporate Network: 1904–1975* (Beverly Hills: Sage Publications, 1982); Johnannes Pennings, *Interlocking Directorates* (San Francisco: Jossey-Bass, 1980).

28. Michael Schwartz, ed., *The Structure of Power in America* (New York and London: Holmes and Meier, 1987), pp. 5–6. Also see Thomas Koenig, Robert Gogel, and Hohn Sonquist, "Models of the Significance of Interlocking Corporate Directorates," *American Journal of Economics and Sociology* 38 (1979): 178–83; David Palmer, "On the Significance of Interlocking Directorates," *Social Science History* 7 (1983): 781–96.

29. Michael Soref, "The Finance Capitalists," in Maurice Zeitlin, ed., *Classes, Class Conflict, and the State* (Cambridge, Mass.: Winthrop, 1980), pp. 60–82.

30. David Kotz, *Bank Control of Large Corporations in the United States* (Berkeley and Los Angeles: University of California Press, 1978). The explanation for this pattern of intercorporate dominance is that banks, insurance companies, and securities firms are able to monopolize avenues of access to capital and capital management. Hence, the less able a nonfinancial corporation is to meet its capital requirements internally, the more dependent it will be on the financial sector. This dependence will be reflected not only through interlocking directors but also in patterns of securities underwriting, bond holdings, stock ownership, asset management relations, and commercial banking relations between the financial and nonfinancial sector. See Robert Fitch and Mary Oppenheimer, "Who Rules the Corporations?" *Socialist Revolution* 1 (1970): no. 4: 73–107; no. 5: 61–114; no. 6: 33–93. As a result of their centralizing role in the capitalist economy, it has often been hypothesized that banks and insurance companies inherently tend to pursue policies that are consonant with the classwide interest of capital. See David M. Kotz, "Finance Capital and Corporate Control," in Richard C. Edwards, Michael Reich, and Thomas E. Weisskopf, eds., *The Capitalist System*, 2nd edition (Englewood Cliffs, N.J.: Prentice-Hall, 1978), pp. 147–58.

31. For an analysis of the single most powerful group, see James C. Knowles, "The Rockefeller Financial Group," in Ralph L. Andreano, ed., *Supercon-centration/Supercorporation*, Module 343, pp. 1–59 (Andover, Mass.: Warner Modular Publications, 1973).

32. Means, *Structure of the American Economy*, pp. 162–63.

33. As a mechanism of intra-class cohesion, the empirical structure of financial groups also suggests three lines of division and conflict within finance capital. There are splits between the financial and non-financial sector, competition between financial groups, and, overlapping with the second division, inter-regional rivalries.

34. Mintz, "United States of America," pp. 217, 218.

35. Schwartz, ed., *The Structure of Power in America*, p. 4.

36. Social status is designated by "every typical component of the life fate of men that is determined by a specific, positive, or negative, social estimation of honor"; Max Weber, "Class, Status, and Party," in Hans H. Gerth and C. Wright Mills, eds., *From Max Weber: Essays in Sociology* (New York: Oxford University Press, 1946), pp. 186–87. As Weber notes, one must hypothesize the analytic separation of economic and social indicators, because property ownership "is not always recognized as a status qualification" or as the only status qualification, even though "in the long run it is, and with extraordinary regularity" (p. 187).

37. Useem, *The Inner Circle*, p. 13.

38. Frank Ackerman, Howard Birnbaum, James Wetzler, and Andrew Zimbalist, "The Extent of Income Inequality in the United States," in Richard C. Edwards, Michael Reich, Thomas E. Weisskopf, eds., *The Capitalist System*, 1st edition (Englewood Cliffs, N.J.: Prentice-Hall, 1972), pp. 211, 209.

39. For figures on the 1980s see U.S. Department of Commerce, Bureau of the Census, *Household Wealth and Ownership* (Washington, D.C.: GPO, 1984); Robert B. Avery and Gregory E. Elliehausen, "Financial Characteristics of High-Income Families," *Federal Reserve Bulletin* 72, no. 3 (March 1986): 163–77.

40. E. Digby Baltzell, *Philadelphia Gentlemen: The Making of a National Upper Class* (New Brunswick: Transaction Publishers, 1989).

41. Domhoff, *Who Rules America?* pp. 16–21; idem, *The Higher Circles*, pp. 9–110.

42. Mintz, "United States of America," p. 210.

43. Useem, *The Inner Circle*, p. 13.

44. Domhoff, *The Higher Circles*, chap. 4.

45. Domhoff, *Who Rules America?* pp. 17–18.

46. Ibid., pp. 19–23; Domhoff, *The Higher Circles*, pp. 24–27; idem, *The Bohemian Grove and Other Retreats: A Study in Ruling-Class Cohesiveness* (New York: Harper and Row, 1974).

47. Domhoff, *The Powers That Be*, pp. 11–12.

48. Miliband, *State in Capitalist Society*, p. 49.

49. Domhoff, *The Powers That Be*, p. 12. The claim by Fred Block ("The Ruling Class Does Not Rule: Notes on the Marxist Theory of the State," *Socialist Revolution* 7, no. 3 [1977], p. 7) that instrumentalist theory "ignores the ideological role of the state" is simply incorrect. Cf. Alan Stone, "Modern Capitalism and the State: How Capitalism Rules," *Monthly Review* 23, no. 1 (May 1971): 31–36.

50. Miliband, *State in Capitalist Society*, p. 54.

51. Ibid., p. 68.

52. In fact, G. William Domhoff ("The Wagner Act and Theories of the State: A New Analysis Based on Class-Segment Theory," *Political Power and Social Theory* 6 [1987]: 159–85) uses power structure analysis to explain an instance, the Wagner Act, in which the state did successfully act against the interests of the capitalist class.

53. See ibid., chap. 2.

54. G. William Domhoff, "Corporate-Liberal Theory and the Social Security Act: A Chapter in the Sociology of Knowledge," *Politics and Society* 15, no. 3 (1986–87): 318. The article is reprinted in idem, *The Power Elite and the State*, chap. 3.

55. Miliband, *State in Capitalist Society*, p. 54.

56. Domhoff, "Corporate-Liberal Theory and the Social Security Act," p. 319.

57. Miliband, *State in Capitalist Society*, p. 55.

58. In the same passage, Miliband notes that capitalists "have never constituted, and do not constitute now, more than a relatively small minority of the state elite as a whole." Ibid., p. 59.

59. Ibid., pp. 56, 48. For recent evidence, see James W. Riddlesperger, Jr., and James D. King, "Elitism and Presidential Appointments," *Social Science Quarterly* 70 (December 1989): 902–10; Richard Zweigenhaft, "Who Represents America?" *Insurgent Sociologist* (Spring, 1975): 119–30; Peter Freitag, "The Cabinet and Big Business," *Social Problems* 23 (1975): 137–52. For historical data see, Beth Mintz, "The President's Cabinet, 1897–1972: A Contribution to the Power Structure Debate," *Insurgent Sociologist* 5 (1975): 131–48.

60. Barbara Ehrenreich and John Ehrenreich, "The Professional Managerial Class," *Radical America* 11 (March–April 1977): 7–31. Ralph Miliband ("State Power and Class Interests," *New Left Review* 138 [March–April 1983], p. 60) elsewhere points to this distinction by noting that the concept of the state "refers to certain people who are in charge of the executive power of the state—presidents, prime ministers, their cabinets, and their top civilian and military advisers."

61. Miliband, *State in Capitalist Society*, p. 119.

62. This problem is particularly acute, for the state "does not, as such, exist" in Miliband's view. Instead, the state is merely an analytic concept that "stands for . . . a number of particular institutions"; ibid., p. 49. This rendition raises serious problems that I think are best resolved through an appeal to corporate liberal historiography. Otherwise, the state deconstructs into an artificial epistemic unity, namely, an ideal type that is externally imposed on disjointed institutions as a necessary condition for understanding them as a coherent historical agent. If so, then studies of individual institutions may well be the proper course for state research. However, as a regularized research practice such an approach would likely yield to a cumulative deconstruction of the state concept.

168   Notes to Pages 29–33

63. Ibid., pp. 72, 75.

64. Block, "The Ruling Class Does Not Rule," p. 10; Ralph Miliband, "State Power and Class Interests," p. 12.

65. David N. Smith, *Who Rules the Universities?* (New York: Monthly Review Press, 1974).

66. Miliband, *State in Capitalist Society*, pp. 120, 123. Domhoff (*Who Rules America?* p. 18) echoes the view that in the United States certain elite institutions such as Harvard, Yale, Princeton, and Columbia "have been absolutely essential in the training of the lawyers, physicians, and intellectuals of the upper class."

67. G. William Domhoff ("State Autonomy and the Privileged Position of Business: An Empirical Attack on a Theoretical Fantasy," *Journal of Political and Military Sociology* 14 [Spring, 1986]: 149–62) correctly argues that such criticisms seem to imply that most scholars have never read more than the first half of Miliband's *State in Capitalist Society*, or ever opened a single book of Domhoff's written after *Who Rules America?*

68. Domhoff, *Who Rules America?* p. 11.

69. Domhoff, *The Powers That Be*, chap. 2. The necessity of pursuing these short-term interests might be explained by the tendency for the rate of profit to fall, particularly in the mature industries of the monopoly sector which have a greater organic composition of capital. This would explain why industries persistently need to seek government protections, exemptions, tax loopholes, and subsidies.

70. Ibid., pp. 26–27.

71. Ibid., p. 53.

72. Ibid., p. 36.

73. Ibid., p. 53.

74. Ibid., p. 46.

75. Murray Edelman, *The Symbolic Uses of Politics* (Urbana: University of Illinois Press, 1976), p. 24.

76. Domhoff (*The Powers That Be*, p. 57) suggests that one might consider "that the sum total of the activities of the special interests *is* class rule." It is possible that special interest pluralism is the political form of class domination characteristic of late capitalism. However, that seems to be too easy and straightforward an answer for most Marxists.

77. McConnell, *Private Power and American Democracy*, pp. 254, 292, 339.

78. Block, "The Ruling Class Does Not Rule," p. 9.

79. Domhoff, *The Powers That Be*, p. 61.

80. Ibid., p. 13. Alvin Gouldner (*The Future of Intellectuals and the Rise of the New Class* [New York: Continuum, 1979], p. 31) notes that, "for the most part, classes themselves do not enter into active political struggle; the active participants in political struggle are usually organizations, parties, associations, vanguards. Classes are cache areas in which these organizations mobilize, re-

cruit, and conscript support and in whose name they legitimate their struggle."

81. Domhoff, *The Higher Circles*, pp. 207–18, 248; idem, *The Powers That Be*, pp. 61–127.

82. Block, "The Ruling Class Does Not Rule," p. 6.

83. Nicos Poulantzas, *State, Power, Socialism* (London: Verso, 1980), pp. 12–13.

84. Useem, *The Inner Circle*, p. 114.

85. Block (*Revising State Theory*) remains unconvinced by this model. Block offers the alternative interpretation that business involvement in major policy reforms could be "a form of damage control; businesspeople are trying to win small concessions on policy proposals that they oppose but are unable to block" (p. 191 fn. 23).

86. Domhoff, *The Powers That Be*, pp. 117–18.

87. Francis Fox Piven and Richard A. Cloward, *Poor People's Movements: Why They Succeed, How They Fail* (New York: Vintage Books, 1977).

88. For example, see G. William Domhoff's analysis of business opposition to the Employment Act of 1946 in *The Power Elite and the State*, chap. 7.

89. Michael Shalev, "The Social Democratic Model and Beyond: Two 'Generations' of Comparative Research on the Welfare State," *Comparative Social Research* 6 (1983): 315–50. Shalev observes that most "income maintenance programs institutionalize links between employment and income (insurance systems) and between labor market status and income (earnings-related benefits), and insofar as they are financed non-progressively and preferably regressively, capital may actually find them beneficial, especially if their purpose is to shield labor from financial risks for which compensation might otherwise be demanded from employers and which in the absence of such a shield might generate discontent with the market system" (p. 325).

90. Miliband, *State in Capitalist Society*, pp. 146–78; Miliband, "State Power and Class Interests," pp. 65–66.

91. Richard M. Titmuss, "The Social Division of Welfare," in his *Essays on the Welfare State* (London: George Allen and Unwin, 1958), pp. 34–55.

92. Walter Korpi, "Social Policy and Distributional Conflict in the Capitalist Democracies: A Preliminary Comparative Framework," *West European Politics* 3 (October 1980), pp. 302–3. The philosophy of corporate liberalism is reconstructed in Martin J. Sklar, *The Corporate Reconstruction of American Capitalism, 1890–1916: The Market, the Law, and Politics* (Cambridge: Cambridge University Press, 1988); R. Jeffrey Lustig, *Corporate Liberalism: The Origins of Modern American Political Theory, 1890–1920* (Berkeley and Los Angeles: University of California Press, 1982); also, Joel H. Spring, *Education and the Rise of the Corporate State* (Boston: Beacon Press, 1972), chap. 1.

93. Korpi, "Social Policy," pp. 302–3.

94. Ibid., p. 299.

95. James Weinstein, *The Corporate Ideal in the Liberal State: 1900–1918* (Boston: Beacon Press, 1968), p. ix.

96. David Horowitz, *The Fate of Midas and Other Essays* (San Francisco: Ramparts Press, 1973), p. 105.

97. Domhoff, *The Powers That Be*, p. xiv.

98. Frances Fox Piven and Richard A. Cloward, *Regulating the Poor: The Functions of Public Welfare* (New York: Vintage Books, 1971), p. xiii.

99. Spring, *Education and the Rise of the Corporate State*, p. xii.

100. Clyde W. Barrow, *Universities and the Capitalist State: Corporate Liberalism and the Reconstruction of American Higher Education, 1894–1928* (Madison: University of Wisconsin Press, 1990).

101. Gosta Esping-Andersen, *Politics against Markets: The Social Democratic Road to Power* (Princeton: Princeton University Press, 1985).

102. Korpi, "Social Policy," p. 307.

103. Shalev, "The Social Democratic Model," p. 319.

104. Korpi, "Social Policy," p. 309.

105. Michael Shalev and Walter Korpi, "Working Class Mobilization and American Exceptionalism," *Economic and Industrial Democracy* 1 (1980): 31–61.

106. Domhoff ("Corporate-Liberal Theory and the Social Security Act," p. 295) persuasively argues that instrumentalism "was misinterpreted as part of a dispute among Marxists concerning who was the most Marxist and whose theories were the most politically useful."

107. Block, *Revising State Theory*, p. 6.

108. Nicos Poulantzas, "The Problem of the Capitalist State," *New Left Review* 58 (November–December 1969), p. 70.

109. Bob Jessop, "Recent Theories of the Capitalist State," p. 361.

110. Lukes, *Power*, p. 54.

111. Block, "The Ruling Class Does Not Rule," p. 320; idem, *Revising State Theory*, pp. 9–11.

112. Theda Skocpol, "Bringing the State Back In: Strategies of Analysis in Current Research," in Peter Evans, Dietrich Rueschemeyer, and Theda Skocpol, eds., *Bringing the State Back In* (Cambridge: Cambridge University Press, 1985), p. 27.

113. Claus Offe, "Structural Problems of the Capitalist State: Class Rule and the Political System. On the Selectiveness of Political Institutions," in Klaus von Beyme, ed., *German Political Studies*, Vol. 1, (Beverly Hills: Sage Publications, 1974), p. 33.

114. Stone, "Modern Capitalism and the State," p. 32; Christopher L. Tomlins, *The State and the Unions: Labor Relations, Law and the Organized Labor Movement in America, 1880–1960* (Cambridge: Cambridge University Press, 1985), p. xiii; Theda Skocpol, "A Brief Response [to G. William Domhoff]," *Politics and Society* 15, no. 3 (1986–1987), p. 331.

115. For example, on the "new business offensive" of the 1970s and 1980s, see Joseph G. Peschek, *Policy Planning Organizations: Elite Agendas and America's Rightward Turn* (Philadelphia: Temple University Press, 1987); Kim

Moody, *An Injury to All: The Decline of American Unionism* (London: Verso, 1988), chap. 6; Thomas Byrne Edsall, *The New Politics of Inequality* (New York: W. W. Norton, 1984), chap. 3.

116. Isaac Balbus, "Modern Capitalism and the State: Ruling Elite Theory vs. Marxist Class Analysis," *Monthly Review* 23, no. 1 (May 1971): 36–46; David Vogel, "The Power of Business in America: A Reappraisal," *British Journal of Political Science* 13, no. 1 (January 1983): 19–43.

117. For example, Poulantzas (*State, Power, Socialism*, p. 13) chastises instrumentalists with the observation "that a number of state functions (e.g., social security) cannot be reduced to political domination alone."

118. See especially the works already cited by G. William Domhoff, Joseph G. Peschek, and Joel Spring, respectively.

119. Tomlins, *The State and the Unions*, p. xiii.

120. Skocpol, "A Brief Response," p. 331.

Chapter 2. Neo-Marxism: The Structuralist Approach

1. For an excellent survey of crisis theory, see James O'Connor, *The Meaning of Crisis: A Theoretical Introduction* (New York: Basil Blackwell, 1987), especially chaps 2–3.

2. Ernest Mandel, *Late Capitalism* (London: Verso, 1978), p. 474.

3. Gold, Lo, and Wright, "Recent Developments, Part I," p. 36; Dunleavy and O'Leary, *Theories of the State*, p. 218.

4. Nicos Poulantzas, *Political Power and Social Classes* (London: Verso, 1978), pp. 1–33; Simon Clarke, "Marxism, Sociology, and Poulantzas' Theory of the State," *Capital and Class* 2 (Summer, 1977): 1–31; Louis Althusser and Etienne Balibar, *Reading Capital* (London: New Left Books, 1970). Balibar observes that "the concept of the 'mode of production' and the concepts immediately related to it thus appear as the first abstract concepts whose validity is not as such limited to a given period or type of society, but on which, on the contrary, the concrete knowledge of this period and type depends" (p. 201).

5. Poulantzas, *Political Power and Social Classes*, p. 42.

6. Goran Therborn, *The Ideology of Power and the Power of Ideology* (London: Verso, 1980), p. 2; Poulantzas, *State, Power, Socialism*, pp. 28–34.

7. Each of these perspectives is elucidated, respectively, in Mandel, *Late Capitalism*; Wright, *Class, Crisis, and the State*; Samir Amin, *Unequal Development* (New York: Monthly Review Press, 1976).

8. The best summary is O'Connor, *The Meaning of Crisis*, chap. 2.

9. Thomas E. Weisskopf, "Marxian Crisis Theory and the Rate of Profit in the Postwar U.S. Economy," *Cambridge Journal of Economics* 3 (1979): 341–78.

10. Erik Olin Wright, "Alternative Perspectives in Marxist Theory of Accumulation and Crisis," in Jesse Schwartz, ed., *The Subtle Anatomy of Capitalism,*

pp. 195–231. (Santa Monica, Calif.: Goodyear Publishing Co., 1977).

11. Nicos Poulantzas, "On Social Classes," *New Left Review* 78 (March–April 1973): 27–54; Erik Olin Wright, "Class Boundaries in Advanced Capitalist Societies," *New Left Review* 98 (July–August 1976): 3–42; Wright, *Class, Crisis and the State*, chap. 2.

12. Hence, Poulantzas (*Political Power and Social Classes*, p. 15) makes the epistemological observation that "the mode of production constitutes an abstract-formal object which does not exist in the strong sense in reality . . . The only thing which really exists is a historically determined *social formation*, i.e., a social whole, in the widest sense, at a given moment in its historical existence: e.g. France under Louis Bonaparte . . . a social formation . . . presents a particular combination, a specific overlapping of several 'pure' modes of production." The best discussions are Barry Hindess and Paul Q. Hirst, *Mode of Production and Social Formation* (London: Macmillan, Ltd., 1977); Amin, *Unequal Development*, pp. 13–26; Barry Hindess and Paul Q. Hirst, *Pre-Capitalist Modes of Production* (London: Routledge and Kegan Paul, 1975), pp. 1–12.

13. Nicos Poulantzas, *Classes in Contemporary Capitalism* (London: Verso, 1978), pp. 22–23; Goran Therborn, *What Does the Ruling Class Do When It Rules?* (London: New Left Books, 1978), p. 148.

14. Poulantzas, *Political Power and Social Classes*, p. 45.

15. Ibid., p. 44; Also see Amy Beth Bridges, "Nicos Poulantzas and the Marxist Theory of the State," *Politics and Society* 2 (1973): 161–90.

16. Clarke, "Marxism, Sociology, and Poulantzas' Theory of the State," p. 18.

17. Poulantzas, *State, Power, Socialism*, p. 17.

18. Poulantzas, *Classes in Contemporary Capitalism*, p. 28.

19. Jill S. Quadagno, "Welfare Capitalism and the Social Security Act of 1935," *American Sociological Review* 49 (October 1984), p. 634.

20. Ibid.

21. Poulantzas, *Political Power and Social Classes*, p. 45.

22. Classic illustrations of this example are Samuel Bowles and Herbert Gintis, *Schooling in Capitalist America* (New York: Basic Books, 1976); Jersome Karabel and A. H. Halsey, eds., *Power and Ideology in Education* (New York: Oxford University Press, 1977); Micheal W. Apple, *Ideology and Curriculum* (London: Routledge and Kegan Paul, 1979).

23. Poulantzas, *Political Power and Social Classes*, p. 50.

24. Ibid., p. 53.

25. Ibid. For an example, see L. S. Mamut, "Questions of Law in Marx's *Capital*," in Bob Jessop, ed., *Karl Marx's Social and Political Thought: Critical Assessments*, Vol. 3 (London: Routledge, Chapman, and Hall, 1990), pp. 95–105; Paul Q. Hirst, *On Law and Ideology* (London: Macmillan Press, Ltd., 1979).

26. Poulantzas, *Political Power and Social Classes*, p. 53.

27. Ibid., p. 54.

28. Poulantzas (*Political Power and Social Classes*, p. 115 fn.) defines an institution as "a system of norms or rules which is socially sanctioned . . . On the other hand, the concept of structure covers the *organizing matrix* of institutions."

29. Gold, Lo, and Wright, "Recent Developments, Part I," p. 36 fn. Cf. Wright (*Class, Crisis and the State*, p. 11 fn.), who observes: ". . . the point of the distinction is to emphasize that there are structural mechanisms which generate immediately encountered reality, and that a Marxist social theory should be grounded in a revelation of the dynamics of those structures, not simply in a generalization about the appearance themselves."

30. Gordon L. Clark and Michael Dear, *State Apparatus: Structures of Language and Legitimacy* (Boston: Allen and Unwin, 1984), p. 41.

31. Therborn, *What Does the Ruling Class Do?* p. 148.

32. Poulantzas, *Political Power and Social Classes*, p. 104.

33. Jessop, *The Capitalist State*, p. 221.

34. Poulantzas, *Political Power and Social Classes*, pp. 52, 104, 106, 115.

35. Ibid., p. 116.

36. Therborn, *What Does the Ruling Class Do?* pp. 35, 151. Clark and Dear (*State Apparatus*, p. 45) observe that "generally speaking, the term 'state apparatus' refers to the set of institutions and organizations through which state power is exercised."

37. Poulantzas, *Political Power and Social Classes*, p. 115 fn.

38. Ibid., p. 115.

39. Jessop, *The Capitalist State*, p. 221. Indeed, Jessop argues that a key methodological guideline in formulating a Marxist theory of the state is a "firm rejection of all attempts to distinguish between 'state power' and 'class power' (whether as descriptive concepts or principles of explanation)," (p. 224).

40. Poulantzas, *Political Power and Social Classes*, p. 115. Similarly, Therborn (*What Does the Ruling Class Do?* p. 132) contends that "the state as such has no power; it is an institution where social power is concentrated and exercised." In this respect, the functional relation of the state to the structure of a social formation is the key conceptual nexus between state power and state institutions.

41. Jessop, *The Capitalist State*, pp. 223–24.

42. Poulantzas, "The Problem of the Capitalist State," p. 73.

43. King, *The State in Modern Society*, p. 77.

44. Gold, Lo, and Wright, "Recent Developments, Part I," p. 38; Block, "The Ruling Class Does Not Rule," p. 7; Clarke, "Marxism, Sociology, and Poulantzas' Theory of the State," pp. 19–20.

45. Bridges, "Nicos Poulantzas," pp. 172, 177.

46. Block, "The Ruling Class Does Not Rule," p. 15.

47. Ernest Mandel, *The Marxist Theory of the State* (New York: Pathfinder Press, 1971), pp. 16–17.

48. Bridges, "Nicos Poulantzas," p. 177.

49. Stephen L. Elkin, *City and Regime in the American Republic* (Chicago: University of Chicago, 1987), see chap. 2.

50. Charles E. Lindblom, "The Market as Prison," *Journal of Politics* 44, no. 2 (May 1982): 324–32. Furthermore, Block ("The Ruling Class Does Not Rule," p. 15) argues that because states are dependent on the overall health of the economy, instead of any one sector of it, state elites are inclined to adopt policies that represent the class interests of capital as a whole.

51. Especially see Lukes, *Power*, chap. 7.

52. Bridges, "Nicos Poulantzas," p. 173.

53. Michael H. Best and William E. Connolly, *The Politicized Economy* (Lexington, Mass.: D. C. Heath, 1976), pp. 174–75.

54. Ibid., p. 175.

55. Adam Przeworski, "Material Interest, Class Compromise, and the Transition to Socialism," *Politics and Society* 10, no. 2 (1980): 125–53.

56. Adam Przeworksi, *Capitalism and Social Democracy* (Cambridge: Cambridge University Press, 1985).

57. Lindblom, "The Market as Prison," p. 330.

58. Ralph Miliband, "The Capitalist State: Reply to Nicos Poulantzas," *New Left Review* 59 (January–February 1970), p. 57.

59. Colin Crouch, "The State, Capital, and Liberal Democracy," in Colin Crouch, ed., *State and Economy in Contemporary Capitalism* (London: Croom Helm, 1979), p. 26.

60. Roger King, "The Political Practice of the Local Capitalist Association," in Roger King, ed., *Capital and Politics* (London: Routledge and Kegan Paul, 1983), pp. 109–10.

61. Crouch, "The State, Capital, and Liberal Democracy," p. 27.

62. Block, "The Ruling Class Does Not Rule," pp. 12–14.

63. For example, see Domhoff's analysis of the Employment Act of 1946 in his "State Autonomy and the Privileged Position of Business," pp. 157–61.

64. Clark and Dear, *State Apparatus*, p. 37.

65. Poulantzas, *Political Power and Social Classes*, p. 52.

66. Dunleavy and O'Leary, *Theories of the State*, p. 249. One of the few examples to appear recently is William F. Grover, *The President as Prisoner: A Structural Critique of the Carter and Reagan Years* (Albany: SUNY Press, 1989). The chief criticism of this work is that it turned out to be "much less about the Presidency (which the author largely sees as epiphenomenal) than about how . . . choices are structured in U.S. society by the omnipresent needs of corporate capitalism"; see Bert A. Rockman, "Review of William F. Grover, *The President as Prisoner*," *American Political Science Review* 84, no. 4 (December 1990), p. 1380.

67. Poulantzas, *State, Power, Socialism*, pp. 123, 128–29.

68. In this vein, Balibar (Althusser and Balibar, *Reading Capital*, pp. 225–26) contends that the scientific method employed in *Capital* confers an axiomatic form on Marxist theory: "This suggests the possibility of an *a priori* science of the modes of production."

69. The work of Goran Therborn is, analytically speaking, a key transitional link between structuralism and the derivationist project; see, especially, Goran Therborn, "The Rule of Capital and the Rise of Democracy," *New Left Review* 103 (May–June 1977): 3–41; and idem, *What Does the Ruling Class Do?*

70. The regulationist school is most notably associated with Michel Aglietta, *A Theory of Capitalist Regulation: The U.S. Experience* (London: New Left Books, 1979); and Alain Lipietz, *Mirages and Miracles: The Crises of Global Fordism* (London: Verso, 1987). The social structure of accumulation school is generally identified with David Gordon, "Stages of Accumulation and Long Economic Cycles," in T. Hopkins and I. Wallerstein, eds., *Processes of the World System* pp. 9–45 (Beverly Hills: Sage Publications, 1980); David M. Gordon, Richard C. Edwards, and Michael Reich, *Segmented Work, Divided Workers* (Cambridge: Cambridge University Press, 1982); James O'Connor, *Accumulation Crisis* (New York: Basil Blackwell, 1984); Samuel Bowles, David M. Gordon, and Thomas E. Weisskopf, "Power and Profits: The Social Structure of Accumulation and the Profitability of the Postwar U.S. Economy," *Review of Radical Political Economics* 18, nos. 1–2 (Spring–Summer, 1986): 132–67. For comparative reviews of the two literatures see, David M. Kotz, "A Comparative Analysis of the Theory of Regulation and the Social Structure of Accumulation Theory," *Science and Society* 54, no. 1 (Spring, 1990): 5–28; also, Haldun Gulalp, "The Stages and Long-Cycles of Capitalist Development," *Review of Radical Political Economics* 21, no. 4 (Spring, 1989): 83–92.

71. Kotz, "A Comparative Analysis," p. 7.

72. Gerard Destanne De Bernis ("On a Marxist Theory of Regulation," *Monthly Review* 41, no. 8 [January 1990]: 28–37) cautions that "our approach is not a complete theoretical system . . . we are extremely aware that a number of very important issues concerning the theory of regulation have not been yet sufficiently analyzed and studied. Among these issues is the building of a multi-stage theory of the role of the state" (p. 36).

73. Jessop, *The Capitalist State*, p. 224.

74. Poulantzas, *Political Power and Social Classes*, p. 132.

75. Poulantzas, *State, Power, Socialism*, p. 134.

76. Ibid., p. 132. This hypothesis is operationalized in Quadagno, "Welfare Capitalism and the Social Security Act of 1935"; and idem, *The Transformation of Old-Age Security: Class and Politics in the American Welfare State* (Chicago: University of Chicago Press, 1988).

77. Jessop, *The Capitalist State*, p. 224. For an excellent example, see Adam Przeworksi, "Social Democracy as a Historical Phenomenon," *New Left Review* 123 (1980): 27–58.

78. Goran Therborn, *Science, Class and Society* (London: New Left Books, 1976), pp. 34–35.

79. Richard C. Edwards, Michael Reich, and Thomas E. Weisskopf, "The Effect of Taxes and Government Spending on Inequality," in Richard C. Edwards, Michael Reich, and Thomas E. Weisskopf, eds., *The Capitalist System*, 1st edition (Englewood Cliffs, N.J.: Prentice-Hall, 1972), p. 236.

80. Also see, Richard C. Edwards, "Who Fares Well in the Welfare State?" in Richard C. Edwards, Michael Reich, and Thomas Weisskopf, eds., *The Capitalist System*, 2nd edition, pp. 307–14; (Englewood Cliffs, N.J.: Prentice-Hall, 1978); Benjamin Page, *Who Gets What from Government* (Berkeley and Los Angeles: University of California Press, 1983), especially chap. 6.

81. Bowles and Gintis, *Schooling in Capitalist America*, pp. 9–11.

82. A recent publication documenting the concentration of wealth is Avery and Elliehausen, "Financial Characteristics of High-Income Families." While the data in this study are not presented in a way that allows them to be included in table 2.2, they confirm that "the most concentrated holdings of assets" by the top 1 percent of the population remain in "non-bank financial assets such as bonds, trust accounts, and stocks" (p. 167).

83. An excellent account of how the market's automatic trigger mechanism introduced "an investment-dependent logic" into income tax policy is Ronald Frederick King, "From Redistributive to Hegemonic Logic: The Transformation of American Tax Politics, 1894–1963," *Politics and Society* 12, no. 1 (1983): 1–52.

84. Poulantzas, *State, Power, Socialism*, p. 135.

85. Poulantzas, "The Problem of the Capitalist State," p. 78.

86. Jessop, *The Capitalist State*, p. 224.

87. Elkin, *City and Regime in the American Republic*, p. 181.

88. Therborn, *Science, Class, and Society*, p. 35.

89. The best analysis of this problem is Gosta Esping-Andersen, Roger Friedland, and Erik Olin Wright, "Modes of Class Struggle and the Capitalist State," *Kapitalistate* 4–5 (1976): 186–220; also see, Przeworski, "Social Democracy as a Historical Phenomenon."

90. George Ross, "Nicos Poulantzas, Eurocommunism, and the Debate on the Theory of the Capitalist State," *Socialist Review* 44 (March 1979), pp. 155–56.

91. Clarke, "Marxism, Sociology, and Poulantzas' Theory of the State," pp. 2, 9, 20.

92. For example, Peter A. Hall, "Patterns of Economic Policy: An Organizational Approach," in Bornstein, Held, and Krieger, eds., *The State in Capitalist Europe*, pp. 21–43.

93. Robert Gordon, "Critical Legal Histories," *Stanford Law Review* 36 (January 1984), p. 84; see especially Fred Block, "Political Choice and the Multiple 'Logics' of Capital," *Theory and Society* 15, nos. 1–2 (1986): 175–90.

94. Dunleavy and O'Leary, *Theories of the State*, p. 256–57; also, Clarke, "Marxism, Sociology, and Poulantzas' Theory of the State," p. 20.

95. Dunleavy and O'Leary, *Theories of the State*, pp. 218–19.

96. Alford and Friedland (*Powers of Theory*, pp. 338–49) provide a compelling critique that, despite their claims to "methodological individualism," rational choice Marxists do not escape a functionalist analysis. See most notably John Elster, "Marxism, Functionalism, Game Theory: The Case for Methodological Individualism," *Theory and Society* 11, no. 4 (July 1982): 453–

82; and Adam Przeworksi and Michael Wallerstein, "The Structure of Class Conflict in Democratic Capitalist Societies," *American Political Science Review* 76, no. 2 (June 1982): 215–38.

97. Jill Quadagno, "Welfare Capitalism and the Social Security Act of 1935."

98. Crouch, "The State, Capital and Liberal Democracy," pp. 13–54.

99. Mary O. Furner and Barry Supple, eds., *The State and Economic Knowledge* (Cambridge: Cambridge University Press, 1990).

100. Robert S. McIntyre and David Wilhelm, *Money for Nothing: The Failure of Corporate Tax Incentives, 1981–1984* (Washington, D.C.: Citizens for Tax Justice, 1986).

101. Corporation for Enterprise Development, *1990 Development Report Card* (Washington, D.C.: Corporation for Enterprise Development, 1990).

102. Block, *Revising State Theory*, chap. 9.

103. In the neoliberal model of a state-capital partnership, the state actively invests in physical and human capital while targeting the emergence of strategic growth sectors with tax subsidies, loans, and direct investment; see David Osborne, *Reinventing Government: The Rise of an Entrepreneurial Public Sector* (Reading, Mass.: Addison-Wesley, 1992); and Peter K. Eisinger, *The Rise of the Entrepreneurial State: State and Local Economic Development Policy in the United States* (Madison: University of Wisconsin Press, 1988). For popular renditions of the neoliberal model see, Robert B. Reich, *The Work of Nations: Preparing Ourselves for 21st Century Capitalism* (New York: Alfred A. Knopf, 1991); Michael S. Dukakis and Rosabeth Moss Kanter, *Creating the Future: The Massachusetts Comeback and Its Promise for America* (New York: Summit Books, 1988); and Paul Tsongas, *A Call to Economic Arms: Forging a New American Mandate* (Boston: The Tsongas Committee, 1991).

104. Samuel Bowles, David M. Gordon, and Thomas E. Weisskopf, *Beyond the Wasteland: A Democratic Alternative to Economic Decline* (Garden City, N.Y.: Anchor Books, 1984); Samuel Bowles, David M. Gordon, and Thomas E. Weisskopf, *After the Wasteland: A Democratic Economics for the Year 2000* (Armonk, N.Y.: M. E. Sharpe, 1990).

105. Martin Carnoy and Derek Shearer, *Economic Democracy: The Challenge of the 1980s* (Armonk, N.Y.: M. E. Sharpe, 1980), chap. 2

Chapter 3. Between Neo-Marxism and Post-Marxism:
The Derivationist Approach

1. Poulantzas, "The Problem of the Capitalist State," pp. 67–78; Miliband, "The Capitalist State: Reply to Poulantzas," pp. 53–60; idem, "Poulantzas and the Capitalist State," *New Left Review* 82 (1973): 83–92; Nicos Poulantzas, "The Capitalist State," *New Left Review* 95 (1976): 63–83.

2. John Holloway and Sol Picciotto, "Introduction: Towards a Materialist Theory of the State," in Holloway and Picciotto, eds., *State and Capital: A Marxist Debate* (Austin: University of Texas Press, 1978), pp. 1–31.

3. Rudolf Sinz, Ana Delgado, and Stephen Leibfried, "Preface" to Elmer Altvater, "Notes on Some Problems of State Interventionism (I)," *Kapitalistate* 1 (1973): 96–97; Sol Picciotto and Hugo Radice, "Capital and State in the World Economy," *Kapitalistate* 1 (1973), p. 56.

4. Holloway and Picciotto, "Introduction: Towards a Materialist Theory of the State," p. 16.

5. Simon Clarke ("State, Class Struggle, and the Reproduction of Capital," *Kapitalistate* 10–11 [1983]: 113–34) disputes the derivationists' reading of *Capital*. Clarke argues, rightly or wrongly, that "Marx offers an analysis of the self-reproduction of the capital relation, within which the social relations of capitalist production are regulated . . . by the operation of the market . . . the implication of Marx's analysis is that the state is not, in the strictest sense, *necessary* to capitalist social reproduction, so that none of the concepts developed in *Capital* presuppose the concept of the state" (pp. 117–18). Clarke reinforces his argument with the claim that "capital did not create the state, either logically or historically" (p. 119).

6. Jessop, "Recent Theories of the Capitalist State," pp. 361–64.

7. Elmer Altvater, "Notes on Some Problems of State Interventionism (I)," *Kapitalistate* 1 (1973): 97–108.

8. Ibid., pp. 101–2; Claudia von Braunmuhl, "On the Analysis of the Bourgeois Nation State within the World Market Context. An Attempt to Develop a Methodological and Theoretical Approach," in Holloway and Picciotto, eds., *State and Capital*, pp. 160–77; Picciotto and Radice, "Capital and State," pp. 56–64.

9. Altvater, "Notes on Some Problems (I)," p. 101.

10. Picciotto and Radice, "Capital and State," p. 56; cf. Alan Wolfe, *The Limits of Legitimacy: Political Contradictions of Contemporary Capitalism* (New York: Free Press, 1977), chap. 1.

11. Cf. Perry Anderson, *Lineages of the Absolutist State* (London: Verso, 1979), especially pp. 397–431; Immanuel Wallerstein, *The World Capitalist System II: Mercantilism and the Consolidation of the European World Economy, 1600–1750* (New York: Academic Press, 1980).

12. Richard Scase, ed., *The State in Western Europe* (New York: St. Martin's Press, 1980), pp. 12–13.

13. Picciotto and Radice, "Capital and State," pp. 56–64.

14. Von Braunmuhl, "On the Analysis of the Bourgeois Nation State," p. 160.

15. Cf. Immanuel Wallerstein, *World Systems Analysis: Theory and Methodology* (Beverly Hills: Sage Publications, 1982); Robert J. S. Ross and Kent C. Trachte, *Global Capitalism: The New Leviathan* (Albany: SUNY Press, 1990).

16. For example, Cheryl Payer, *The Debt Trap: The IMF and the Third World* (New York: Monthly Review Press, 1975).

17. See Peter J. Katzenstein, ed., *Between Power and Plenty: Foreign Economic Policies of Advanced Industrial Societies* (Madison: University of Wisconsin Press, 1978).

18. Peter Cocks, "Towards a Marxist Theory of European Integration," *International Organization* 34, no. 1 (Winter, 1984): 1–40; John Holloway, *Social Policy Harmonisation in the European Community* (Westmead, England: Gower Press, 1981).

19. Kees van der Pijl, "The International Level" in Bottomore and Brym, eds., *The Capitalist Class*, pp. 237–66.

20. Jessop, "Recent Theories of the Capitalist State," pp. 364–67.

21. Joachim Hirsch, "The State Apparatus and Social Reproduction: Elements of a Theory of the Bourgeois State," in Holloway and Picciotto, eds., *State and Capital*, pp. 57–107; Heide Gerstenberger, "Class Conflict, Competition and State Functions," Holloway and Picciotto, eds., *State and Capital*, pp. 148–59.

22. Hirsch, "The State Apparatus and Social Reproduction," p. 61; Anderson, *Lineages of the Absolutist State*, p. 430: "*All* modes of production in class societies prior to capitalism extract surplus labour from the immediate producers by means of extra-economic coercion. Capitalism is the first mode of production in history in which the means whereby the surplus is pumped out of the direct producer is 'purely' economic in form—the wage contract."

23. Clarke ("State, Class Struggle, and the Reproduction of Capital") also challenges Hirsch's derivation of the state. Clarke argues that, contrary to expectations, Hirsch fails to emphasize that the historical development of class *struggle* necessitates a collective instrument of domination. Clarke (p. 119) observes that "if there were no class struggle, if the working class were willing to submit passively to their subordination to capitalist social relations, there would be no state."

24. Hirsch, "The State Apparatus and Social Reproduction," p. 61.

25. Ibid., p. 59.

26. Ibid., p. 83.

27. Ibid., p. 75.

28. Gerstenberger, "Class Conflict, Competition, and State Functions," p. 148.

29. Clarke ("State, Class Struggle, and the Reproduction of Capital," p. 119) correctly points out that the derivationists' concept of class struggle finally "makes possible the transition from the level of abstraction to the real world."

30. Scase, *The State in Western Europe*, pp. 16ff.

31. Hirsch, "The State Apparatus and Social Reproduction," p. 65.

32. Ibid., p. 76.

33. Scase, *The State in Western Europe*, p. 14.

34. Clarke, "State, Class Struggle, and the Reproduction of Capital," p. 116: "All that exists is a particular resolution of conflicting interests."

35. Scase, *The State in Western Europe*, p. 13.

36. Gerstenberger, "Class Conflict, Competition, and State Functions,"

p. 158. Gerstenberger goes on to qualify her statement by noting: "Not that the interests of capital are not in general implemented; but in a concrete analysis we should not assume in advance as a certainty that in a concrete case the ensuring state activity will further possibilities for accumulation of national capital to the fullest extent possible under capitalist conditions."

37. Scase, *The State in Western Europe*, p. 19.

38. Hirsch, "The State Apparatus and Social Reproduction," p. 101; cf. Crouch, "The State, Capital and Liberal Democracy," pp. 13–54.

39. Hirsch, "The State Apparatus and Social Reproduction," p. 100.

40. Scase, *The State in Western Europe*, p. 200.

41. Pierre Birnbaum, "The State in Contemporary France," in Scase, ed., *The State in Western Europe*, pp. 94–114.

42. Carlo Donolo, "Social Change and Transformation of the State in Italy," in Scase, ed., *The State in Western Europe*, pp. 164–96.

43. Hirsch, "The State Apparatus and Social Reproduction," p. 100.

44. Gerstenberger, "Class Conflict, Competition, and State Functions," p. 159.

45. Goran Therborn's "Rule of Capital and the Rise of Democracy" offers a brilliant derivation of Western democracies. Therborn concludes that democracy is primarily a political phenomenon that is neither necessary nor necessarily functional to the rule of capital.

46. Gough, *The Political Economy of the Welfare State*. I do not mean to imply that Gough is a derivationist, strictly speaking, only that his analysis is compatible with one of its central theoretical conclusions.

47. Picciotto and Radice, "Capital and State," p. 67.

48. Holloway and Picciotto, "Introduction: Towards a Materialist Theory of the State," p. 22.

49. Bernhard Blanke, Ulrich Jurgens, and Hans Kastendiek, "The Relationship between the Political and Economic as a Point of Departure for a Materialist Analysis of the Bourgeois State," *International Journal of Politics* 6 (1976): 68–126.

50. Bernhard Blanke, Ulrich Jurgens, and Hans Kastendiek, "On the Current Marxist Discussion on the Analysis of Form and Function of the Bourgeois State: Reflections on the Relationship of Politics to Economics," Holloway and Picciotto, eds., *State and Capital*, pp. 108–47.

51. Ibid., p. 119.

52. Gerstenberger, "Class Conflict, Competition, and State Functions," p. 158.

53. Ibid., p. 157; italics mine.

54. Holloway and Picciotto, "Introduction: Towards a Materialist Theory of the State," p. 30.

Chapter 4. Post-Marxism I: The Systems-Analytic Approach

1. O'Connor, *The Meaning of Crisis*. On the crisis of liberal democracy, see Michel J. Crozier, Samuel P. Huntington, and Joji Watanuki, eds., *The Crisis of Democracy* (New York: New York University Press, 1975). On the fiscal crisis of the welfare state, see Logue, "The Welfare State"; James O'Connor, *The Fiscal Crisis of the State* (New York: St. Martin's Press, 1973). On the cultural crisis of capitalism see Daniel Bell, *The Cultural Contradictions of Capitalism* (New York: Basic Books, 1976).

2. Holloway and Picciotto, "Introduction: Towards a Materialist Theory of the State," p. 10.

3. Offe, *Contradictions*, p. 35.

4. Ibid., p. 37; Jurgen Habermas, *Legitimation Crisis* (Boston: Beacon Press, 1975), p. 49.

5. Offe, *Contradictions*, p. 37.

6. Ibid., p. 132.

7. Ibid., p. 116 fn. 15.

8. Ibid., pp. 88–89.

9. Ibid., p. 100.

10. Claus Offe (*Disorganized Capitalism* [Cambridge, Mass.: M.I.T. Press, 1985], p. 6) poses the central analytic question of post-Marxist analysis: "Do the procedures, patterns of organization, and institutional mechanisms that supposedly mediate and maintain a dynamic balance between social power and political authority . . . actually *fail* to perform this function?"

11. For example, Jurgen Habermas (*Toward a Rational Society* [Boston: Beacon Press, 1970], p. 90) identifies his objective "to construct a conceptual model of institutional change brought about by the extension of subsystems of purposive-rational action" (i.e., the economic system) to the normative spheres of the life-world (i.e., politics and culture).

12. Offe, *Disorganized Capitalism*, p. 53.

13. Offe, *Contradictions*, pp. 92–93.

14. Offe, *Disorganized Capitalism*, p. 2. Offe's methodological premise is that power "is an attribute not of actors, but of modes of interaction" (ibid., p. 1). For a more extensive discussion see ibid., pp. 10–51.

15. Cf. Polanyi, *The Great Transformation*.

16. For example, Samuel Bowles and Herbert Gintis, "The Crisis of Liberal Democratic Capitalism: The Case of the United States," *Politics and Society* 11, no. 1 (1982): 51–93.

17. Offe, *Contradictions*, p. 98. Similarly, Offe argues that "social policy is the state's manner of effecting the lasting transformation of non-wage laborers into wage-laborers" (ibid., p. 92).

18. Offe's discussion of pre-Keynesian state forms is quite sketchy; see *Disorganized Capitalism*, pp. 4–5.

19. For a brief description of the welfare state, see Douglas Rae, "The Egalitarian State: Notes on a System of Contradictory Ideals," in Stephen R.

Graubard, ed., *The State*, pp. 37–54 (New York: W. W. Norton, 1979). For a more extensive historical analysis see Peter Flora, ed., *Growth to Limits: The Western European Welfare States since World War II* (New York: Walter de Gruyter, 1986).

20. Claus Offe, "The Theory of the Capitalist State and the Problem of Policy Formation," in Leon Lindberg, ed., *Stress and Contradiction in Modern Capitalism* (Lexington, Mass.: D. C. Heath, 1975), p. 125; idem, *Contradictions*, pp. 88–89.

21. Offe, "Structural Problems of the Capitalist State."

22. Offe, "Theory of the Capitalist State," p. 126.

23. Elkin, *City and Regime in the American Republic*, p. 18.

24. Offe, "Theory of the Capitalist State," p. 126.

25. Offe, "Structural Problems of the Capitalist State," pp. 39–40; Sabine Sardei-Biermann, Jens Christiansen, Knuth Dohse, "Class Domination and the Political System: A Critical Interpretation of Recent Contributions by Claus Offe," *Kapitalistate* 2 (1973): 60–69.

26. Offe, *Contradictions*, p. 126.

27. Offe, "Theory of the Capitalist State," p. 127; idem, "Structural Problems of the Capitalist State," p. 47.

28. The best analysis is still Edelman's *Symbolic Use of Politics*, where he observes that "the most intensive dissemination of symbols commonly attends the enactment of legislation which is most meaningless in its effect upon resource allocation" (p. 29).

29. Offe, *Contradictions*, p. 49.

30. Ibid.

31. Claus Offe, "The Abolition of Market Control and the Problem of Legitimacy (I)," *Kapitalistate* 1 (1973): 109–16.

32. Offe, *Contradictions*, p. 50.

33. Karl Hinrichs, Claus Offe, and Helmut Wiesenthal, "The Crisis of the Welfare State and Alternative Modes of Work Redistribution," *Thesis Eleven* 10–11 (1984–85): 37–55.

34. Offe, *Contradictions*, p. 61.

35. Ibid., pp. 51, 61.

36. Habermas, *Legitimation Crisis*, Part 2, chaps. 1–8; also, Dunleavy and O'Leary, *Theories of the State*, pp. 259–70.

37. Habermas, *Legitimation Crisis*, p. 2.

38. Dunleavy and O'Leary (*Theories of the State*, p. 264) note poignantly how the idea that an old-fashioned economic crisis could not occur in advanced capitalism began to seem "slightly quaint in the 1980s, even though Habermas does not completely rule out the possibility of an economic crisis in advanced capitalism."

39. O'Connor's *Meaning of Crisis* provides an excellent comprehensive survey of the crisis-theory literature.

40. O'Connor, *Fiscal Crisis of the State*; idem, "Summary of the Theory of the Fiscal Crisis," *Kapitalistate* 1 (1973): 79–83.

41. O'Connor ("Summary of the Theory," p. 79) also links this mandate to the dependency principle: ". . . a state that ignores the many and varied problems involving accumulation and profits is self-destructive—it risks drying up the source of its own power, the surplus production capacity of the economic system and the taxes that are drawn from this surplus."

42. Gough, *The Political Economy of the Welfare State*.

43. O'Connor, "Summary of the Theory," p. 79.

44. Ibid., p. 82.

45. Scott Lehigh and Frank Phillips, "House Leaders Push Budget with Receivership Warnings," *Boston Globe*, May 16, 1991, p. 1.

46. Offe, "Abolition of Market Control (I)," pp. 114–15.

47. For instance, one could argue that the legitimacy of due process rules in the U.S. legal procedure rests on their functional effectiveness. The dominant social assumption is that the application of due process by jurists will insure that the innocent are acquitted without jeopardizing the conviction of the guilty. When that social assumption is undermined by the perception that the guilty consistently go free because of "procedural technicalities" then the legitimacy of due process rules is eroded.

48. In Massachusetts state politics this dichotomy has surfaced in the state Democratic party as a schism between so-called process liberals and substance liberals.

49. Offe, *Disorganized Capitalism*, pp. 303–7; Habermas, *Legitimation Crisis*, p. 47; Sardei-Biermann, Christiansen, and Dohse, "Class Domination and the Political System," pp. 65–66.

50. King, "From Redistributive to Hegemonic Logic."

51. O'Connor, "Summary of the Theory," p. 83.

52. Cf. Bell, *The Cultural Contradictions of Capitalism*.

53. Habermas, *Legitimation Crisis*, pp. 47–48.

54. Claus Offe, "Political Authority and Class Structures: An Analysis of Late Capitalist Societies," *International Journal of Sociology* 2 (1972): 73–108.

55. Andre Gorz, *Critique of Economic Reason* (London: Verso, 1989), chaps. 8–9; cf. Ronald Inglehart, *The Silent Revolution: Changing Values and Political Styles among Western Publics* (Princeton: Princeton University Press, 1977).

56. Joachim Hirsch, "The Fordist Security State and New Social Movements," *Kapitalistate* 10–11 (1983): 75–87; Gorz, *Critique of Economic Reason*; Alain Touraine, *The Post-Industrial Society* (New York: Random House, 1971); Offe, *Disorganized Capitalism*, chaps. 2, 4.

57. Karl Marx, *Grundrisse: Foundations of the Critique of Political Economy*, trans. Martin Nicholaus (New York: Vintage Books, 1973); Jurgen Habermas, *Knowledge and Human Interests* (Boston: Beacon Press, 1971), p. 47; Andre Gorz, *Farewell to the Working Class: An Essay on Postindustrial Socialism* (Boston: South End Press, 1982).

58. Claus Offe, "Advanced Capitalism and the Welfare State," *Politics and Society* 2 (1972): 479–88.

59. Cf. Barry Bluestone and Bennett Harrison, *The Deindustrialization of America* (New York: Basic Books, 1982).

60. Offe, *Disorganized Capitalism*, p. 3.

61. Hirsch, "The Fordist Security State," pp. 83–85.

62. Offe, *Disorganized Capitalism*, pp. 101–28.

63. For example, cf. Gorz, *Farewell to the Working Class* with Daniel Bell, *The Coming of Postindustrial Society* (New York: Basic Books, 1973).

64. Offe, *Contradictions*, p. 40.

65. Claus Offe, "The Abolition of Market Control and the Problem of Legitimacy (II)," *Kapitalistate* 2 (1973): 73–75.

66. Offe, *Contradictions*, p. 40.

67. Cf. Mancur Olson, *The Rise and Decline of Nations* (New Haven: Yale University Press, 1984).

68. Hinrichs, Offe, and Wiesenthal, "The Crisis of the Welfare State," p. 51.

69. Claus Offe, "Challenging the Boundaries of Institutional Politics: Social Movements since the 1960's," in Charles S. Maier, ed., *Changing Boundaries of the Political*, pp. 63–105 (Cambridge: Cambridge University Press, 1987); Ernesto Laclau and Chantal Mouffe, *Hegemony and Socialist Strategy* (London: Verso, 1985); Carl Boggs, *Social Movements and Political Power: Emerging Forms of Radicalism in the West* (Philadelphia: Temple University Press, 1986); Alain Touraine, *Return of the Actor* (Minneapolis: University of Minnesota Press, 1988).

70. Offe, *Contradictions*, p. 42.

71. Thus, Alford and Friedland (*Powers of Theory*, p. 435) note that for Offe "the most intense political conflicts are increasingly located in these non-commodified institutions and not in the capitalist economy per se. The conflicts potentially threaten the commodity form as the primary social relation."

72. C. Pierson, "New Theories of the State and Civil Society," *British Journal of Sociology* 18, no. 4 (1984): 563–71.

73. Habermas, *Legitimation Crisis*, p. 49; Offe, *Disorganized Capitalism*, p. 6.

74. Habermas, *Legitimation Crisis*, p. 49.

75. Offe, *Contradictions*, p. 46.

76. Ibid., p. 115 fn. 7.

77. Habermas, *Toward a Rational Society*, pp. 108–9.

78. Offe, *Contradictions*, p. 35.

79. See Carnoy, *The State and Political Theory*, p. 220.

80. Offe, *Contradictions*, p. 51.

81. Sardei-Biermann, Christiansen, and Dohse, "Class Domination and the Political System," p. 67.

82. David A. Gold, Clarence Y. H. Lo, and Erik Olin Wright, "Recent Developments in Marxist Theories of the Capitalist State, Part II," *Monthly Review* 27, no. 6 (November 1975), p. 38.

83. Offe, *Contradictions*, pp. 51–52.

84. Ibid., pp. 88–89.

85. Ibid., pp. 119–20.

86. Harry Eckstein, "On the 'Science' of the State," in Graubard, ed., *The State*, p. 15.

87. Johannes Berger and Claus Offe, "Functionalism vs. Rational Choice? Some Questions Concerning the Rationality of Choosing One or the Other," *Theory and Society* 11, no. 4 (July 1982), p. 521. My italics.

88. Offe, *Contradictions*, p. 120.

89. Ibid., p. 121.

90. Offe, "Theory of the Capitalist State," p. 127.

91. Offe, *Contradictions*, p. 120.

92. Ibid., pp. 125–26.

93. Ibid., p. 115 fn. 7.

94. Ibid., pp. 101–2.

95. Ibid., p. 102.

96. Ibid., pp. 105, 109; see also Jean L. Cohen, "Between Crisis Management and Social Movements: The Place of Institutional Reform," *Telos* 52 (1982): 21–40, especially pp. 22–26.

97. Berger and Offe, "Functionalism vs. Rational Choice?" p. 524.

98. Offe (*Contradictions*, pp. 115–16 fn. 7) notes that to explain the choice between functionally equivalent solutions to structural problems shifts the explanatory emphasis onto "the given alignments and processes of conflict and consensus arising from concrete actors and situations." Also, Berger and Offe, "Functionalism vs. Rational Choice," p. 522.

99. Offe, *Contradictions*, p. 258.

100. Offe acknowledges that "the initial boom period of the neo-Marxist study of the state is over by now, and that its conceptual rigidities, deductive speculations and failure to come to grips with empirical and historical details and national peculiarities of the various late capitalist states hurt the intellectual appeal of the new paradigm."

101. A concise survey of this literature is Thomas F. Mayer, "In Defense of Analytical Marxism," *Science and Society* 53, no. 4 (Winter, 1989–90): 416–41.

102. Offe, *Contradictions*, p. 159.

103. Ibid., p. 257.

104. For example, Weinstein, *The Corporate Ideal*, pp. xiii–xv; Barrow, *Universities and the Capitalist State*, chaps. 3–5.

105. David Easton, *The Analysis of Political Structure* (New York: Routledge and Kegan Paul, 1990).

106. Held and Krieger ("Theories of the State: Some Competing Claims)," in Bornstein, Held, and Krieger, eds., *The State in Capitalist Europe*, p. 19) agree with Offe that state policies are limited to crisis management, but point out that "the capacity of a regime to maneuver is enhanced by its ability to displace the effects of economic problems onto vulnerable groups, for instance,

the elderly, consumers, the sick, non-unionized, non-white, and so on, and onto vulnerable regions."

107. O'Connor, *Fiscal Crisis of the State*, p. 221.

108. Cf. Spring, *Education and the Rise of the Corporate State*; Barrow, *Universities and the Capitalist State*.

109. Weinstein, *The Corporate Ideal*.

110. King, *The State in Modern Society*, p. 82.

111. William Connolly, ed., *Legitimacy and the State* (Oxford: Basil Blackwell, 1984).

112. Theda Skocpol, *States and Social Revolution* (Cambridge: Cambridge University Press, 1979), p. 16.

113. King, *The State in Modern Society*, p. 82.

114. Certainly, this principle was long understood by Marxist scholars studying the Third World. Dependency theory, theories of dependent development, and world-systems analysis all posit this asymmetry as a basic concept.

115. Block (*Revising State Theory*, p. 173) observes that "as competition mounts within that world economy, there are powerful pressures to reduce the level of taxes and social welfare in any particular country toward the lowest international common denominator."

116. Clarke, "State, Class Struggle, and the Reproduction of Capital," p. 114.

117. For instance, see Suzanne Gordon, *Prisoners of Men's Dreams* (Boston: Little, Brown and Co., 1991).

118. Boggs, *Social Movements and Political Power*, p. 247.

119. Gorz (*Farewell to the Working Class*, p. 67) points out that the neoproletariat is a nonlaboring group "whose social activity yields no power," while such a condition objectively strips it of "the means to take power, nor does it feel called upon to do so."

120. Habermas, *Toward a Rational Society*, p. 110; Boris Frankel (*Postindustrial Utopians* [Madison: University of Wisconsin Press, 1987]) draws the same conclusion. Cf. Claus Offe, "New Social Movements: Challenging the Boundaries of Institutional Politics," *Social Research* 52, no. 4 (Winter, 1985): 817–68, especially pp. 855ff.

121. Hirsch, "The State Apparatus and Social Reproduction," p. 84.

122. King, *The State in Modern Society*, p. 82. For examples of these new capacities see: Morton Halperin, *The Lawless State* (New York: Penguin Books, 1976); Gregg Barak, ed., *Crimes by the Capitalist State* (Albany: SUNY Press, 1991).

123. Gorz, *Critique of Economic Reason*, p. 242.

Chapter 5. Post-Marxism II:
The Organizational Realist Approach

1. Karen Orren and Stephen Skowronek ("Editors' Preface," *Studies in American Political Development*, Vol. 1 [New Haven: Yale University Press,

1986], p. vii) define the "new institutionalism" as a research agenda which seeks to use "the work of the recent past as a new point of departure from which to specify more closely the complex patterns of state-society relations." Its major theoretical claim is "that institutions have an independent and formative influence on politics," while methodologically it emphasizes history as "the dimension necessary for understanding institutions as they operate under varying conditions."

2. I have drawn the term "organizational realism" from Theda Skocpol's *States and Social Revolutions* (p. 31), where she suggests that her methodological approach to the state "might appropriately be labeled 'organizational' and 'realist.' " I am presenting organizational realism as a post-Marxist variant of the new institutionalism. For a summary introduction to the literature see, Theda Skocpol, "Bringing the State Back In."

3. Theda Skocpol and Edwin Amenta, "States and Social Policies," *Annual Review of Sociology* 12 (1986), p. 131; cf. the similar definitions in John A. Hall and G. John Ikenberry, *The State* (Minneapolis: University of Minnesota Press, 1989), pp. 1–2; and Gianfranco Poggi, *The State: Its Nature, Development and Prospects* (Stanford: Stanford University Press, 1990), pp. 19–33.

4. Fred Block, "Beyond Relative Autonomy: State Managers as Historical Subjects," *Socialist Register* 14 (1980): 227–42; Lynn G. Zucker, "Institutional Theories of Organization," *Annual Review of Sociology* 13 (1987): 443–64; James G. March and Johan P. Olsen, "The New Institutionalism: Organizational Factors in Political Life," *American Political Science Review* 78, no. 3 (September 1984): 734–49, especially p. 747.

5. Skocpol, "Bringing the State Back In," p. 8. For example, see the excellent collection of articles in Bornstein, Held, and Krieger, *The State in Capitalist Europe*; also, the essays in Katzenstein, ed., *Between Power and Plenty*.

6. Peter B. Evans, Dietrich Rueschemeyer, and Theda Skocpol, "On the Road toward a More Adequate Understanding of the State," in Evans, Rueschemeyer, and Skocpol, eds., *Bringing the State Back In*, p. 348.

7. Ibid., p. 347.

8. Theda Skocpol, "A Critical Review of Barrington Moore's Social Origins of Dictatorship and Democracy," *Politics and Society* 4 (1973): 18; also see, Skocpol, *States and Social Revolution*, p. 28.

9. Skocpol, *States and Social Revolution*, p. 25.

10. Block, "Beyond Relative Autonomy," pp. 228–29.

11. Skocpol, *States and Social Revolutions*, p. 31.

12. Skocpol, "Bringing the State Back In," p. 9.

13. Skocpol, *States and Social Revolution*, p. 29. Similarly, Block ("Beyond Relative Autonomy," p. 229) argues: "As Weber insisted, the heart of that [i.e., state] power is the monopoly over the means of violence, which is the basis on which the managers of the state apparatus are able to force compliance with their wishes." Likewise, Poggi (*The State*, p. 5) insists that "what we should consider as unique to political power, as conceptually intrinsic to it, is control over the means of violence."

14. Skocpol, *States and Social Revolution*, p. 29.

15. Ibid., p. 30.

16. The approach clearly takes off from the assumption that capitalist classes are, in general, politically dominant. The approach logically relies on the assumption, for its polemical force, that in most cases the state does secure or (at a minimum) does not act against capitalistic interests. Otherwise, an empirical argument that the state sometimes may act against the capitalist class would be of no theoretical importance; see Gabriel A. Almond, "The Return to the State," *American Political Science Review* 82, no. 3 (September 1988): 853–74.

17. Skocpol, *States and Social Revolution*, p. 29; see also Charles Tilly, "Reflections on the History of European State Making," in Charles Tilly, ed., *The Formation of National States in Western Europe* (Princeton: Princeton University Press, 1975), pp. 1–99.

18. Skocpol, *States and Social Revolution*, p. 30.

19. Poggi, *The State*, pp. 96–97.

20. Block, "Beyond Relative Autonomy," pp. 232–34.

21. Skocpol, *States and Social Revolution*, p. 30.

22. Ibid., p. 31.

23. Skocpol, "Bringing the State Back In," p. 9.

24. Ibid.

25. Ellen Kay Trimberger, *Revolution from Above* (New Brunswick, N.J.: Transaction Books, 1978), p. 4.

26. Alfred Stepan, *The State and Society* (Princeton: Princeton University Press, 1978).

27. Skocpol, "Bringing the State Back In," p. 10.

28. Ibid., p. 11; cf. N. Hamilton, *The Limits of State Autonomy: Post-Revolutionary Mexico* (Princeton: Princeton University Press, 1982).

29. Skocpol, "Bringing the State Back In," p. 14.

30. Ibid., p. 11.

31. Stephen Skowronek, *Building a New American State: The Expansion of National Administrative Capacities, 1877–1920* (Cambridge: Cambridge University Press, 1982), p. 19.

32. Ibid., p. 20.

33. Ibid., p. 24.

34. Ibid., p. 31.

35. Richard Bensel (*Yankee Leviathan: The Origins of Central State Authority in America, 1859–1877* [Cambridge: Cambridge University Press, 1990], pp. 99–125) develops a highly useful comparative taxonomy of state strength that builds on Skowronek's earlier work.

36. Wolfe, *The Limits of Legitimacy*, pp. 146–75.

37. Theda Skocpol, "Political Response to Capitalist Crisis: Neo-Marxist Theories of the State and the Case of the New Deal," *Politics and Society* 10 (1980), p. 200. This last generalization of Skocpol's leaves open the question of class content. Whether interventionist policies are directed toward securing

the general interests of capital, whether they are directed toward the socialization of production, or whether they are directed toward merely securing the autonomous power of state elites is viewed as a historically contingent event.

38. Skocpol, "Bringing the State Back In," p. 19; cf. Charles Tilly, *From Mobilization to Revolution* (New York: Addison-Wesley, 1981).

39. Jerry Lembcke (*Capitalist Development and Class Capacities: Marxist Theory and Union Organization* [Westport, Conn.: Greenwood Press, 1988], p. 4) develops an analytic framework which argues that "*working-class* capacity is [also] . . . observable as an *organizational* variable."

40. Skocpol, "Bringing the State Back In," p. 8.

41. Evans, Rueschemeyer, and Skocpol, "On the Road toward a More Adequate Understanding of the State," p. 351.

42. Margaret Weir and Theda Skocpol, "State Structures and Social Keynesianism: Responses to the Great Depression in Sweden and the United States," *International Journal of Sociology* 26 (1983): 4–29. Similarly, Margaret Weir, Ann Shola Orloff, and Theda Skocpol (eds., *The Politics of Social Policy in the United States* [Princeton: Princeton University Press, 1988], p. 19) characterize American state structure as extremely weak based on the absence of centralization and the lack of internal coordination between state activities (i.e., federalism and separation of powers).

43. See Skocpol, "Political Response to Capitalist Crisis," for this analysis.

44. Skocpol, "Bringing the State Back In," p. 12.

45. Korpi, "Social Policy," pp. 296–316; Shalev, "The Social Democratic Model," pp. 315–51.

46. Weir and Skocpol, "State Structures and Social Keynesianism," p. 5.

47. Skocpol, "Bringing the State Back In," p. 13.

48. Ibid., p. 17.

49. Weir, Orloff, Skocpol, *Politics of Social Policy*, p. 431. Italics mine in both quotes.

50. Skocpol, "Bringing the State Back In," p. 14.

51. Michael M. Atkinson and William D. Coleman, "Strong States and Weak States: Sectoral Policy Networks in Advanced Capitalist Economies," *British Journal of Political Science* 19, no. 1 (January 1989): 47–67. For examples of the uneven capacities of states to implement and administer industrial policies, see: Maurice Wright, "Policy Community, Policy Network and Comparative Industrial Policies," *Political Studies* 36 (1988): 593–612; and S. Wilks and M. Wright, eds., *Comparative Government-Industry Relations* (Oxford: Clarendon Press, 1987).

52. Evans, Rueschemeyer, and Skocpol, "On the Road toward a More Adequate Understanding of the State," p. 351.

53. Ibid., p. 355.

54. Theda Skocpol and Kenneth Finegold, "State Capacity and Economic Intervention in the Early New Deal," *Political Science Quarterly* 97, no. 2 (Summer, 1982): 255–78, quotation on p. 274.

55. Ibid., p. 275.

56. Ibid., p. 276; cf. Skocpol and Finegold's argument with Shalev and Korpi, "Working Class Mobilization and American Exceptionalism."

57. Skocpol and Finegold, "State Capacity and Economic Intervention," p. 278.

58. Skocpol, "Political Response to Capitalist Crisis," p. 156.

59. See Domhoff, *The Higher Circles*, p. 207–18, for his full account of the Social Security Act; and idem, "Corporate-Liberal Theory and the Social Security Act," for his polemical rejoinder to Skocpol and Quadagno. See Theda Skocpol and John Ikenberry, "The Political Formation of the American Welfare State in Historical and Comparative Perspective," *Comparative Social Research* 6 (1983): 87–148, for the statist account; Theda Skocpol and Edwin Amenta, "Did Capitalists Shape Social Security?" *American Sociological Review* 50 (August 1985): 572–75, for the statist response to Quadagno; and Skocpol, "A Brief Response," pp. 331–32, for the response to Domhoff. Finally, see Quadagno, "Welfare Capitalism and the Social Security Act of 1935"; and idem, *The Transformation of Old-Age Security*, for the structuralist account of social security; Jill S. Quadagno, "Two Models of Welfare State Development: Reply to Skocpol and Amenta," *American Sociological Review* 50 (August 1985): 575–77; G. William Domhoff, "On 'Welfare Capitalism' and the Social Security Act of 1935," *American Sociological Review* 51 (June 1986): 445–46.

60. A second round of polemics, almost identical with those over the Social Security Act, has recently been concluded on the National Labor Relations Act. See Domhoff, *The Power Elite and the State*, chap. 4; and Thomas Ferguson, "From Normalcy to New Deal: Industrial Structure, Party Competition, and American Public Policy in the Great Depression," *International Organization* 38 (1984): 41–94, for the corporate liberal argument; see Michael Goldfield, "Worker Insurgency, Radical Organization, and New Deal Labor Legislation," *American Political Science Review* 83, no. 4 (December 1989): 1257–82, where he emphasizes the role of class struggle and labor insurgency; and Theda Skocpol and Kenneth Finegold, "Explaining New Deal Labor Policy," *American Political Science Review* 84, no. 4 (December 1990): 1297–304, for a response by organizational realists.

61. Skocpol, "A Brief Response," pp. 331–32.

62. Domhoff, "Corporate-Liberal Theory and the Social Security Act," p. 296.

63. Quadagno, "Welfare Capitalism and the Social Security Act of 1935," p. 646.

64. Domhoff, "Corporate-Liberal Theory and the Social Security Act," p. 317.

65. Ibid., pp. 309–10.

66. Ibid. This dispute is largely a question of theoretical emphasis and only partly a question of empirical evidence.

67. Ibid., p. 310. Italics mine in the first quote.

68. Block, *Revising State Theory*, p. 15.

69. Gouldner, *The Future of Intellectuals*, p. 31. Likewise, Carnoy (*The*

State and Political Theory, p. 220) observes that "classes do not act as classes, only as groups and organizations in particular class-structured social situations."

70. For example, see Poulantzas, "On Social Classes," p. 40 for the structuralists view that intellectuals are a "social category" who *themselves belong to classes.*"

71. Skocpol, "Bringing the State Back In," p. 27. More recently, Weir, Orloff, and Skocpol (*Politics of Social Policy*, pp. 21–22) have attributed the inability of either class to organize effectively to the impact of federalism and the fragmentation of American state power.

72. Goldfield, "Worker Insurgency, Radical Organization, and New Deal Labor Legislation," p. 1263. Goldfield concludes, in the case of the National Labor Relations Act, that the political power of academic policy experts and middle-class liberal reformers "was derived from their connections to certain capitalists who often sustained their activities or from their acting as brokers for conservative and moderate labor leaders of the labor movement . . . They had narrow room for maneuvering, usually being buffetted by events and social forces" (p. 1269).

73. Ibid., p. 1263; Skocpol, "A Brief Response," p. 331. Weir, Orloff, and Skocpol (*Politics of Social Policy*, p. 14) have recently reiterated the claim that corporate liberalism's "proponents have failed to demonstrate convincingly that genuine groups or categories of capitalists—as opposed to a handful of maverick individuals not representative of any class or industrial sector—actually supported mandatory public pensions or social insurance."

74. Skocpol, "A Brief Response," p. 331.

75. Skocpol and Amenta, "Did Capitalists Shape Social Security?" p. 574.

76. Ibid.

77. Poulantzas, *State, Power, Socialism*, p. 133.

78. Ibid., p. 132.

79. Quadagno, "Welfare Capitalism and the Social Security Act of 1935," p. 645.

80. Ibid., p. 646.

81. Weir, Orloff, and Skocpol, *Politics of Social Policy*, p. 25.

82. Ibid., pp. 25–26. Support for this claim is found in Martha Derthick, *Policy Making for Social Security* (Washington, D.C.: Brookings Institution, 1985).

83. Weir, Orloff, and Skocpol, *Politics of Social Policy*, p. 432.

84. Kenneth Finegold, "From Agrarianism to Adjustment: The Political Origins of New Deal Agricultural Policy," *Politics and Society* 11 (1982): 1–27.

85. Ibid., p. 1.

86. Ibid., p. 25.

87. George E. Paulsen, "The Federal Trade Commission versus the National Recovery Administration, 1935," *Social Science Quarterly* 70, no. 1 (March 1989): 149–63, quotation on p. 160.

88. Ibid., p. 161.

192   Notes to Pages 143–145

89. Paul Cammack, "Review Article: Bringing the State Back In?" *British Journal of Political Science* 19, no. 2 (April 1989), p. 278.

90. Skocpol and Finegold, "State Capacity and Economic Intervention," p. 258.

91. Cammack, "Review Article," p. 278. Gregory Hooks ("From an Autonomous to a Captured State Agency: The Decline of the New Deal in Agriculture," *American Sociological Review* 55 [February 1990]: 29–43) has attempted to salvage Skocpol and Finegold's thesis by arguing that "even the capture of the USDA, an out-come anticipated by society-centered accounts, can only be understood by analyzing the state and its institutions" (p. 40). Yet, even though he studiously tries to avoid the conclusion, Hooks concedes that New Deal reformers were unable to sustain their policies because they "lacked a viable base in society" (p. 35).

92. For example, Edwin Amenta and Bruce G. Carruthers, "The Formative Years of U.S. Social Spending Policies: Theories of the Welfare State and the American States during the Great Depression," *American Sociological Review* 53 (1988): 661–78; and Stanely DeViney, "Characteristics of the State and the Expansion of Public Social Expenditures," *Comparative Social Research* 6 (1983): 151–73.

93. Stanley Vittoz's *New Deal Labor Policy and the American Industrial Economy* (Chapel Hill: University of North Carolina Press, 1987) exemplifies the difficulties of sorting out the different class sources and legislative origins of public policy. The book is an "attempt to provide a systematic description and analysis of New Deal labor policy in the context of [Vittoz's] deeper concern about the need for a broadly applicable integrated theory of the state, politics, and class," and, yet, its implications for the state are indeterminate, ambiguous, and contradictory. The result is that despite being highly sensitive to this theoretical issue "the book does not provide an elaborate theoretical framework of the sort called for above" (p. 9).

94. Block, *Revising State Theory*, p. 16.

95. Ibid., p. 21.

96. Jessop, *State Theory*, p. 316.

97. Timothy Mitchell, "The Limits of the State: Beyond Statist Approaches and Their Critics," *American Political Science Review* 85, no. 1 (March 1991): 77–96. For instance, see the essays in Charles S. Maier, ed., *Changing Boundaries of the Political* (Cambridge, Mass.: Harvard University Press, 1987).

98. Hall and Ikenberry, *The State*, pp. 14, 95–96; see also, for example, Clyde W. Barrow, "Corporate Liberalism, Finance Hegemony, and Central State Intervention in the Reconstruction of American Higher Education," *Studies in American Political Development* 6 (June 1992): 240–64.

99. Paul Q. Hirst, ed., *The Pluralist Theory of the State* (London: Routledge and Kegan Paul, 1989), pp. 1–46.

100. Jessop, *State Theory*, p. 316.

101. Poggi, *The State*, p. 184. Italics mine.

102. For example, see Richard Rose, *The Postmodern Presidency: The White House Meets the World* (Chatham, N.J.: Chatham House, 1988).

103. Poggi, *The State*, p. 184.

Chapter 6. The Antinomies of Marxist Political Theory

1. Cf. O'Connor, *The Meaning of Crisis*.

2. Gold, Lo, and Wright, "Recent Developments, Part I," p. 31.

3. Jessop (*The Capitalist State*, p. 221) observes that "state power is capitalist to the extent that it creates, maintains, or restores the conditions required for capital accumulation in a given situation and it is non-capitalist to the extent those conditions are not realized."

4. Anthony Giddens, *Central Problems in Social Theory: Action, Structure and Contradiction in Social Analysis* (Berkeley and Los Angeles: University of California Press, 1979), p. 111.

5. Callinicos, *Making History*, chaps. 1–2.

6. Giddens, *Central Problems in Social Theory*, p. 55.

7. Ibid., p. 56.

8. For example, Domhoff (*The Powers That Be*, p. xii) claims to provide only a framework "for considering the specific processes through which the ruling class dominates the government and underlying population within the territory or 'state' known as the United States."

9. For example, see Miliband, *State in Capitalist Society*.

10. Offe, "Structural Problems of the Capitalist State," p. 32.

11. Ibid., p. 33.

12. Giddens, *Central Problems in Social Theory*, pp. 64–66.

13. Callinicos, *Making History*, p. 39.

14. Wright, *Class, Crisis, and the State*, chap. 1.

15. Giddens, *Central Problems in Social Theory*, p. 111.

16. The classic structuralist reading is Etienne Balibar, "On the Basic Concepts of Historical Materialism," in Louis Althusser and Etienne Balibar, *Reading Capital*, pp. 199–308 (London: New Left Books, 1970).

17. Callinicos, *Making History*, p. 39: ". . . to say that a society has a structure is to say that there are limits to the extent to which it may vary without becoming an instance of a different kind of society."

18. The critical theory matrix has a methodological counterpart in mainstream social science. The four dominant non-Marxian approaches to the state are pluralism (power structure analysis), structural functionalism, systems analysis, and institutionalism (organizational realism). For example, see, respectively, Dahl, *Who Governs?*; Gabriel A. Almond, *Comparative Politics: System, Process, and Policy* (Boston: Little, Brown and Co., 1978); David Easton, *A Systems Analysis of Political Life* (Chicago: University of Chicago

Press, 1979); Samuel P. Huntington, *Political Order in Changing Societies* (New Haven: Yale University Press, 1968). Conversely, Miliband and Domhoff's instrumentalist approach has often been criticized by structuralists for accepting the methodological premises of a liberal-pluralist–behavioral paradigm; see Gold, Lo, and Wright, "Recent Developments, Part I," pp. 33–35. Similarly, Simon Clarke ("Marxism, Sociology, and Poulantzas' Theory of the State," pp. 9–13) observes that structuralist theory grafts the Marxist concept of class struggle onto "the theory of society developed by structural-functionalism, and above all by Talcott Parsons" (p. 9). On the other hand, as Fred Block (*Revising State Theory*, pp. 171–72) observes, Offe and O'Connor's accumulation-legitimation thesis is an analytic "mirror image of conservative arguments about interference with free markets." Finally, Hall and Ikenberry (*The State*, pp. 9–12) note that organizational realism is indebted analytically to a concept of the state drawn from the conservative realist approach.

19. For a similar concept of "paradigm" see J. G. A. Pocock, *Politics, Language and Time* (New York: Atheneum, 1973), p. 277.

20. Callinicos, *Making History*, p. 4.

21. Alford and Friedland, *Powers of Theory*, p. 390.

22. Ibid., pp. xiii–xiv.

23. Ibid., p. xiii. Quite the contrary, in their discussions of Marxian approaches, Alford and Friedland (ibid., p. 271 fn. 1) covertly note the suppression of competing assumptions: "Our own approach is to retain the assumption of contradictory institutional logics but to drop the assumption that they are hierarchically ordered in a deterministic fashion, which actually incorporates elements of a managerial [i.e., what I have called organizational] epistemology into a presumably dialectical method."

24. Lukes, *Power*; Block, "The Ruling Class Does Not Rule."

25. Block conceptualizes the same phenomena as levels, which he refers to, respectively, as decision-making, subsidiary structural mechanisms, and major structural mechanisms. Lukes's terminology is less precise, but he uses the same conceptual apparatus.

26. Alford and Friedland, *Powers of Theory*, pp. 4–5.

27. Ibid., p. 393.

28. Fred Block's "major structural mechanism" and Claus Offe's "dependency principle" are the obvious candidates to supply this deficiency. I have already addressed the shortcomings of these concepts, respectively, in chapter 2 and chapter 4.

29. Alford and Friedland, *Powers of Theory*, p. 287. In another passage, Alford and Friedland concede that they "believe the perspectives to be incompatible at all three levels of analysis" (p. 393).

30. Ibid., p. 3.

31. Ibid., p. 441.

32. Jessop, *The Capitalist State*, pp. 11, 212–43. Callinicos's attempt to bridge the action-structure methodological antinomy resulted in seven method-

ological guidelines to be followed in the construction of an "adequate" theory of the state, see *Making History*, pp. 235–37.

33. Jessop, *The Capitalist State*, p. 252.

34. Jessop, *State Theory*, p. 366.

35. Ibid., p. 367.

36. Held and Krieger, "Theories of the State," pp. 18–19.

37. Carnoy, *The State and Political Theory*, p. 255.

38. Thomas S. Kuhn, *The Structure of Scientific Revolutions*, 2nd edition (Chicago: University of Chicago Press, 1970), pp. 23–24.

39. Ibid., p. 24. Note in this passage that Kuhn refers explicitly to a paradigm's capacity to generate multiple theories. In other words, paradigms are diffuse and loosely constructed conceptual constellations which allow for the formulation of more than one theoretical approach, particularly when that conceptual axis is welded to competing philosophies of science (i.e., methodological axes). On the other hand, as with any structure, no paradigm is capable of infinite development without changing into something different (i.e., a paradigm shift).

40. Ibid., p. 24.

41. Ibid., p. 24.

Sources Consulted

Ackerman, Frank, Howard Birnbaum, James Wetzler, and Andrew Zimbalist. "The Extent of Income Inequality in the United States." In Richard C. Edwards, Michael Reich, and Thomas Weisskopf, eds., *The Capitalist System*, 1st edition, pp. 207–18. Englewood Cliffs, N.J.: Prentice-Hall, 1972.

Aglietta, Michel. *A Theory of Capitalist Regulation: The U.S. Experience.* London: New Left Books, 1979.

Alford, Robert R., and Roger Friedland. *Powers of Theory: Capitalism, the State, and Democracy.* Cambridge: Cambridge University Press, 1985.

Almond, Gabriel A. *Comparative Politics: System, Process, and Policy.* Boston: Little, Brown and Co., 1978.

Almond, Gabriel A. "The Return to the State." *American Political Science Review* 82, no. 3 (September 1988): 853–74.

Althusser, Louis, and Etienne Balibar. *Reading Capital.* London: New Left Books, 1970.

Altvater, Elmer. "Notes on Some Problems of State Interventionism (I)." *Kapitalistate* 1 (1973): 97–108.

Altvater, Elmer. "Notes on Some Problems of State Interventionism (II)." *Kapitalistate* 2 (1973): 76–83.

Amenta, Edwin, and Bruce G. Carruthers. "The Formative Years of U.S. Social Spending Policies: Theories of the Welfare State and the American States during the Great Depression." *American Sociological Review* 53 (1988): 661–78.

Amin, Samir. *Unequal Development.* New York: Monthly Review Press, 1976.

Anderson, Perry. *Lineages of the Absolutist State.* London: Verso, 1979.

Apple, Michael W. *Ideology and Curriculum.* London: Routledge and Kegan Paul, 1979.

Atkinson, Michael M., and William D. Coleman. "Strong States and Weak States: Sectoral Policy Networks in Advanced Capitalist Economies." *British Journal of Political Science* 19, no. 1 (January 1989): 47–67.

Avery, Robert B., and Gregory E. Elliehausen. "Financial Characteristics of High-Income Families." *Federal Reserve Bulletin* 72, no. 3 (March 1986): 163–77.

Balbus, Isaac. "Modern Capitalism and the State: Ruling Elite Theory vs. Marxist Class Analysis." *Monthly Review* 23, no. 1 (May 1971): 36–46.

Balibar, Etienne. "On the Basic Concepts of Historical Materialism." In Louis Althusser and Etienne Balibar, *Reading Capital*, pp. 199–308. London: New Left Books, 1970.

197

Baltzell, E. Digby. *Philadelphia Gentlemen: The Making of a National Upper Class*. New Brunswick: Transaction Publishers, 1989.

Barak, Gregg, ed. *Crimes by the Capitalist State*. Albany: SUNY Press, 1991.

Baran, Paul A., and Paul M. Sweezy. *Monopoly Capital: An Essay on the American Economic and Social Order*. New York: Monthly Review Press, 1966.

Barrow, Clyde W. *Universities and the Capitalist State: Corporate Liberalism and the Reconstruction of American Higher Education, 1894–1928*. Madison: University of Wisconsin Press, 1990.

Barrow, Clyde W. "Corporate Liberalism, Finance Hegemony, and Central State Intervention in the Reconstruction of American Higher Education." *Studies in American Political Development* 6 (June 1992): 240–64.

Bell, Daniel. *The Coming of Postindustrial Society*. New York: Basic Books, 1973.

Bell, Daniel. *The Cultural Contradictions of Capitalism*. New York: Basic Books, 1976.

Bensel, Richard. *Yankee Leviathan: The Origins of Central State Authority in America, 1859–1877*. Cambridge: Cambridge University Press, 1990.

Berger, Johannes, and Claus Offe. 1982. "Functionalism vs. Rational Choice? Some Questions Concerning the Rationality of Choosing One or the Other." *Theory and Society* 11, no. 4 (July 1982): 521–26.

Bernstein, Eduard. *Evolutionary Socialism*. New York: Schocken Books, 1961.

Bernstein, Richard J. *The Restructuring of Social and Political Theory*. Philadelphia: University of Pennsylvania Press, 1976.

Bernstein, Richard J. *Beyond Objectivism and Relativism*. Philadelphia: University of Pennsylvania Press, 1983.

Best, Michael H., and William E. Connolly. *The Politicized Economy*. Lexington, Mass.: D. C. Heath, 1976.

Birnbaum, Pierre. "The State in Contemporary France." In Richard Scase, ed., *The State in Western Europe*, pp. 94–114. New York: St. Martin's Press, 1980.

Blanke, Bernhard, Ulrich Jurgens, and Hans Kastendiek. "The Relationship between the Political and Economic as a Point of Departure for a Materialist Analysis of the Bourgeois State." *International Journal of Politics* 6 (1976): 68–126.

Blanke, Bernhard, Ulrich Jurgens, and Hans Kastendiek. "On the Current Marxist Discussion on the Analysis of Form and Function of the Bourgeois State: Reflections on the Relationship of Politics to Economics." In John Holloway and Sol Picciotto, eds., *State and Capital: A Marxist Debate*, pp. 108–47. Austin: University of Texas Press, 1978.

Block, Fred L. "The Ruling Class Does Not Rule: Notes on the Marxist Theory of the State." *Socialist Revolution* 7, no. 3 (1977): 6–28.

Block, Fred B. "Beyond Relative Autonomy: State Managers as Historical Subjects." *Socialist Register* 14 (1980): 227–42.

Block, Fred. "Political Choice and the Multiple 'Logics' of Capital." *Theory and Society* 15, nos. 1–2 (1986): 175–90.

Block, Fred. *Revising State Theory*. Philadelphia: Temple University Press, 1987.

Bluestone, Barry, and Bennett Harrison. *The Deindustrialization of America*. New York: Basic Books, 1982.

Boggs, Carl. *Social Movements and Political Power: Emerging Forms of Radicalism in the West*. Philadelphia: Temple University Press, 1986.

Bornstein, Stephen, David Held, and Joel Krieger. *The State in Capitalist Europe: A Casebook*. Boston: George Allen and Unwin, 1984.

Bottomore, Tom B. *Classes in Modern Society*. New York: Vintage Books, 1966.

Bowles, Samuel, and Herbert Gintis. *Schooling in Capitalist America*. New York: Basic Books, 1976.

Bowles, Samuel, and Herbert Gintis. "The Crisis of Liberal Democratic Capitalism: The Case of the United States." *Politics and Society* 11, no. 1 (1982): 51–93.

Bowles, Samuel, David M. Gordon, and Thomas E. Weisskopf. *Beyond the Wasteland: A Democratic Alternative to Economic Decline*. Garden City, N.Y.: Anchor Books, 1984.

Bowles, Samuel, David M. Gordon, and Thomas E. Weisskopf. "Power and Profits: The Social Structure of Accumulation and the Profitability of the Postwar U.S. Economy." *Review of Radical Political Economics* 18, nos. 1–2 (Spring–Summer, 1986): 132–67.

Bowles, Samuel, David M. Gordon, and Thomas E. Weisskopf. *After the Wasteland: A Democratic Economics for the Year 2000*. Armonk, N.Y.: M. E. Sharpe, 1990.

Bridges, Amy Beth. "Nicos Poulantzas and the Marxist Theory of the State." *Politics and Society* 2 (1973): 161–90.

Callinicos, Alex. *Making History: Agency, Structure and Change in Social Theory*. Ithaca: Cornell University Press, 1988.

Cammack, Paul. "Review Article: Bringing the State Back In?" *British Journal of Political Science* 19, no. 2 (April 1989): 261–90.

Carnoy, Martin. *The State and Political Theory*. Princeton: Princeton University Press, 1984.

Carnoy, Martin, and Derek Shearer. *Economic Democracy: The Challenge of the 1980s*. Armonk, N.Y.: M. E. Sharpe, 1980.

Clark, Gordon L., and Michael Dear. 1984. *State Apparatus: Structures of Language and Legitimacy*. Boston: Allen and Unwin, 1984.

Clarke, Simon. "Marxism, Sociology, and Poulantzas' Theory of the State." *Capital and Class* 2 (Summer, 1977): 1–31.

Clarke, Simon. "State, Class Struggle, and the Reproduction of Capital." *Kapitalistate* 10–11 (1983): 113–34.

Cocks, Peter. "Towards a Marxist Theory of European Integration." *International Organization* 34, no. 1 (Winter, 1984): 1–40.

Cohen, Jean L. "Between Crisis Management and Social Movements: The Place of Institutional Reform." *Telos* 52 (1982): 21–40.

Connolly, William, ed. *Legitimacy and the State*. Oxford: Basil Blackwell, 1984.

Corporation for Enterprise Development. *1990 Development Report Card.* Washington, D.C.: Corporation for Enterprise Development, 1990.

Crouch, Colin. "The State, Capital, and Liberal Democracy." In Colin Crouch, ed., *State and Economy in Contemporary Capitalism*, pp. 13–54. London: Croom Helm, 1979.

Crozier, Michel J., Samuel P. Huntington, and Joji Watanuki, eds. *The Crisis of Democracy.* New York: New York University Press, 1975.

Dahl, Robert A. "A Critique of the Ruling Elite Model." *American Political Science Review* 52 (1958): 463–69.

Dahl, Robert A. *Who Governs? Democracy and Power in an American City.* New Haven: Yale University Press, 1961.

Dahl, Robert A. *Polyarchy.* New Haven: Yale University Press, 1971.

Dahl, Robert A. *A Preface to Economic Democracy.* New Haven: Yale University Press, 1985.

De Bernis, Gerard Destanne. "On a Marxist Theory of Regulation." *Monthly Review* 41, no. 8 (January 1990): 28–37.

Derthick, Martha. *Policy Making for Social Security.* Washington, D.C.: Brookings Institution, 1985.

DeViney, Stanley. "Characteristics of the State and the Expansion of Public Social Expenditures." *Comparative Social Research* 6 (1983): 151–73.

Domhoff, G. William. *Who Rules America?* Englewood Cliffs, N.J.: Prentice-Hall, 1967.

Domhoff, G. William. *The Higher Circles: The Governing Class in America.* New York: Vintage Books, 1970.

Domhoff, G. William. *The Bohemian Grove and Other Retreats: A Study in Ruling-Class Cohesiveness.* New York: Harper and Row, 1974.

Domhoff, G. William. *Who Really Rules?* New Brunswick: Transaction, 1978.

Domhoff, G. William. *The Powers That Be: Processes of Ruling Class Domination in America.* New York: Vintage Books, 1979.

Domhoff, G. William. *Power Structure Research.* Beverly Hills: Sage Publications, 1980.

Domhoff, G. William. "State Autonomy and the Privileged Position of Business: An Empirical Attack on a Theoretical Fantasy." *Journal of Political and Military Sociology* 14 (Spring, 1986): 149–62.

Domhoff, G. William. "On 'Welfare Capitalism' and the Social Security Act of 1935." *American Sociological Review* 51 (June 1986): 445–46.

Domhoff, G. William. "Corporate-Liberal Theory and the Social Security Act: A Chapter in the Sociology of Knowledge." *Politics and Society* 15, no. 3 (1986–87): 295–330.

Domhoff, G. William. "The Wagner Act and Theories of the State: A New Analysis Based on Class-Segment Theory." *Political Power and Social Theory* 6 (1987): 159–85.

Domhoff, G. William. *The Power Elite and the State.* New York: Aldine de Gruyter, 1990.

Donolo, Carlo. "Social Change and Transformation of the State in Italy." In

Richard Scase, ed., *The State in Western Europe*, pp. 164–96. New York: St. Martin's Press, 1980.

Draper, Hal. *Karl Marx's Theory of Revolution*, Vol. 1. New York: Monthly Review Press, 1977.

Dukakis, Michael S., and Rosabeth Moss Kanter. *Creating the Future: The Massachusetts Comeback and Its Promise for America*. New York: Summit Books, 1988.

Dunleavy, Patrick, and Brendan O'Leary. *Theories of the State*. New York: Macmillan, 1987.

Easton, David. *A Systems Analysis of Political Life*. Chicago: University of Chicago Press, 1979.

Easton, David. *The Analysis of Political Structure*. New York: Routledge and Kegan Paul, 1990.

Eckstein, Harry. "On the 'Science' of the State." In Stephen R. Graubard, ed., *The State*, pp. 1–20. New York: W. W. Norton, 1979.

Edelman, Murray. *The Symbolic Uses of Politics*. Urbana: University of Illinois Press, 1976.

Edsall, Thomas Byrne. *The New Politics of Inequality*. New York: W. W. Norton, 1984.

Edwards, Richard C. "Who Fares Well in the Welfare State?" In Richard C. Edwards, Michael Reich, and Thomas Weisskopf, eds., *The Capitalist System*, 2nd edition, pp. 307–14. Englewood Cliffs, N.J.: Prentice-Hall, 1978.

Edwards, Richard C., Michael Reich, and Thomas Weisskopf, eds. *The Capitalist System*, 2nd edition. Englewood Cliffs, N.J.: Prentice-Hall, 1978.

Edwards, Richard C., Michael Reich, and Thomas Weisskopf. "The Effect of Taxes and Government Spending on Inequality." In Richard C. Edwards, Michael Reich, and Thomas Weisskopf, eds., *The Capitalist System*, 1st edition, pp. 236–38. Englewood Cliffs, N.J.: Prentice-Hall, 1972.

Ehrenreich, Barbara, and John Ehrenreich. "The Professional Managerial Class." *Radical America* 11 (March–April 1977): 7–31.

Eisinger, Peter K. *The Rise of the Entrepreneurial State: State and Local Economic Development Policy in the United States*. Madison: University of Wisconsin Press, 1988.

Elkin, Stephen L. *City and Regime in the American Republic*. Chicago: University of Chicago, 1987.

Elster, John. "Marxism, Functionalism, Game Theory: The Case for Methodological Individualism." *Theory and Society* 11, no. 4 (July 1982): 453–82.

Esping-Andersen, Gosta. *Politics against Markets: The Social Democratic Road to Power*. Princeton: Princeton University Press, 1985.

Esping-Andersen, Gosta, Roger Friedland, and Erik Olin Wright. "Modes of Class Struggle and the Capitalist State." *Kapitalistate* 4–5 (1976): 186–220.

Evans, Peter B., Dietrich Rueschemeyer, and Theda Skocpol. "On the Road toward a More Adequate Understanding of the State." In Peter Evans, Dietrich Rueschemeyer, and Theda Skocpol, eds., *Bringing the State Back In*, pp. 347–66. Cambridge: Cambridge University Press, 1985.

Fay, Brian. *Social Theory and Political Practice*. London: George Allen and Unwin, 1975.

Ferguson, Thomas. "From Normalcy to New Deal: Industrial Structure, Party Competition, and American Public Policy in the Great Depression." *International Organization* 38 (1984): 41–94.

Finegold, Kenneth. "From Agrarianism to Adjustment: The Political Origins of New Deal Agricultural Policy." *Politics and Society* 11 (1982): 1–27.

Fitch, Robert, and Mary Oppenheimer. "Who Rules the Corporations?" *Socialist Revolution* 1 (1970): no. 4: 73–107; no. 5: 61–114; no. 6: 33–93.

Flora, Peter, ed. *Growth to Limits: The Western European Welfare States since World War II*. New York: Walter de Gruyter, 1986.

Frankel, Boris. *The Postindustrial Utopians*. Madison: University of Wisconsin Press, 1987.

Freitag, Peter. "The Cabinet and Big Business." *Social Problems* 23 (1975): 137–52.

Furner, Mary O., and Barry Supple, eds. *The State and Economic Knowledge*. Cambridge: Cambridge University Press, 1990.

Gallie, W. B. "Essentially Contested Concepts." *Proceedings of the Aristotelian Society* 56 (1955–56): 167–98.

Gerstenberger, Heide. "Class Conflict, Competition and State Functions." In John Holloway and Sol Picciotto, eds., *State and Capital: A Marxist Debate*, pp. 148–59. Austin: University of Texas Press, 1978.

Giddens, Anthony. *Central Problems in Social Theory: Action, Structure and Contradiction in Social Analysis*. Berkeley and Los Angeles: University of California Press, 1979.

Girardin, Jean-Claude. "On the Marxist Theory of the State." *Politics and Society* 5, no. 1 (1973): 193–223.

Gold, David A., Clarence Y. H. Lo, and Erik Olin Wright. "Recent Developments in Marxist Theories of the Capitalist State, Part I." *Monthly Review* 27, no. 5 (October 1975): 29–43.

Gold, David A., Clarence Y. H. Lo, and Erik Olin Wright. "Recent Developments in Marxist Theories of the Capitalist State, Part II." *Monthly Review* 27, no. 6 (November 1975): 36–51.

Goldfield, Michael. "Worker Insurgency, Radical Organization, and New Deal Labor Legislation." *American Political Science Review* 83, no. 4 (December 1989): 1257–82.

Gordon, David. "Stages of Accumulation and Long Economic Cycles." In T. Hopkins and I. Wallerstein, eds., *Processes of the World System*, pp. 9–45. Beverly Hills: Sage Publications, 1980.

Gordon, David M., Richard C. Edwards, and Michael Reich. *Segmented Work, Divided Workers*. Cambridge: Cambridge University Press, 1982.

Gordon, Robert. "Critical Legal Histories." *Stanford Law Review* 36 (January 1984): 57–125.

Gordon, Suzanne. *Prisoners of Men's Dreams*. Boston: Little, Brown and Co., 1991.

Gorz, Andre. *Farewell to the Working Class: An Essay on Postindustrial Social-ism*. Boston: South End Press, 1982.

Gorz, Andre. *Critique of Economic Reason*. London: Verso, 1989.

Gough, Ian. *The Political Economy of the Welfare State*. London: Macmillan Press, Ltd., 1979.

Gouldner, Alvin. *The Future of Intellectuals and the Rise of the New Class*. New York: Continuum, 1979.

Grafstein, Robert. "A Realist Foundation for Essentially Contested Political Concepts." *Western Political Quarterly* 41 (March 1988): 9–28.

Gray, John. "On the Contestability of Social and Political Concepts." *Political Theory 5*, no. 3 (August 1977): 331–48.

Grover, William F. *The President as Prisoner: A Structural Critique of the Carter and Reagan Years*. Albany: SUNY Press, 1989.

Gulalp, Haldun. "The Stages and Long-Cycles of Capitalist Development." *Review of Radical Political Economics* 21, no. 4 (Spring, 1989): 83–92.

Habermas, Jurgen. *Toward a Rational Society*. Boston: Beacon Press, 1970.

Habermas, Jurgen. *Knowledge and Human Interests*. Boston: Beacon Press, 1971.

Habermas, Jurgen. *Legitimation Crisis*. Boston: Beacon Press, 1975.

Hall, John A., and G. John Ikenberry. *The State*. Minneapolis: University of Minnesota Press, 1989.

Hall, Peter A. "Patterns of Economic Policy: An Organizational Approach." In Stephen Bornstein, David Held, and Joel Krieger, eds., *The State in Capitalist Europe: A Casebook* pp. 21–43. Cambridge, Mass.: George Allen and Unwin, 1984.

Halperin, Morton. *The Lawless State*. New York: Penguin Books, 1976.

Hamilton, N. *The Limits of State Autonomy: Post-Revolutionary Mexico*. Princeton: Princeton University Press, 1982.

Hanson, Russell L. *The Democratic Imagination in America*. Princeton: Princeton University Press, 1985.

Held, David, and Joel Krieger. "Theories of the State: Some Competing Claims." In Stephen Bornstein, David Held, and Joel Krieger, eds., *The State in Capitalist Europe*, pp. 1–20. Boston: George Allen and Unwin, 1984.

Hindess, Barry, and Paul Q. Hirst. *Pre-Capitalist Modes of Production*. London: Routledge and Kegan Paul, 1975.

Hindess, Barry, and Paul Q. Hirst. *Mode of Production and Social Formation*. London: Macmillan Press, Ltd., 1977.

Hinrichs, Karl, Claus Offe, and Helmut Wiesenthal. "The Crisis of the Welfare State and Alternative Modes of Work Redistribution." *Thesis Eleven* 10–11 (1984–85): 37–55.

Hirsch, Joachim. "The State Apparatus and Social Reproduction: Elements of a Theory of the Bourgeois State." In John Holloway and Sol Picciotto, eds., *State and Capital: A Marxist Debate*, pp. 57–107. Austin: University of Texas Press, 1978.

Hirsch, Joachim. "The Fordist Security State and New Social Movements." *Kapitalistate* 10–11 (1983): 75–87.

Hirst, Paul Q. *On Law and Ideology.* London: Macmillan Press, Ltd., 1979.

Hirst, Paul Q., ed. *The Pluralist Theory of the State.* London: Routledge and Kegan Paul, 1989.

Holloway, John. *Social Policy Harmonisation in the European Community.* Westmead, England: Gower Press, 1981.

Holloway, John, and Sol Picciotto. "Introduction: Towards a Materialist Theory of the State." In John Holloway and Sol Picciotto, eds., *State and Capital: A Marxist Debate,* pp. 1–31. Austin: University of Texas Press, 1978.

Hooks, Gregory. "From an Autonomous to a Captured State Agency: The Decline of the New Deal in Agriculture." *American Sociological Review* 55 (February 1990): 29–43.

Horowitz, David. *The Fate of Midas and Other Essays.* San Francisco: Ramparts Press, 1973.

Hunter, Floyd. *Community Power Structure.* Chapel Hill: University of North Carolina Press, 1953.

Huntington, Samuel P. *Political Order in Changing Societies.* New Haven: Yale University Press, 1968.

Inglehart, Ronald. *The Silent Revolution: Changing Values and Political Styles among Western Publics.* Princeton: Princeton University Press, 1977.

Jessop, Bob. "Recent Theories of the Capitalist State." *Cambridge Journal of Economics* 1 (1977): 353–72.

Jessop, Bob. *The Capitalist State: Marxist Theories and Methods.* New York: New York University Press, 1982.

Jessop, Bob. "Accumulation Strategies, State Forms, and Hegemonic Projects." *Kapitalistate* 10–11 (1983): 89–112.

Jessop, Bob. *State Theory: Putting Capitalist States in Their Place.* Cambridge: Polity Press, 1990.

Johnson, Gene, and Beth Mintz, eds. *Networks of Power: Organizational Actors at the National, Corporate, and Community Levels.* New York: Aldine, 1988.

Karabel, Jerome, and A. H. Halsey, eds. *Power and Ideology in Education.* New York: Oxford University Press, 1977.

Katzenstein, Peter J., ed. *Between Power and Plenty: Foreign Economic Policies of Advanced Industrial Societies.* Madison: University of Wisconsin Press, 1978.

King, Roger. "The Political Practice of the Local Capitalist Association." In Roger King, ed., *Capital and Politics,* pp. 107–31. London: Routledge and Kegan Paul, 1983.

King, Roger. *The State in Modern Society.* Chatham, N.J.: Chatham House Publishers, 1986.

King, Ronald Frederick. "From Redistributive to Hegemonic Logic: The Transformation of American Tax Politics, 1894–1963." *Politics and Society* 12, no. 1 (1983): 1–52.

Knowles, James C. "The Rockefeller Financial Group." In Ralph L. Andreano, ed., *Superconcentration/Supercorporation*, Module 343, pp. 1–59. Andover, Mass.: Warner Modular Publications, 1973.

Koenig, Thomas, Robert Gogel, and Hohn Sonquist. "Models of the Significance of Interlocking Corporate Directorates." *American Journal of Economics and Sociology* 38 (1979): 178–83.

Korpi, Walter. "Social Policy and Distributional Conflict in the Capitalist Democracies: A Preliminary Comparative Framework." *Western European Politics* 3 (October 1980): 296–316.

Kotz, David M. "Finance Capital and Corporate Control" In Richard C. Edwards, Michael Reich, and Thomas E. Weisskopf, eds., *The Capitalist System*, 2nd edition, pp. 147–58. Englewood Cliffs, N.J.: Prentice-Hall, 1978.

Kotz, David M. *Bank Control of Large Corporations in the United States.* Berkeley and Los Angeles: University of California Press, 1978.

Kotz, David M. "A Comparative Analysis of the Theory of Regulation and the Social Structure of Accumulation Theory." *Science and Society* 54, no. 1 (Spring, 1990): 5–28.

Kuhn, Thomas S. *The Structure of Scientific Revolutions*, 2nd edition. Chicago: University of Chicago Press, 1970.

Laclau, Ernesto, and Chantal Mouffe. *Hegemony and Socialist Strategy.* London: Verso, 1985.

Lampman, Robert J. *The Share of Top Wealth Holders in National Wealth.* Princeton: Princeton University Press, 1962.

Lehigh, Scott, and Frank Phillips. "House Leaders Push Budget with Receivership Warnings." *Boston Globe*, May 16, 1991, p. 1.

Lehman, Edward W. "The Theory of the State versus the State of Theory." *American Sociological Review* 53 (December 1988): 807–23.

Lembcke, Jerry. *Capitalist Development and Class Capacities: Marxist Theory and Union Organization.* Westport, Conn.: Greenwood Press, 1988.

Lindblom, Charles E. "The Market as Prison." *Journal of Politics* 44, no. 2 (May 1982): 324–32.

Lipietz, Alain. *Mirages and Miracles: The Crises of Global Fordism.* London: Verso, 1987.

Logue, John. "The Welfare State: Victim of Its Success." In Stephen R. Graubard, ed., *The State*, pp. 69–88. New York: W. W. Norton, 1979.

Lukács, Georg. *History and Class Consciousness.* Cambridge, Mass.: M.I.T. Press, 1971.

Lukes, Steven. *Power: A Radical View.* London: Macmillan Press, Ltd., 1974.

Lustig, R. Jeffrey. *Corporate Liberalism: The Origins of Modern American Political Theory, 1890–1920.* Berkeley and Los Angeles: University of California Press, 1982.

McConnell, Grant. *Private Power and American Democracy.* New York: Alfred A. Knopf, 1966.

McIntyre, Robert S., and David Wilhelm. *Money for Nothing: The Failure of Corporate Tax Incentives, 1981–84.* Washington, D.C.: Citizens for Tax Justice, 1986.

Maier, Charles S., ed., *Changing Boundaries of the Political.* Cambridge, Mass.: Harvard University Press, 1987.

Mamut, L. S. "Questions of Law in Marx's *Capital.*" In Bob Jessop, ed., *Karl Marx's Social and Political Thought: Critical Assessments,* Vol. 3, pp. 95–105. London: Routledge, Chapman, and Hall, 1990.

Mandel, Ernest. *The Marxist Theory of the State.* New York: Pathfinder Press, 1971.

Mandel, Ernest. *Late Capitalism.* London: Verso, 1978.

Mannheim, Karl. *Ideology and Utopia.* New York: Harcourt, Brace, Jovanovich, 1936.

March, James G., and Johan P. Olsen. "The New Institutionalism: Organizational Factors in Political Life." *American Political Science Review* 78, no. 3 (September 1984): 734–49.

Marx, Karl. *Capital,* Vol. 1, trans. Samuel Moore and Edward Aveling. New York: Modern Library, 1906.

Marx, Karl. *Grundrisse: Foundations of the Critique of Political Economy,* trans. Martin Nicholaus. New York: Vintage Books, 1973.

Mason, Edward S. *Economic Concentration and the Monopoly Problem.* New York: Atheneum, 1964.

Mason, Edward. *The Modern Corporation.* New York: Atheneum, 1969.

Mayer, Thomas F. "In Defense of Analytical Marxism." *Science and Society* 53, no. 4 (Winter, 1989–90): 416–41.

Means, Gardiner C. *The Structure of the American Economy.* Washington, D.C.: GPO, 1939.

Miliband, Ralph. *The State in Capitalist Society.* New York: Basic Books, 1969.

Miliband, Ralph. "The Capitalist State: Reply to Nicos Poulantzas." *New Left Review* 59 (January–February 1970): 53–60.

Miliband, Ralph. "Poulantzas and the Capitalist State." *New Left Review* 82 (1973): 83–92.

Miliband, Ralph. "State Power and Class Interests." *New Left Review* 138 (March–April 1983): 37–68.

Mills, C. Wright. *The Marxists.* New York: Dell, 1962.

Mintz, Beth. "The President's Cabinet, 1897–1972: A Contribution to the Power Structure Debate." *Insurgent Sociologist* 5 (1975): 131–48.

Mintz, Beth. "United States of America." In Tom Bottomore and Robert J. Brym, eds., *The Capitalist Class: An International Study,* pp. 207–36. Washington Square, N.Y.: New York University Press, 1989.

Mintz, Beth, and Michael Schwartz. *The Power Structure of American Business.* Chicago: University of Chicago Press, 1985.

Mitchell, Timothy. "The Limits of the State: Beyond Statist Approaches and Their Critics." *American Political Science Review* 85, no. 1 (March 1991): 77–96.

Mizruchi, Mark. *The American Corporate Network: 1904–1975*. Beverly Hills: Sage Publications, 1982.

Moody, Kim. *An Injury to All: The Decline of American Unionism*. London: Verso, 1988.

O'Connor, James. *The Fiscal Crisis of the State*. New York: St. Martin's Press, 1973.

O'Connor, James. *Accumulation Crisis*. New York: Basil Blackwell, 1984.

O'Connor, James. *The Meaning of Crisis: A Theoretical Introduction*. New York: Basil Blackwell, 1987.

O'Connor, Jim. "Summary of the Theory of the Fiscal Crisis." *Kapitalistate* 1 (1973): 79–83.

Offe, Claus. "Advanced Capitalism and the Welfare State." *Politics and Society* 2 (1972): 479–88.

Offe, Claus. "Political Authority and Class Structures: An Analysis of Late Capitalist Societies." *International Journal of Sociology* 2 (1972): 73–108.

Offe, Claus. "The Abolition of Market Control and the Problem of Legitimacy (I)." *Kapitalistate* 1 (1973): 109–16.

Offe, Claus. "The Abolition of Market Control and the Problem of Legitimacy (II)." *Kapitalistate* 2 (1973): 73–75.

Offe, Claus. "Structural Problems of the Capitalist State: Class Rule and the Political System. On the Selectiveness of Political Institutions." In Klaus von Beyme, ed., *German Political Studies*, Vol. 1, pp. 31–57. Beverly Hills: Sage Publications, 1974.

Offe, Claus. "The Theory of the Capitalist State and the Problem of Policy Formation." In Leon Lindberg, ed., *Stress and Contradiction in Modern Capitalism*, pp. 125–144. Lexington, Mass.: D. C. Heath, 1975.

Offe, Claus. *Contradictions of the Welfare State*. Cambridge, Mass.: M.I.T. Press, 1984.

Offe, Claus. *Disorganized Capitalism*. Cambridge, Mass.: M.I.T. Press, 1985.

Offe, Claus. "New Social Movements: Challenging the Boundaries of Institutional Politics." *Social Research* 52, no. 4 (Winter, 1985): 817–68.

Offe, Claus. "Challenging the Boundaries of Institutional Politics: Social Movements since the 1960's." In Charles S. Maier, ed., *Changing Boundaries of the Political*, pp. 63–105. Cambridge: Cambridge University Press, 1987.

Olson, Mancur. *The Rise and Decline of Nations*. New Haven: Yale University Press, 1984.

Orren, Karen, and Stephen Skowronek. "Editors' Preface." *Studies in American Political Development*, Vol. 1. New Haven: Yale University Press, 1986.

Osborne, David. *Reinventing Government: The Rise of an Entrepreneurial Public Sector*. Reading, Mass.: Addison-Wesley, 1992.

Page, Benjamin. *Who Gets What from Government*. Berkeley and Los Angeles: University of California Press, 1983.

Palmer, David. "On the Significance of Interlocking Directorates." *Social Science History* 7 (1983): 781–96.

Paulsen, George E. "The Federal Trade Commission versus the National Recovery Administration, 1935." *Social Science Quarterly* 70, no. 1 (March 1989): 149–63.

Payer, Cheryl. *The Debt Trap: The IMF and the Third World.* New York: Monthly Review Press, 1975.

Pennings, Johannes. *Interlocking Directorates.* San Francisco: Jossey-Bass, 1980.

Peschek, Joseph G. *Policy Planning Organizations: Elite Agendas and America's Rightward Turn.* Philadelphia: Temple University Press, 1987.

Picciotto, Sol, and Hugo Radice. "Capital and State in the World Economy." *Kapitalistate* 1 (1973): 56–68.

Pierson, C. "New Theories of the State and Civil Society." *British Journal of Sociology* 18, no. 4 (1984): 563–71.

Piore, Michael J., and Charles F. Sabel. *The Second Industrial Divide.* New York: Basic Books, 1984.

Piven, Frances Fox, and Richard A. Cloward. *Poor People's Movements: Why They Succeed, How They Fail.* New York: Vintage Books, 1977.

Piven, Francis Fox, and Richard A. Cloward. *Poor People's Movements: Why They Succeed, How They Fail.* New York: Vintage Books, 1977.

Pocock, J. G. A. *Politics, Language and Time.* New York: Atheneum, 1973.

Poggi, Gianfranco. *The State: Its Nature, Development and Prospects.* Stanford: Stanford University Press, 1990.

Polanyi, Karl. *The Great Transformation.* Boston: Beacon Press, 1949.

Poulantzas, Nicos. "The Problem of the Capitalist State." *New Left Review* 58 (November–December 1969): 67–78.

Poulantzas, Nicos. "On Social Classes." *New Left Review* 78 (March–April 1973): 27–54.

Poulantzas, Nicos. "The Capitalist State." *New Left Review* 95 (1976): 63–83.

Poulantzas, Nicos. *Classes in Contemporary Capitalism.* London: Verso, 1978.

Poulantzas, Nicos. *Political Power and Social Classes.* London: Verso, 1978.

Poulantzas, Nicos. *State, Power, Socialism.* London: Verso, 1980.

Przeworski, Adam. "Material Interest, Class Compromise, and the Transition to Socialism." *Politics and Society* 10, no. 2 (1980): 125–53.

Przeworski, Adam. "Social Democracy as a Historical Phenomenon." *New Left Review* 123 (1980): 27–58.

Przeworski, Adam. *Capitalism and Social Democracy.* Cambridge: Cambridge University Press, 1985.

Przeworski, Adam, and Michael Wallerstein. "The Structure of Class Conflict in Democratic Capitalist Societies." *American Political Science Review* 76, no. 2 (June 1982): 215–38.

Quadagno, Jill S. "Welfare Capitalism and the Social Security Act of 1935." *American Sociological Review* 49 (October 1984): 632–47.

Quadagno, Jill S. "Two Models of Welfare State Development: Reply to Skocpol and Amenta." *American Sociological Review* 50 (August 1985): 575–77.

Quadagno, Jill S. *The Transformation of Old-Age Security: Class and Politics in the American Welfare State.* Chicago: University of Chicago Press, 1988.

Rae, Douglas. "The Egalitarian State: Notes on a System of Contradictory Ideals." In Stephen R. Graubard, ed., *The State*, pp. 37–54. New York: W. W. Norton, 1979.

Reich, Robert B. *The Work of Nations: Preparing Ourselves for 21st Century Capitalism.* New York: Alfred A. Knopf, 1991.

Riddlesperger, James W., Jr., and James D. King. "Elitism and Presidential Appointments." *Social Science Quarterly* 70 (December 1989): 902–10.

Rockman, Bert A. "Review of William F. Grover, *The President as Prisoner*." *American Political Science Review* 84, no. 4 (December 1990): 1380.

Rose, Richard. *The Postmodern Presidency: The White House Meets the World.* Chatham, N.J.: Chatham House, 1988.

Ross, George. "Nicos Poulantzas, Eurocommunism, and the Debate on the Theory of the Capitalist State." *Socialist Review* 44 (March 1979): 143–58.

Ross, Robert J. S., and Kent C. Trachte. *Global Capitalism: The New Leviathan.* Albany: SUNY Press, 1990.

Roth, Paul. *Meaning and Method in the Social Sciences: A Case for Methodological Pluralism.* Ithaca: Cornell University Press, 1987.

Sardei-Biermann, Sabine, Jens Christiansen, and Knuth Dohse. "Class Domination and the Political System: A Critical Interpretation of Recent Contributions by Claus Offe." *Kapitalistate* 2 (1973): 60–69.

Scase, Richard, ed. *The State in Western Europe.* New York: St. Martin's Press, 1980.

Schneider, Saundra K. "The Sequential Development of Social Programs in the Eighteen Welfare States." *Comparative Social Research* 5 (1982): 195–219.

Schwartz, Michael, ed. *The Structure of Power in America.* New York and London: Holmes and Meier, 1987.

Shalev, Michael. "The Social Democratic Model and Beyond: Two 'Generations' of Comparative Research on the Welfare State." *Comparative Social Research* 6 (1983): 315–51.

Shalev, Michael, and Walter Korpi. "Working Class Mobilization and American Exceptionalism." *Economic and Industrial Democracy* 1 (1980): 31–61.

Sinz, Rudolf, Ana Delgado, and Stephen Leibfried. "Preface" to Elmer Altvater, "Notes on Some Problems of State Interventionism (I)." *Kapitalistate* 1 (1973): 96–97.

Sklar, Martin J. *The Corporate Reconstruction of American Capitalism, 1890–1916: The Market, the Law, and Politics.* Cambridge: Cambridge University Press, 1988.

Skocpol, Theda. "A Critical Review of Barrington Moore's Social Origins of Dictatorship and Democracy." *Politics and Society* 4 (1973): 1–34.

Skocpol, Theda. *States and Social Revolution.* Cambridge: Cambridge University Press, 1979.

Skocpol, Theda. "Political Response to Capitalist Crisis: Neo-Marxist Theories of the State and the Case of the New Deal." *Politics and Society* 10 (1980): 155–201.

Skocpol, Theda. "Bringing the State Back In: Strategies of Analysis in Current Research." In Peter Evans, Dietrich Rueschemeyer, and Theda Skocpol, eds., *Bringing the State Back In*, pp. 3–43. Cambridge: Cambridge University Press, 1985.

Skocpol, Theda. "A Brief Response [to G. William Domhoff]." *Politics and Society* 15, no. 3 (1986–87): 331–32.

Skocpol, Theda. "The Dead End of Metatheory: Review of *Powers of Theory: Capitalism, the State, and Democracy*, by Robert R. Alford and Roger Friedland." *Contemporary Sociology* 16 (1987): 10–12.

Skocpol, Theda, and Edwin Amenta. "Did Capitalists Shape Social Security?" *American Sociological Review* 50 (August 1985): 572–75.

Skocpol, Theda, and Edwin Amenta. "States and Social Policies." *Annual Review of Sociology* 12 (1986): 131–57.

Skocpol, Theda, and Kenneth Finegold. "State Capacity and Economic Intervention in the Early New Deal." *Political Science Quarterly* 97, no. 2 (Summer, 1982): 255–78.

Skocpol, Theda, and Kenneth Finegold. "Explaining New Deal Labor Policy." *American Political Science Review* 84, no. 4 (December 1990): 1297–304.

Skocpol, Theda, and John Ikenberry. "The Political Formation of the American Welfare State in Historical and Comparative Perspective." *Comparative Social Research* 6 (1983): 87–148.

Skowronek, Stephen. *Building a New American State: The Expansion of National Administrative Capacities, 1877–1920*. Cambridge: Cambridge University Press, 1982.

Smith, David N. *Who Rules the Universities?* New York: Monthly Review Press, 1974.

Soref, Michael. "The Finance Capitalists." In Maurice Zeitlin, ed., *Classes, Class Conflict, and the State*, pp. 60–82. Cambridge, Mass.: Winthrop, 1980.

Spring, Joel H. *Education and the Rise of the Corporate State*. Boston: Beacon Press, 1972.

Stepan, Alfred. *The State and Society*. Princeton: Princeton University Press, 1978.

Stinchcombe, Arthur L. "The Functional Theory of Social Insurance." *Politics and Society* 14, no. 4 (1985): 411–30.

Stokman, Frans, Rolf Ziegler, and John Scott, eds. *Networks of Corporate Power*. Cambridge: Polity Press, 1984.

Stone, Alan. "Modern Capitalism and the State: How Capitalism Rules." *Monthly Review* 23, no. 1 (May 1971): 31–36.

Sweezy, Paul. *The Theory of Capitalist Development*. New York: Monthly Review Press, 1942.

Therborn, Goran. *Science, Class and Society*. London: New Left Books, 1976.

Therborn, Goran. "The Rule of Capital and the Rise of Democracy." *New Left Review* 103 (May–June 1977): 3–41.

Therborn, Goran. *What Does the Ruling Class Do When It Rules?* London: New Left Books, 1978.

Therborn, Goran. *The Ideology of Power and the Power of Ideology.* London: Verso, 1980.

Tilly, Charles. "Reflections on the History of European State Making." In Charles Tilly, ed., *The Formation of National States in Western Europe*, pp. 1–99. Princeton: Princeton University Press, 1975.

Tilly, Charles. *From Mobilization to Revolution.* New York: Addison-Wesley, 1981.

Titmuss, Richard M. "The Social Division of Welfare." In *Essays on the Welfare State*, pp. 34–55. London: George Allen and Unwin, 1958.

Tomlins, Christopher L. *The State and the Unions: Labor Relations, Law and the Organized Labor Movement in America, 1880–1960.* Cambridge: Cambridge University Press, 1985.

Touraine, Alain. *The Post-Industrial Society.* New York: Random House, 1971.

Touraine, Alain. *Return of the Actor.* Minneapolis: University of Minnesota Press, 1988.

Trimberger, Ellen Kay. *Revolution from Above.* New Brunswick, N.J.: Transaction Books, 1978.

Tsongas, Paul. *A Call to Economic Arms: Forging a New American Mandate.* Boston: The Tsongas Committee, 1991.

Tucker, Robert C., ed. *The Marx-Engels Reader*, 2nd edition. New York: W. W. Norton, 1978.

U.S. Department of Commerce, Bureau of the Census. *Household Wealth and Ownership.* Washington, D.C.: GPO, 1984.

Useem, Michael. *The Inner Circle: Large Corporations and the Rise of Business Political Activity in the U.S. and U.K.* Oxford: Oxford University Press, 1984.

van der Pijl, Kees. "The International Level." In Tom Bottomore and Robert J. Brym, eds., *The Capitalist Class: An International Study*, pp. 237–66. Washington Square, N.Y.: New York University Press, 1989.

Vittoz, Stanley. *New Deal Labor Policy and the American Industrial Economy.* Chapel Hill: University of North Carolina Press, 1987.

Vogel, David. "The Power of Business in America: A Reappraisal." *British Journal of Political Science* 13, no. 1 (January 1983): 19–43.

von Braunmuhl, Claudia. "On the Analysis of the Bourgeois Nation State within the World Market Context. An Attempt to Develop a Methodological and Theoretical Approach." In John Holloway and Sol Picciotto, eds., *State and Capital: A Marxist Debate*, pp. 160–77. Austin: University of Texas Press, 1978.

Wallerstein, Immanuel. *The World Capitalist System II: Mercantilism and the*

Consolidation of the European World Economy, 1600–1750. New York: Academic Press, 1980.

Wallerstein, Immanuel. *World Systems Analysis: Theory and Methodology.* Beverly Hills: Sage Publications, 1982.

Warren, Mark E. "What Is Political Theory/Philosophy?" *PS: Political Science and Politics* 22 (September 1989): 606–12.

Weber, Max. "Class, Status, and Party." In Hans H. Gerth and C. Wright Mills, eds., *From Max Weber: Essays in Sociology,* pp. 180–95. New York: Oxford University Press, 1946.

Weber, Max. "The Quantitative Development of Administrative Tasks." In Hans H. Gerth and C. Wright Mills, eds., *From Max Weber: Essays in Sociology,* pp. 209–11. New York: Oxford University Press, 1946.

Weber, Max. "Qualitative Changes of Administrative Tasks." In Hans H. Gerth and C. Wright Mills, eds., *From Max Weber: Essays in Sociology,* pp. 212–14. New York: Oxford University Press, 1946.

Weber, Max. *The Methodology of the Social Sciences.* New York: Free Press, 1949.

Weinstein, James. *The Corporate Ideal in the Liberal State: 1900–1918.* Boston: Beacon Press, 1968.

Weir, Margaret, and Theda Skocpol. "State Structures and Social Keynesianism: Responses to the Great Depression in Sweden and the United States." *International Journal of Sociology* 26 (1983): 4–29.

Weir, Margaret, Ann Shola Orloff, and Theda Skocpol, eds. *The Politics of Social Policy in the United States.* Princeton: Princeton University Press, 1988.

Weisskopf, Thomas E. "Marxian Crisis Theory and the Rate of Profit in the Postwar U.S. Economy." *Cambridge Journal of Economics* 3 (1979): 341–78.

Wilks, S., and M. Wright, eds. *Comparative Government-Industry Relations.* Oxford: Clarendon Press, 1987.

Wolfe, Alan. *The Limits of Legitimacy: Political Contradictions of Contemporary Capitalism.* New York: Free Press, 1977.

Wright, Erik Olin. "Class Boundaries in Advanced Capitalist Societies." *New Left Review* 98 (July–August 1976): 3–42.

Wright, Erik Olin. "Alternative Perspectives in Marxist Theory of Accumulation and Crisis." In Jesse Schwartz, ed., *The Subtle Anatomy of Capitalism,* pp. 195–231. Santa Monica, Calif.: Goodyear Publishing Co., 1977.

Wright, Erik Olin. *Class, Crisis and the State.* London: New Left Books, 1978.

Wright, Erik Olin. *Class Structure and Income Determination.* New York: Academic Press, 1979.

Wright, Maurice. "Policy Community, Policy Network and Comparative Industrial Policies." *Political Studies* 36 (1988): 593–612.

Zeitlin, Maurice. *The Large Corporation and Contemporary Classes.* New Brunswick, N.J.: Rutgers University Press, 1989.

Zeitlin, Maurice. "Corporate Ownership and Control: The Large Corporation and the Capitalist Class." *American Journal of Sociology* 79, no. 5 (1974): 1073–119.

Zucker, Lynne G. "Institutional Theories of Organization." *Annual Review of Sociology* 13 (1987): 443–64.

Zweigenhaft, Richard. "Who Represents America?" *Insurgent Sociologist* (Spring, 1975): 119–30.

Index

Accumulation. *See* Capitalist accumulation

Action. *See* Agency

Agency: in state theory, 46, 72, 119–20, 147–48, 185*n98*. *See also* Political theory

Agricultural Adjustment Act: and state autonomy, 134–36, 142–43, 192*n91*

Alford, Robert R.: on state theory, 9, 12, 152–53

Altvater, Elmer: on logic of capital, 79–85 *passim;* mentioned, 85, 86, 90, 102, 106

Amenta, Edwin, 140

American Association for Labor Legislation, 137–41 *passim*

Baltzell, E. Digby, 22

Baran, Paul: on monopoly capital, 17; on financial groups, 18

Bernstein, Eduard: on Marxist methodology, 11

Best, Michael H.: on functional constraint mechanisms, 60–61

Birnbaum, Pierre, 89

Blanke, Bernhard, 94

Block, Fred: on special interests of capital, 32–33; on major structural mechanism 59, 60, 73–75 *passim,* 152, 174–75, 186*n114,* 186*n115;* on subsidiary structural mechanisms, 62–63, 152; on corporate liberal model, 138, 169*n85;* mentioned, 58, 129, 143. *See also* Business confidence

Boggs, Carl: on new social groups, 123

Bourgeoisie. *See* Capitalist class

Bowles, Samuel H.: on education policy, 67–68

Bridges, Amy Beth: on functional constraint mechanisms, 58–59, 60

Brown, Edmund G., Jr., 61

Bush, George, 74

Business confidence: as a functional constraint mechanism, 60–62, 73–75, 101–3, 122, 142–43, 174*n50,* 174*n66,* 183*n41,* 186*n114,* 186*n115;* and social investment, 76, 177*n103*

Business Council, 33, 37, 38, 137–39 *passim*

Business Roundtable, 33, 36

Callinicos, Alex, 149

Cammack, Paul, 143

Capital flight. *See* Business confidence

Capitalist accumulation: and mixed economy, 6, 40–41, 91; General Law of, 16, 164*n13;* crises of, 52, 182*n38;* models of, 74–76, 79–85; globalization of, 83–85, 90, 93. *See also* Crisis

Capitalist class: defined, 17; as an upper class, 22–24, 166*n36;* special interests of, 30–32, 52, 90, 168*n69,* 179*n34;* inner circle of, 33–34; long-term and general interests of, 40, 47, 78–85 *passim,* 90–91, 101, 102, 114, 142, 167*n52,* 168*n76,* 174*n50,* 179–80*n36,* 191*n71. See also* Financial Groups, Income distribution

Carey, Hugh, 61

Carnoy, Martin, 156

Case studies. *See* Agricultural Adjustment Act, National Industrial Recovery Act, National Labor Relations Act, Policy analysis, Social Security Act of 1935.

Chamber of Commerce, 38, 39

89 *passim,* 124; mentioned, 90–93
passim, 99
Holloway, John: 94–95 *passim*

Ideology. *See* Legitimacy, Political theory
Imperialism: defined, 87
Income distribution: and social policy,
5–6, 22, 176*n82;* and social democracy, 42, 169*n89;* and income tax,
67–68
Income tax: and income distribution,
67–68; and business confidence, 74–75
Infrastructure. *See* Social investment
Intellectuals: and power elite, 33–35;
and social democracy, 38; as policy
experts, 131–39 *passim,* 142, 191*n72;*
mentioned, 53
Interlocking directorates: defined, 18–
19; mentioned, 46, 165*n30. See also*
Capitalist class, Financial Groups,
Policy-planning organizations

Jessop, Bob: on instrumentalism, 46;
on state power, 57, 67, 154, 173*n39,*
193*n3;* on revolution, 69; on state autonomy, 144; on metatheory, 153–56;
mentioned, 89
Jurgens, Ulrich, 94

Kastendiek, Hans, 94
King, Roger: on functional constraint
mechanisms, 58, 62, 121
Korpi, Walter: on social policy, 41–42;
on social democratic model, 44–45
Krieger, Joel, 156
Kuhn, Thomas S.: on anomalies, 50; on
paradigms, 156–57, 195*n39*

Labor market: and education, 6, 43–44,
55–56, 67–68; as a power-generating
mechanism, 56, 86, 98–99, 110, 112–
13, 123–24, 179*n22,* 179*n23,* 181*n17;*
and new social groups, 110–13, 123,
184*n71,* 186*n119*
LaRouche, Lyndon, 47
Legitimacy: defined, 25; and ideological
concealment mechanisms, 101, 118,
182*n28;* and social consumption, 106,
121–22; and procedural rules, 183*n47*

Lindblom, Charles, 58, 60, 61, 73, 74
Lo, Clarence, 16, 56, 117
Lukács, George, 11
Lukes, Steven: on methodology, 46–47;
mentioned, 152

McConnell, Grant: on special interests of
capital, 32–33
Maintenance function: discussed, 51–52,
70, 73, 80, 85–86, 91, 96, 99, 100–2
passim; failure of, 103–4. *See* Business
confidence, Capitalist class, Crisis,
Legitimacy
Mandel, Ernest, 51, 59
Marx, Karl: on Principle of Commodification, 15; on General Law of Capitalist Accumulation, 16, 164*n13;* and
state theory, 41, 70, 78, 178*n5;* on tendency for the rate of profit to fall, 52;
on technology, 110; mentioned, 123
Marxism. *See* Plain Marxism, Political
theory, Rational choice Marxism,
Regulation theory, Social structure of
accumulation theory
Metatheory. *See* Political theory
Miliband, Ralph: Miliband-Poulantzas
debate, 3, 45–47, 58, 77–78; on ruling
class, 16, 27; on state autonomy, 26; on
state managers, 28–30; mentioned, 3,
48, 58, 77, 78
Mintz, Beth: on capitalist class, 18, 23
Mitchell, Timothy, 144
Mode of production: concept of, 171*n4,*
172*n12,* 174*n68,* 179*n22. See also*
Social formation

National Association of Manufacturers,
38, 39
National Industrial Recovery Act, 134–36
National Labor Relations Act, 49
National Recovery Administration,
135–36, 142–43
Neoproletariat: defined, 111, 123–24;
powerlessness of, 186*n119. See also*
New social groups, Servile class
New institutionalism: defined, 186–87*n1*
New social groups: as a surplus population, 110–14, 185*n106,* 186*n119;* and
distributional interests, 123, 184*n71*